JAMES B. DUKE: MASTER BUILDER

JOHN WILBER JENKINS

James B. Duke
Master Builder

by

John Wilber Jenkins

The Story of Tobacco, Development of Southern and Canadian Water-Power and the Creation of a University.

Books for Business
New York - Hong Kong

James B. Duke: Master Builder

by
John Wilber Jenkins

ISBN: 0-89499-059-4

Copyright © 2001 by Books for Business

Reprinted from the 1927 edition

Books for Business
New York - Hong Kong
http://www.BusinessBooksInternational.com

All rights reserved, including the right to reproduce this book, or portions thereof, in any form.

In order to make original editions of historical works available to scholars at an economical price, this facsimile of the original edition of 1927 is reproduced from the best available copy and has been digitally enhanced to improve legibility, but the text remains unaltered to retain historical authenticity.

INTRODUCTION

"America has many merchant princes and captains of industry, but only three industrial kings: John D. Rockefeller in Oil, Andrew Carnegie in Steel, and James B. Duke in Tobacco," a financial writer recorded in *Leslie's Weekly* more than twenty years ago. That was the judgment of others, in and out of Wall Street. Opinions may differ as to relative rank, but certainly no men ever occupied more commanding positions in their respective branches of the nation's business. And it is significant that, in time, these three became America's foremost philanthropists.

Their careers were not unlike. All were self-made, rising unaided from poverty to power and wealth— the tall York State boy, going West, getting his start in a grocery store and eventually merging rivers of oil into a golden stream; the canny little Scotchman, turning from a telegrapher's key to the mastery of steel; and the robust Southern farmer lad who, beginning by flailing out tobacco on a log-barn floor, came to dominate the world's tobacco trade. Each created the extensive machinery of production and distribution which extended his trade into new and untried fields; and each of them devoted as earnest thought to the disposition of his fortune as he had to its accumulation.

Few will agree with Mr. Carnegie, that "To die rich is to die disgraced"; but feudal fortunes are no longer in favor. Men of wider vision have a burning desire to do something for others, to leave behind them some monumental beneficence that will go on serving humanity for generations. That has been the saving grace of our large fortunes. Greed has not been banished.

INTRODUCTION

We have our share of selfishness and avarice. But in no other time or country has wealth seemed so conscious of its responsibilities or contributed so liberally to the general welfare. Giving on so vast a scale is something new in the world.

In a single generation we have seen American industries grow from comparatively small beginnings to the largest enterprises ever known, with a capacity that seems almost limitless, supplying home markets and carrying our trade around the globe.

Measuring by millions, in capital, dividends, output, trade balances, this unparalleled commercial development, we are inclined to lose sight of the human element. Yet these mammoth industries were created by individuals as truly as were the blacksmith shops and country stores of other days, most of them by men who began without a dollar and worked their way up from the ranks. As a rule they were principally the creation of some one man, more far-seeing and enterprising than his competitors, who had the daring and ability to carry through undertakings which others hesitated to attempt.

Whatever their faults or virtues, these men loom large in the history of our time, for they must undeniably be counted among the makers of America, the America of to-day in which we live and have our being. Among the outstanding figures in commerce and finance there have been few as enterprising or successful as James B. Duke, and hardly one whose career presents more vivid contrasts.

Born on a farm so poor that his family could hardly wring a living from its soil, reared in a section impoverished by war and "reconstruction," he became one of the largest manufacturers of his day. Working in the fields, beating out tobacco in an old barn, eventually

INTRODUCTION

he revolutionized the industry and controlled the larger part of the entire tobacco trade.

Driving through the country with his father in a covered wagon, learning his first lessons in trade by bartering at cross-road stores, he became one of the masters of merchandising. Bernard M. Baruch and others have called him "America's greatest merchant." Having but scant schooling himself, never considering college training essential to business success, he made a princely gift to education and furnished the means to create a great university.

Mr. Duke has been called "almost the last of the log-cabin millionaires"—a misnomer, for he was not born in a log cabin and never lived in one, save for a few months after the Civil War. He was long ago designated as "The Tobacco King," a title he may have deserved, but never relished. Numbered for thirty years among our "Captains of Industry," few of that group were less known to the general public and more than once he has been termed perhaps "the least known of America's men of large wealth and influence."

It was not, in fact, until the announcement of his gift of $40,000,000 to establish a university, build up hospitals in his native South, and provide for orphans and for aged ministers in their declining years, that the nation at large came to realize something of the part he had played in his generation and the generous spirit that led him to devote his means to humanity.

There were reasons for this. Shunning the limelight, he had an innate modesty that amounted almost to shyness with strangers. One of the largest of advertisers, spending millions in exploiting his products, he cared nothing for personal prominence.

Luxury meant little to him. Leisure he never enjoyed. The thought of retirement, of "taking things

INTRODUCTION

easy," hardly entered his mind. Fond of doing things, that was his life, and there was never time enough for all he wished to do.

Tall, rugged, red-headed, big mentally and physically, there was something granite, unbreakable, in his make-up. "He was like one of Cromwell's 'Old Ironsides,'" a friend remarked. With the dignity and reserve of the Puritans and much of their rigid belief, there was in his personality none of their hesitant caution or narrowness of view. In business matters his mind swept over States and continents, and the space of years. Taking what seemed at times tremendous chances, he staked millions without a tremor on enterprises which others considered risky if not reckless, but of which he had not a shadow of doubt.

Few men were more severely assailed in the long and stormy periods of anti-trust agitation, yet his indifference to criticism was proverbial. "I never saw any one so unconcerned about attacks," one of his associates said. "Making no reply himself, he would tell us to 'pay no attention to them.'"

"Tobacco is the poor man's luxury," was a favorite saying of his. "Where else can he get so much enjoyment for his five or ten cents?" Never losing sight of the fellow who cannot afford to pay more than a nickel or a dime for his smoke, catering especially to the masses, no man did more to make the tobacco trade one of the country's largest industries. Devoting his later years to hydro-electric development, he was privileged to see water-power become our mightiest source of electric energy.

Determined from boyhood to "be a rich man," wealth was to him not an end but a means. "Money makes jobs for men" was the keynote of his financial philosophy. Stimulating ambition, providing work for

INTRODUCTION

the energetic, inspiring men to make the most of themselves was, from his point of view, the truest philanthropy. And this idea lay behind his benefactions as well as business enterprises.

"Is there any satisfaction in just having a million dollars?" a newspaper man, Ben Dixon McNeill, asked Mr. Duke, in perhaps the longest interview he ever gave for publication.

"Not a dinged bit," was the emphatic reply.

"Not any satisfaction in four hundred millions even, the sheer power that comes with that much money?"

"Not a dinged bit."

"Then what do you want with four hundred millions? How much money ought one to have?"

Enough for a comfortable home, for food, clothes and other necessities, sufficient to meet personal wants and carry on business. That was all any man really needed. No reply was made to the first question; that was over-estimating his fortune. But possessing the larger part of that sum, whether he "wanted" it or not, the answer was given when he established the Duke Endowment.

Finding his greatest pleasure in providing work for thousands; in having business associates and employees share in his prosperity; in opening wider markets for farm products and developing thriving industries, he thoroughly enjoyed the saying that he had "made more millionaires than any other man in this country."

Years ago, when one of his attorneys, William R. Perkins, asked what in his opinion was the greatest thing he had accomplished, Mr. Duke said it was bringing together in the American Tobacco Company such a capable group of men that when the combination was dismembered they were easily able to conduct the separate companies without injury to the industry.

INTRODUCTION

Neither bricks nor mortar, capital or corporations make a business or institution, was his view; the most important factor is the men who run it.

After the trust for education and philanthropy was created Mr. Perkins asked, "What do you say now is the greatest thing you have done?"

"The Duke Endowment," he replied; "because through it I do not merely bring men together, I make men."

The need of the world, he declared, to which all other needs are subservient, is men—real men, upright, downright, all-right men. It was not as merchant, manufacturer or industrial developer that Mr. Duke preferred to be remembered, but as, most of all, a maker of men.

In building up his water-power enterprises two definite objects were kept in view: First, developing industries by furnishing an adequate supply of electric current at low cost; second, providing an unfailing and increasing source of dividends for the support and extension of his philanthropies.

Differing in many respects from other foundations, the Duke Endowment is not only perpetual but cumulative, stimulating giving by others, inspiring people to help themselves in maintaining educational, religious, medical and charitable institutions. The provision by which twenty per cent of the income is to be set aside, reinvested and added to the principal will in time double the original gift, increasing the fund to $80,000,000. With the $17,000,000 specifically devised and the residuary estate bequeathed to the Endowment and Duke University, his benefactions will, in years to come, reach a total of more than $100,000,000.

Based on a utility that will last as long as water flows and industry demands its power, safeguarded

INTRODUCTION

against waste or dissipation of funds, constantly increasing in principal with means for ever-broadening service, Mr. Duke sought to make his Endowment as enduring as wisdom could foresee or forethought provide.

Starting at the very bottom, with bare hands, he climbed to the heights of commercial and financial power. Realizing his boyish dreams and the ambitions of his later years, perhaps his greatest satisfaction, in the end, was in feeling that the wheels of industry he had set in motion would never stop turning; that they would go on, driving factories and railways, building up towns and cities, colleges, churches, hospitals, supporting ministers and orphans, long after he had passed away.

Is not such a personality well worth knowing, such a career all the more worth recounting because it is so unfamiliar to most of his fellow countrymen?

CONTENTS

	PAGE
INTRODUCTION	V

CHAPTER ONE
EARLY DAYS ON A SOUTHERN FARM 19

CHAPTER TWO
IN THE SWEEPING TIDE OF WAR 34

CHAPTER THREE
FROM LOG BARN AND COVERED WAGON TO GREAT FACTORIES AND WORLD TRADE 44

CHAPTER FOUR
THE RISE OF "GOLDEN BELT" TOBACCO 55

CHAPTER FIVE
MAKING CIGARETTES BY THE MILLION 65

CHAPTER SIX
THE YOUNGEST DUKE INVADES NEW YORK . . . 73

CHAPTER SEVEN
FOUNDING THE AMERICAN TOBACCO CO. 85

CHAPTER EIGHT
A WALL STREET BATTLE IN WHICH THE LOSER WON . . 99

CHAPTER NINE
MANY COMPANIES IN ONE, WITH DUKE IN FULL CONTROL . 111

CHAPTER TEN
BRITISH AND AMERICANS IN A WORLD-WIDE ALLIANCE . . 124

CHAPTER ELEVEN
DISSOLVING THE COMBINE—SETTING UP NEW COMPANIES . 146

CONTENTS

CHAPTER TWELVE
JOBS FOR MEN AND MEN FOR JOBS 161

CHAPTER THIRTEEN
HARNESSING RIVERS TO SERVE SOUTHERN INDUSTRIES . . 172

CHAPTER FOURTEEN
TAMING THE WATERS OF THE SAGUENAY 185

CHAPTER FIFTEEN
CREATING A WONDERLAND—HOMES IN CITY AND COUNTRY . 194

CHAPTER SIXTEEN
THE MAN AS OTHERS SAW HIM 203

CHAPTER SEVENTEEN
A BUSINESS MAN'S VIEW OF WAR PROBLEMS 218

CHAPTER EIGHTEEN
TRINITY—NEW LIFE IN AN OLD COLLEGE 231

CHAPTER NINETEEN
TRUE FRIENDS OF THE COLORED RACE 244

CHAPTER TWENTY
MILLIONS FOR EDUCATION, HOSPITALS, CHURCHES AND ORPHANS 251

CHAPTER TWENTY-ONE
AS HE CAME TO THE END OF HIS DAYS 258

CHAPTER TWENTY-TWO
BRINGING INTO BEING A MODERN UNIVERSITY . . . 269
INDENTURE AND DEED OF TRUST ESTABLISHING THE DUKE ENDOWMENT 281

ILLUSTRATIONS

		FACING PAGE
1.	PORTRAIT OF JAMES B. DUKE	*Frontispiece*
2.	WASHINGTON DUKE, FOUNDER OF THE FAMILY FORTUNES	20
3.	ARTELIA RONEY DUKE, MOTHER OF JAMES AND BENJAMIN	24
4.	THE OLD HOMESTEAD NEAR DURHAM WHERE JAMES DUKE WAS BORN	32
5.	BENJAMIN N. DUKE	36
6.	LOG BARN THAT WAS THE DUKES' FIRST FACTORY	44
7.	DURHAM PLANT THAT MADE CIGARETTES BY MILLIONS	44
8.	THE RISING YOUNG TOBACCO MAGNATE	74
9.	MRS. JAMES B. DUKE	96
10.	DORIS DUKE, JAMES DUKE'S ONLY CHILD	104
11.	BRITISH-AMERICAN BANQUET MENU—CABLES SENT BY DUKE	128
12.	GREAT FALLS AND FISHING CREEK STATIONS, SOUTH CAROLINA	174
13.	THE MOUNTAIN ISLAND POWER PLANT, NEAR CHARLOTTE	174
14.	NINETY-NINE ISLANDS STATION, ON BROAD RIVER	180
15.	RHODHISS STATION AND COTTON MILLS	180
16.	ISLE MALIGNE, THE 540,000-HORSEPOWER STATION ON THE SAGUENAY	186
17.	OFFICIALS OF POWER AND ALUMINUM COMPANIES WITH MR. DUKE ON HIS LAST VISIT TO CANADA, JULY, 1925	188
18.	45,000-HORSEPOWER HYDRO-TURBINE, ISLE MALIGNE, CANADA	192
19.	A GLIMPSE OF "DUKE FARMS," THE WONDERLAND CREATED IN NEW JERSEY	196
20.	"ROUGH POINT," THE SEASIDE ESTATE AT NEWPORT	200
21.	THE FIFTH AVENUE MANSION, OVERLOOKING CENTRAL PARK	200

ILLUSTRATIONS

		FACING PAGE
22.	TRINITY COLLEGE LIBRARY	232
23.	"EAST DUKE" BUILDING	232
24.	THE COORDINATE COLLEGE FOR WOMEN, DUKE UNIVERSITY, WHICH WILL INCLUDE TRINITY BUILDINGS	242
25.	CHAPEL CAMPUS—CENTRAL BUILDINGS PLANNED FOR DUKE UNIVERSITY	252
26.	DUKE UNIVERSITY STUDENTS, THE GUARD OF HONOR AT ITS FOUNDER'S FUNERAL	260
27.	CHAPEL TOWER AND ADMINISTRATION BUILDING	270
28.	INTERIOR OF CHAPEL, DUKE UNIVERSITY	270
29.	MEDICAL SCHOOL AND HOSPITAL, ONE OF THE MAJOR GROUPS OF UNIVERSITY BUILDINGS	274
30.	TYPICAL DORMITORY GROUP, ARCHITECT'S DESIGN	276
31.	THE UNION CLOISTERS—DUKE UNIVERSITY	276

JAMES B. DUKE:
MASTER BUILDER

CHAPTER ONE
Early Days on a Southern Farm

THE old farm, near Durham, N. C., where the "Duke boys," as the neighbors still call them, were born and reared, is to-day very much as it was seventy years ago. The weathered two-story frame house; the "front room" and parlor, the big kitchen with its stone fire-place, and the well-house in the rear are in daily use. The log-barn in which they began tobacco manufacture has vanished, but their first plank factory stands, firm as the day it was finished, built, as the present owner points out, of solid timber and lumber, put together mainly with wooden pegs.

Up under the roof of the farm-house is the boys' room, which "Buck" and "Ben" occupied as youngsters. From the low windows, looking across the yard, can be seen the tall steel towers of the high-tension lines, transmitting electric current from the water-powers they developed, the wires running across the fields where they raised their first tobacco. The village which was scarcely more than a railway station in their childhood has grown into a flourishing city with suburbs extending in every direction, and not far away is the broad campus of Duke University, covering the acreage of a dozen plantations.

A plain country homestead this, like thousands through the Carolinas, and its occupants had even fewer advantages than the average farmer's boy.

Coming into the world on December 23, 1856, the youngest member of the family was christened James Buchanan, in honor of the veteran Pennsylvanian who had recently been elected President. His father, Washington Duke, had been twice married. Miss Mary C. Clinton, his first wife, who was the

JAMES B. DUKE

daughter of Jesse and Rachel Vickers Clinton, of Orange County, N. C., and the mother of his two elder sons, Sydney T., who lived to the age of fourteen, and Brodie L. Duke, died November 18, 1847.

Five years later, on December 9, 1852, Mr. Duke was married again, to Miss Artelia Roney, daughter of John and Mary Roney of Alamance County, who was the mother of his three younger children—Mary E., who became Mrs. Robert E. Lyon, of Durham; Benjamin N. and James B., known to his intimates as "Buck" Duke, the brothers who, in partnership with their father, built up the firm of W. Duke, Sons and Company.

Artelia Roney Duke died on August 20, 1858, when her last born was a babe in arms. Her life centering in home and family, her keenest regret was that she could not survive to see her little ones grow to maturity. But she left upon them the impress of her own high character, her deep sense of duty, and that disposition to help others which was her moving spirit.

"Telia" Roney is remembered by those who knew her as one of the prettiest girls in Alamance. Having a pleasing voice she sang in the choir at Pisgah Church, near her home, and it was there that her future husband caught his first glimpse of her. Desire to hear a favorite Methodist preacher led Mr. Duke to journey to the neighboring county. Enjoying the sermon, but being even more attracted by the young lady in the choir, he was introduced to her that day, soon began calling regularly, and before many months rolled by had won her heart and hand. Married in the Roney home, which stands north of Big Falls, now Hopedale Mill, their six years of married life were supremely

WASHINGTON DUKE, FOUNDER OF THE FAMILY FORTUNES

EARLY DAYS

happy, and her early death was the family's greatest sorrow.

The unknown mothers of well-known men—will the world ever realize what a debt it owes to them? The younger Dukes had hardly the faintest recollection of their mother, their only knowledge of her being gained from what their father and relatives told them. They knew that she was a woman of unusual attractiveness, of superior qualities of mind and heart; that she came of the Roneys and Trollingers, families identified with the county from its earliest settlement; that she had given her life to her children, who had inherited from her some of their best characteristics. But they had not even a picture of her.

She had been lying more than half a century in the country graveyard beside Haw River before they found a likeness of her. After long search a quaint daguerreotype, discovered in the home of a Trollinger descendant, was identified by her one surviving brother, who said, "Surely, that's Telia," as he looked upon the long-vanished face. That faded picture was treasured by her sons as one of the few links binding them to their mother.

Erecting at Elon College, as a tribute to her memory, a handsome Science Building bearing her name, they installed in the place of honor an oil painting of Artelia Duke, reproduced from that ancient daguerreotype resurrected after so many years.

His mother passing away before his remembrance, James' affections turned to his father, whose homely maxims, to the end of life, he never tired of quoting.

"My father told me never to start any job I didn't intend to finish," he would remark in a business conference where millions were involved.

JAMES B. DUKE

"My daddy wouldn't have done that, and I won't do it either," was his frequent comment in turning down some proposition not considered sound.

Valuing more than any other part of his inheritance the eminent common sense and unfailing consideration of the parent who, amid difficulties and hardships, had literally dug his living out of the soil and laid the foundation of the family fortunes, his father held first place in his heart.

A man of unusual force and strong character, Washington Duke, born December 20, 1820, in the Bahama section of Orange, that is now part of Durham County, was the son of Taylor Duke, whose family had settled originally in Virginia. His mother, before her marriage Miss Dicie Jones, was from Granville, a neighboring county. Of English and Scotch-Irish blood on his father's side, his mother of Welsh descent, Mr. Duke came of sturdy, God-fearing people, the pioneer stock which settled the Southern colonies and set their stamp upon its civilization.

Looked up to and respected by his neighbors, Taylor Duke was a man of standing in his community. One evidence of this was his election as captain of the militia, then quite an honor. "Muster days" were great occasions when the volunteer soldiers gathered for review. The War of 1812 was fresh in the minds of men, traditions of the Revolution clustered around Hillsboro, the county seat, and there were still living those who remembered the Red-Coats of Cornwallis and the Continentals who fought at Guilford Court House, not far away. Captain Duke must have made a brave figure at the head of his company, and this was not his only distinction, for he served for many years as deputy sheriff, charged with the enforcement of law and order.

EARLY DAYS

Large families were the rule in Eastern Orange, and Taylor Duke's was no exception. He was the father of ten children, of whom Washington was the youngest. William J., the eldest, died at his home near Durham in 1884. Mary, wife of James Stagg, survived until 1881. Anna, wife of John Clinton, died in 1848, Amelia, wife of James Riggs, in 1846. Kirkland, the second son, died in 1864, Malinda, the fourth daughter, in 1874. James T., who lived to a ripe old age, was a resident of Tennessee. Brodie passed away in 1844, while yet a young man. Robert died while serving in the Confederate army in 1863. Washington, last-born of the ten, reached the age of 84, his long life ending on May 8, 1905.

With such a large flock to provide for, every member of the family was used to hard work from childhood. They did not mind that, for all farmers' children worked, except those of the few big planters who had slaves by the score.

The Dukes were far from rich, and there were times when it was not easy to "get along." But their neighbors were no better off, many of them not so fortunate. Owning their land, they grew wheat and corn sufficient for food and provender, and enough cotton and tobacco to bring in a few dollars in the fall. Their cows furnished milk and butter in abundance. The women folk raised flocks of chickens, and turkeys to grace the table at Thanksgiving, Christmas or when the minister came to visit them. Pigs were fed from the crib and kitchen, furnishing pork and hams, and at "hog killing" time the neighborhood reveled in hog and hominy, pig jowls and turnip salad, lights, liver and "hasslets," as well as hams and bacon.

Money was scarce and clothing by no means plentiful. There was little to spend on luxuries or personal

JAMES B. DUKE

adornment. Men of means had their broadcloth suits and beaver hats, their wives and daughters silks and satins; but these were rare and kept for occasions. Ready-made clothing was unknown. On the spinning wheels in nearly every farm-house housewives spun the yarn from cotton picked from their own fields and wool sheared from their own sheep, which was woven into cloth on hand-looms, or knit into stockings and comforters by the busy hands of women whose needles seldom rested. Men wore the stout brown "butternut," and women cotton homespun in summer and the warmer woolens in winter time.

Plowing, hoeing, sowing wheat, cultivating corn, cotton or tobacco, laboring in the fields, farmers worked in their shirt-sleeves, wearing the oldest trousers they possessed. Tailors and dress-makers plied their trade in the larger towns, but they were patronized almost entirely by the wealthy. Women in the country made their own clothes and those of their men folk, as they had since colonial days. "Store bought" goods were rarities, valued highly and carefully cut and sewed, when they could be afforded. Outworn suits of fathers were "made over" for boys, and mothers' dresses were turned and reduced for the girls. Some boys hardly knew what it was to have a new suit until they were almost grown.

Luxuries were few and amusements, as the boys and girls of our day know them, almost non-existent. But there was plenty to eat and enough to wear, and no one suffered for lack of food or clothing.

Work from dawn to dusk was the daily portion. There was no eight-hour day for the farmer boy. Wakened before dawn, there were horses and mules, cattle and hogs to feed and water, wood to chop, fires to kindle, numerous chores to be done. Breakfast by

ARTELIA RONEY DUKE, MOTHER OF JAMES B. AND BENJAMIN

EARLY DAYS

candle-light, for gas and electricity were still far in the future, and even the oil lamps, burning "kerosene," were not in use until years later. Into the fields at the crack of day, following the plow or handling heavy hoes until noon, when the blast of the dinner horn called them to the mid-day meal. Laboring away all the long, hot afternoon, until the last light died away. Feeding cattle and stock, milking the cows, looking after barns and corn-cribs, bringing in water and wood. Supper served hot, with biscuits and cornbread, fried meat, buttermilk and potatoes—wholesome food for hungry men.

The strenuous day ended, they were ready enough for bed, and sound sleep. "Early to bed and early to rise" was no mere maxim but a rule of life. If it did not make boys wealthy and wise, it did promote health and inure strength and endurance.

On such a farm, some twelve miles from Hillsboro, Washington Duke was reared. There were not many advantages, educational or otherwise, for youngsters in that region. Schools were few and far between. Most of them were rude log houses, where classes were taught for two or three months in winter or spring, when the pupils were not employed in the fields. Competent teachers were rare, and instruction principally confined to the three R's. If a boy could read and write and "figure" fairly well, that was sufficient. Private schools, good ones in some of the towns, existed, but they were mainly for the children of the well-to-do. Here and there an "academy" which ran to Greek and Latin gave some grounding in literature and history. But there was scarcely what could be termed a public school system. Frowning upon "free schools," the wealthier property-owners resented even the insignificant taxes levied for their support. As for

JAMES B. DUKE

higher education, a poor boy might get that as best he could. Some did make their way through academy and university, by slaving and sacrifice, but the vast majority did not consider it worth the struggle.

A few colleges, of more or less merit, existed, but they were, as a rule, struggling institutions with small attendance. Going to college was beyond the dreams of the average youth. North Carolina possessed a flourishing university, the oldest State institution of the kind, established soon after the Revolution. That was at Chapel Hill, less than a day's drive from the Duke home. But it might have been a thousand miles away, so far as Taylor Duke's sons were concerned. They could not afford to go there, or afford the high-school training necessary for entrance. Philosophers tell us that men value most things they do not possess or those of which they have been deprived. Perhaps it was this remembrance of the sparse opportunities of his boyhood that led Washington Duke, when fortune favored him, to give so liberally to education.

Learning little from teachers, spending not more than six months of his life in school, he was not uneducated, if education means knowing things worth while; for he acquired a vast fund of practical knowledge that is not found in books. Laboring with his brothers on the farm, he grew to manhood with a heritage of clean blood, a strong physique, a capacity for clear thinking, and the courage that surmounts difficulties.

As an early History of Durham described his education, he was "graduated with high distinction at the—Plow Handles, an institution which is the bone and sinew of our great republican nationality; an institution upon which the perpetuity of our greatness as a people is based, and from which our greatest men have

EARLY DAYS

come to bless the world, and leave behind them a halo of imperishable glory."

If that is too high praise of the plow-handles, it is not too high a commendation of men like the elder Duke, for these sons of the soil, from Abraham Lincoln down, have been the country's mainstay and dependence. And the farmer and manufacturer had about him much of the rugged strength of character and homely wisdom which distinguished the great War President.

Like the prophets of old, the fear of God was in his heart. Religion a vital thing to him, a part of his daily life, he was devoted to his church and its ministers.

"My old daddy always said," James Duke often remarked, "that if he amounted to anything in life it was due to the Methodist circuit riders who frequently visited his home and whose preaching and counsel brought out the best that was in him. If I amount to anything in this world I owe it to my daddy and the Methodist Church."

In the year 1827, earlier chronicles relate, a pale-faced, timid boy of seven made his way into the old-fashioned Methodist chapel near his home, and joined the Sunday School at "Mount Bethel." Finding there the inspiration of earnest teachers, the companionship for which he hungered, he made friendships which lasted through life.

To encourage regular attendance the teachers presented each pupil a card, bearing some verse of scripture. Mr. Duke was fond of recalling, long years after, the first card he received. "Remember thy creator in the days of thy youth" was the inscription, indelibly impressed upon his mind.

Three years later, at the age of ten, he was converted at a revival service, and joined the Methodist Church. His father and mother being serious-minded, devout Methodists who seldom missed a service, to their children, as well as themselves, Mount Bethel was the brightest spot in their existence.

The social as well as religious center of the neighborhood, the country church was the gathering-place of residents for miles around. There they met on Sundays not only to hear the preacher and join in the songs of Zion, but to exchange the news and gossip of crops, politics and neighborhood happenings. "Quarterly meetings," revivals and camp meetings were events to be looked forward to, and afterwards remembered.

Going to church was something no country boy or girl would willingly miss. Father, mother and children piled into the buggies and wagons, dressed in their Sunday best—"go-to-meeting clothes" the negroes termed them—and however the boys might shift along in one-gallus trousers, plowing during the week, and the girls wear slat sun-bonnets and faded ginghams at their house-work, on Sundays they were decked out in the best they could afford. Sunday school was a weekly affair, but few churches could have preaching even every other week. Oftener, it was once a month. Churches were widely separated. Some circuits embraced almost an entire county.

"Circuit rider" was no idle designation for Methodist ministers a century ago. Many times they rode twenty or thirty miles to fill appointments. Few of them could afford buggies or teams. A familiar sight was the gaunt itinerant, mounted on a raw-boned horse, his personal belongings and books in his saddlebags, and his Bible in his hand.

"Mighty men of God" were these circuit riders who carried the gospel to the rural regions of the Carolinas.

EARLY DAYS

Fired with the burning zeal of John Wesley and Francis Asbury, they had no shadow of doubt as to their mission or belief. Saving souls was the business of their lives. Thundering forth their solemn warnings, they called sinners to repentance.

"Ministers" and "clergymen" were not fitting terms for them. They were preachers, preaching the simple gospel handed down from Calvary, "Christ and Him crucified"; speaking with authority, and not as the scribes.

Born orators, preaching with a fire and force that were compelling, ministers and laymen alike would have scorned one who "read his lines." Most of them had never written a sermon in their lives. Unlearned as they may have been in letters and theology, they knew the Scriptures and preached religion, undiluted and undefiled.

Their congregations held the same strenuous belief. Religion was one of the chief concerns of daily life. The Bible was their guide and comforter; many read it "from cover to cover" every year. Lots of passages were hard to understand, of course, but they believed every word of it, from Genesis to Revelations. Religious experience was not foreign to them. Oppressed by the sense of sin, they "wrestled with God." A man knew when he was forgiven, at peace with his Maker. "Conversion," turning from sin to righteousness, was as real as any event of existence. Parents were not satisfied until their sons and daughters were "brought to God."

How the rafters rang, when the preacher gave out the hymn and some ardent brother lifted the tune! There was no choir in those days, no organ to swell the note. But when the congregation joined in sing-

JAMES B. DUKE

ing these stirring hymns, voicing their hopes and fears, there was a thrill no paid choir could ever bring.

> "How firm a foundation,
> Ye saints of the Lord!"

The foundations on which they stood could never crumble.

"Rock of ages, cleft for me"—a refuge it was from every ill and care.

Faith was the basis of their belief, faith in God and Man, never lost or shaken, through all the years. Imperfect enough—for they would be the last to pose as saints or claim perfection—there was something about this "old-time religion" which produced men of larger stature and firmer confidence, leading them to do more for their fellows. It touched the hearts of men and women, and rough and uncultured as many were, there dwelt in them an inner light that could not be dimmed. Can science or scholarship, higher criticism or philosophy compare in strength and comfort with this Faith of our Fathers?

Washington Duke had this faith, and transmitted it to his children, often speaking of these preachers and how deeply they influenced his life. Their treasure, he knew, was laid up in heaven. They had none on earth. Scarcely able to exist on their scanty incomes, few were able to lay by anything for declining years. Old age found them in poverty and want, with no means of support.

In providing for those worn out in ministerial service, for their widows and children, James Duke was endeavoring to repay in some measure the debt owed to them. Duke University, the funds to provide for aged ministers and maintain churches in rural districts are monuments to these self-sacrificing itinerants.

EARLY DAYS

Reaching the age of twenty-one, Washington Duke left his father's roof to make his own way in the world with hardly a dollar of his own. Renting the land of others, for four years he was a tenant farmer, then managed to accumulate enough to buy a small tract of land. Year by year adding to his holdings, at the outbreak of the Civil War he owned three hundred acres. No small achievement, for the average farm in the vicinity then as now was only ninety acres. What he accomplished in later years, making millions in manufacturing, was merely applying the same energy and enterprise on a larger scale.

When Mrs. Duke died, in 1858, her sisters, Miss Elizabeth Roney, whom the youngsters affectionately called "Aunt Betty," and Miss Anne Roney, came into the home to care for the little ones. Supporting a family of a half-dozen was not always easy, hardships were not infrequent, but the farmer was doing well in a material way, building up a property of some value, until war came and almost swept it away.

Taking an interest in the affairs of the community, the Dukes were particularly active in church work. William J., Washington's elder brother, who had been converted at a Methodist cross-roads picnic gathering, had been walking five miles to church on Sundays, he and his wife each carrying a child. Seeking some place of worship nearer home, he built a large arbor, of leafy boughs over a framework of posts and poles, where arbor services and camp meetings could be held. For two or three years, possibly more, between 1836 and 1840, these arbor services continued, William Duke entertaining as many visitors as could be accommodated in his home, the others camping in the woods around. Then, setting aside an acre of land, he built a log church called Hebron, more familiarly known as

JAMES B. DUKE

Duke's Chapel. Both arbor and church services were conducted by a local preacher who was also a farmer and cotton-mill owner, Thomas W. Holden, father of William W. Holden, who became Governor of North Carolina. Another son, Rev. Lucius M. Holden, was later pastor of the congregation.

The Dukes naturally felt a deep interest in the church founded by "Uncle Billy," who was sometimes referred to as "Uncle Billy of the Old Ship," his favorite song being "The Old Ship of Zion." Attending services there in earlier years, they contributed to its support continuously, and there is now under construction at old Hebron a new Duke's Chapel which will be perhaps the finest country church in the State—a model structure of its kind.

But that was not the only house of worship the family attended. One mile east of Durham, near Washington Duke's home, stood a Methodist Chapel known as "Orange Grove." Organized in 1830 in a schoolhouse, as the result of a revival conducted by Rev. Willis Haynes and Rev. David Nicholson, five years later the building, used jointly for church and school, was burned by a miscreant, Jefferson Dillard, who "fled for parts unknown."

Replaced by a larger chapel, by 1860 this structure was also outgrown and the congregation moved to Durham, a grove at the edge of the town being purchased and a frame building erected. Contributing to its erection and support, the elder Dukes were among the stewards and with their families attended services there.

The times were exciting. North and South drifting apart, there was widespread talk of armed conflict. Democrats were divided, Whigs at sea, scarcely knowing where to turn. Buchanan was in the White House, but the lately born Republican party, having nominated

THE OLD HOMESTEAD NEAR DURHAM WHERE JAMES DUKE WAS BORN

EARLY DAYS

Abraham Lincoln for President, was sweeping through the Northern States.

Feeling ran high, politics were discussed wherever men gathered, and could not be kept out of the churches. Secession was the burning issue. The Lincoln and Douglas debates fresh in the public mind, citizens were eager to hear both sides of the question.

The Methodist chapel in Durham was the scene of a notable debate. The orators themselves were eminent enough to attract any audience. On one side, advocating the preservation of the Union, was William A. Graham, who after serving as governor and United States senator, had been Secretary of the Navy in President Fillmore's cabinet, and had been nominated eight years before for Vice President, on the ticket with General Winfield Scott. Opposing him was Henry E. Nash, an eloquent speaker and ardent advocate of secession. A contest memorable but indecisive.

The congregation was divided. Rev. J. B. Alford, the pastor, and a majority of the Methodists were fiery secessionists, the Dukes and others strong for the Union. A trying time, with neighbors at odds, families disagreeing, the entire community seethed with discussion, and over all was the shadow of what many even then were terming the "irrepressible conflict."

CHAPTER TWO

In the Sweeping Tide of War

FORTY-ONE years old at the outbreak of the Civil War, believing firmly in a united country, Washington Duke looked upon the disruption as needless strife, a deplorable struggle that could end only in disaster. Up to that time a consistent Democrat, naming his youngest son for a Democratic President, he was deeply and conscientiously opposed to secession, as were not a few of his fellow citizens, including men of prominence.

North Carolina was one of the last of the Southern States to secede, and it was at Raleigh, not many miles from his home, that the Ordinance of Secession was adopted on May 20, 1861.

Not in sympathy with the Confederacy or approving armed resistance, when called Mr. Duke responded and did his part as a private in the ranks. Going into the army meant the breaking up of his home. The oldest son, Brodie, entered the Confederate service. But the others, "Ben" and "Buck," and his daughter Mary, were too young to have anything to do with war. There was no one to keep the farm going or care for the children at the home place. So they were sent to their Grandfather Roney's, in Alamance County, to be cared for by aunts, grandparents and their colored nurse. Opposed to slavery, Mr. Duke owned one slave, a girl named Caroline. Serving in the home, she assisted in "looking after" the children, and remained with them during the war.

Entering the Confederate army in 1863, Mr. Duke was sent to Camp Holmes, and placed on guard duty. Transferred to the navy and ordered to South Carolina, he served on a ship which was one of the defenses

IN THE TIDE OF WAR

of Charleston harbor, taking part in the heavy bombardments at James Island. Thus for a time he was in sight of the spot where the firing on Fort Sumter precipitated the War between the States.

Later again transferred, this time to the artillery, he was sent to Virginia and attached to Battery Brook, one of the defenses of Richmond, near Drury's Bluff. Becoming an expert gunner, he was placed in charge of a battery and promoted to orderly sergeant. Serving there until the city was abandoned, he filed south with his ragged comrades as they watched the burning capital of the Confederacy, and not so fortunate as the majority, was captured by the Federals and sent to Libby Prison. But a few weeks later, after Lee surrendered at Appomattox and the bloody struggle ended, he was released from captivity.

Transported to North Carolina, but to a point nowhere near his own locality, he was sent by the Federal authorities to New Bern, in the southeastern part of the State. Deposited there with no money or means of transportation, walking was the only way to reach home, and he walked the entire distance, 135 miles. Going on foot from town to town, foraging for food, sleeping wherever night overtook them, the discharged Confederates made their way as best they could. Impoverished, many families in dire need, the farmers along the way were kind enough to the soldiers, ready to divide their last crust with the veterans; but it was a long and weary march for the war-worn "Tar Heels."

The Duke youngsters had led a quiet existence while their father was in the army. Ben and Buck were sturdy little fellows, popular with playmates, and their sister Mary, those who knew her say, "was as fine a girl as ever lived." The boys were kept busy doing chores around the house, barns and stables, and helping in the fields, while Mary was occupied with household affairs. All three attended school in winter, going first to the log schoolhouse at Harden's and later to Pisgah Church, where school was held.

"Many's the time I played bull-pen with Ben and Buck," recalls F. P. Rogers, one of their schoolmates, who at 75 was still keeping the neighborhood general store. "How they would duck and dodge to keep from being hit by the ball!"

Buck was "pigeon-toed" in his youth, Mr. Rogers relates, and this handicap often caused him to get hit in the game, which was great fun for the other players. He had to wear special shoes, which were made for him by De Shavers, a half-breed Indian, who made most of the shoes worn in that section. "My, they were rough, hard shoes to wear!" exclaimed Mr. Rogers, who recalled that Buck later had his feet corrected by surgery and had as firm a footing as any of them.

Impatient to get things done, Buck even in childhood was inclined to hurry the process. One incident that occurred when he was a little fellow was a standing joke in the family. Raising chickens was one of his occupations. An old hen that was his special care had been "setting" for an unconscionably long time, and when at last the eggs began hatching, there was a terrific squawking in the barn-yard. Out his aunts ran, to learn what was the matter. There was Buck, hatless and breathless, battling with the enraged mother. The biddies not emerging rapidly enough for him, he had taken the hen from her nest and was plucking off the egg-shells, lifting out the chicks as fast as he came to them.

"You'll kill the poor little things," he was told. Surprised and penitent, Buck explained that he was

BENJAMIN N. DUKE

IN THE TIDE OF WAR

just "helping them get out." But that was his last attempt to interfere with a setting hen.

Growing tobacco in summer, attending school in winter, school-boy games, going to church on Sunday, visits to the neighbors and occasional trips to town were their only recreations. But life was not without its hardships.

War had cast its shadow over this region, as it had over the entire South. Practically all the able-bodied men and many boys hardly big enough to hold a gun had gone to the front. Only the old folks, women and children were left. North Carolina, with a military population of 115,000, had furnished more than 125,000 troops to the Confederacy. The losses had been terrible. Nearly every family was in mourning for some son or father who had fallen.

The conflict had been to most of them a mysterious, far-off thing, the nearest battlefields, until near the end, being in Virginia or Tennessee. But before the strife was over the residents of this section were to see soldiers by thousands, feel the thrill of marching regiments, and, as well, get a taste of the destruction that follows in the wake of moving armies. For big events revolved around Durham. Its vicinity was the scene of Johnston's surrender to Sherman, the final collapse of the Confederacy.

Having marched through Georgia to the sea, Sherman swept his way through the Carolinas, moving toward Virginia to form a junction with Grant's army. But the fall of Richmond and Lee's surrender changed his plans. Johnston, with his army of 30,000 giving battle at Bentonsville, fighting stubbornly at every step, was the only opposing force remaining. Sherman turned toward Johnston, who had fallen back on Raleigh to protect the State capital. Outnumbered,

JAMES B. DUKE

the Confederates retreated toward Hillsboro, passing within a few miles of the Duke farm. Occupying Raleigh, Sherman sent Kilpatrick, with his cavalry, in pursuit.

Jefferson Davis and his cabinet, driven from Virginia, had taken refuge in Greensboro, fifty miles away. As the Federals approached the capital Governor Zebulon B. Vance sent peace commissioners, under a flag of truce, to treat with Sherman. On the same day Johnston was summoned to Greensboro to confer with President Davis. Seated around the conference table were Judah P. Benjamin, Secretary of State; S. R. Mallory, Secretary of the Navy; John H. Reagan, Postmaster General, and General P. G. T. Beauregard. Knowing conditions were desperate, Johnston presumed he had been called to consider the best way to end hostilities. He was amazed when Mr. Davis declared that he would, in two or three weeks, have a large force in the field, proposing to call out all the enrolled men whom the Conscript Bureau had been unable to bring into the army.

Secretary of War Breckenridge arrived a few hours later, confirming the rumors of Lee's surrender. Mr. Davis immediately called a second conference. Johnston urged making overtures for peace at once. The Confederate President asked the members of his Cabinet for their opinions. Breckenridge, Mallory and Reagan, General Johnston relates, "thought the war was decided against us, and that it was absolutely necessary to make peace." But Secretary Benjamin violently opposed such action, making a fervid speech for continuing the war. Mr. Davis hesitated to attempt overtures, feeling that the Federal Government would probably reject any terms he might offer, but finally

IN THE TIDE OF WAR

consented to permit General Johnston to initiate negotiations with Sherman.

Replying promptly, Sherman proposed an armistice on the same terms which Grant had offered Lee at Appomattox. Delayed in transmission, the message did not reach Johnston until the 16th. General Wade Hampton then arranged an interview between the commanding generals, to take place half way between the picket lines of the two armies.

Though providing for surrender of military forces and the ending of the Confederacy, the terms proposed by Johnston, to which Sherman gave favorable consideration, were liberal, guaranteeing protection of Southern citizens in their political and property rights, and granting immunity from prosecution or penalties for participation in the war. Had these terms been accepted, the hardships and terrors of "Reconstruction" might have been avoided, bitter hatreds abated, and history changed for a generation. But at that very moment a tragedy occurred which horrified the country and prevented any concessions to the stricken South, any treatment save that of a conquered enemy. That was the assassination of President Lincoln.

There is no more graphic story of these events, recounted in Dr. Boyd's history of Durham, than is given by General Sherman himself in his "Memoirs":

"I ordered a car and locomotive to be prepared to convey me up to Durham's at eight o'clock of the morning of the 17th. Just as we were entering the car, the telegraph operator, whose office was upstairs in the depot building, ran down to me and said that he was at that instant of time receiving a most important dispatch in cipher from Morehead City, which I ought to see. I held the train for nearly half an hour, when he returned with the message translated and written out. It was from Mr. Stanton, announcing the assassination of Mr.

JAMES B. DUKE

Lincoln, the attempt on the life of Mr. Seward and son, and a suspicion that a like fate was designed for General Grant and all the principal officers of the government.

"Dreading the effect of such a message at that critical instant, I asked the operator if any one besides himself had seen it; he answered no. I then bade him not to reveal the contents by word or look till I came back, which I proposed to do the same afternoon. The train then started, and, as we passed Morris Station, General Logan, commanding the Fiftieth Corps, came into my car, and I told him I wanted to see him, as I had something very important to communicate.

"We reached Durham's, 26 miles, about 10 A.M., where General Kilpatrick had a squadron of cavalry drawn up to receive me," said General Sherman. "We passed into the house in which he had his headquarters, and soon after mounted some horses, which he had prepared for myself and staff. General Kilpatrick sent a man ahead with a white flag, followed by a small platoon, behind which we rode, and were followed by the rest of the escort. We rode up the Hillsboro road for about five miles, when our flag-bearer discovered another coming to meet him. They met, and word was passed back to us that General Johnston was near at hand, when we rode forward and met General Johnston on horseback, riding side by side with General Wade Hampton. We shook hands and introduced our respective attendants. I asked if there was a place convenient where we could be private, and General Johnston said he had passed a small farmhouse a short distance back, when we rode back to it side by side, our staff officers and escorts following.

"We soon reached the house of a Mr. Bennett, dismounted, and left our horses with orderlies in the road. Our officers, on foot, passed into the yard, and General Johnston and I entered the small farmhouse. We asked the farmer if we could have the use of his house for a few minutes, and he and his wife withdrew into a small log house, which stood close by."

This house, a log and timber structure, at the forks of the road, three and a half miles from Durham, stood, an interesting landmark, until 1921, when it was destroyed by fire. Only the chimneys and foundation remain, but the spot has been marked by a bronze tablet bearing this inscription:

THE BENNETT HOUSE

Generals J. E. Johnston and Sherman met here at noon April 17, 1865, to discuss terms of surrender. They met in this house again on April 18 and wrote and signed a "Basis of Agreement." President Johnson rejected the terms and sent orders to Sherman to give Johnston till the 24th or resume hostilities.

On the evening of April 25, Gen. Johnston asked for another interview with Sherman.

On the 26th at 2 P.M. the Generals met in the Bennett House and signed the terms of a "military convention" under which 36,817 Confederate soldiers in North Carolina and 52,453 in Georgia and Florida laid down their arms.

What strange turns events take! It was William T. Sherman, most feared and hated of Northern generals, who in this cabin signed the "Basis of Agreement," proposing the restoration of the Southern States to the Union, and favorable treatment of their people. In this General Sherman believed he was carrying out the policy of Lincoln who, he said, had, in numerous letters and telegrams, urged him to make terms with civil authorities, governors and legislatures. But Lincoln lay dead in Washington, stricken down by the bullet of John Wilkes Booth. The reins of government were in other hands. Public sentiment in the North was so aroused that even a Southern-born President could not stem the tide. The Executive who, under a compulsion that was irresistible, rejected these liberal terms and rebuked Sherman for submitting them, was Andrew Johnson, a native of North Carolina, born and

JAMES B. DUKE

reared in Raleigh, within a stone's throw of Sherman's headquarters.

While the armies were camped around, and these eventful happenings were taking place so near their home, the Duke boys were miles away. The foraging soldiers raided their farm, sweeping it clean of food and provender, taking off everything they thought worth carrying away. But the boys were not there. They were at Grandpa Roney's up in Alamance, and missed all the excitement. As Benjamin recalled, long afterward, "We never saw the Yankees."

They had troubles enough of their own. The fall of Richmond meant less to them than did the fact that their father had been captured in the retreat from that city. Later they learned he was in Libby Prison, and though in time released, there were weeks of waiting before his children could greet the parent from whom they had been separated for two years.

Dark days these were for every one. Sorrow over the fall of the Confederacy was mitigated, however, by the fact that the war was over. Wives, mothers, children with thankfulness and tears of joy welcomed home their loved ones who had been so long exposed to its perils. The shadow of death was at last lifted. Poverty stricken, the Dukes and their neighbors were glad to be alive, able to return to the pursuits of peace.

Food was by no means plentiful, clothing had been patched and mended as long as it would hold together. Sugar was a rarity. Some children, like the Dukes, had almost forgotten the taste of it. Coffee had long since passed from the family tables, only the richest being able to afford this luxury. The poor drank chickory as a substitute, and "sassafras tea," made from the roots of the sassafras shrub.

Neither the returning soldiers nor the civilian popu-

IN THE TIDE OF WAR

lation had any money. Long before hostilities ended Confederate currency had declined until $500 was required to buy a $30 cow, a pair of boots or a silk dress cost $1,000 and sugar and coffee went as high as $100 a pound. Following the surrender the currency was absolutely worthless, as were also the Confederate bonds, in which men of means had invested millions. The banks, their funds invested in Confederate and State bonds, their deposits in Confederate money, all failed. There was no stable currency, and practically no capital.

The armies had swept live-stock from the plantations, commandeering horses and mules for cavalry and transport service, cattle, hogs and sheep for food for the troops. On some farms there was hardly a chicken left. The slaves were freed, and in their newfound freedom were naturally not inclined to work. The accustomed labor supply gone or reduced to a fraction of its former effectiveness, cotton culture was for the time being impracticable.

Some crop that could be raised without any great amount of labor was sought by farmers, some industry which did not require large capital by business men. Tobacco answered both requirements, and proved their salvation.

CHAPTER THREE

From Log Barn and Covered Wagon to Great Factories and World Trade

Two blind army mules which had been given him and fifty cents in cash constituted Mr. Duke's entire working capital when the war ended. A five-dollar Confederate note had been swapped with a Yankee trooper for the precious half-dollar.

Better off at that than many of his neighbors, for hungry, footsore, almost in rags, service in the army had not broken his physique or spirit, the head of the family accepted conditions as they were and set at work to better them.

Gathering his children together, he brought them back to the home place. But his farm had been sold on credit to a neighbor, the purchaser could not pay for it and would not be ousted. Months elapsed before the owners regained possession. In the meantime a working agreement was made with the occupant by which the Dukes resumed farming, receiving a share of the crops and some return for their labor.

Room for Mary, the daughter, was provided in the farm-house; but there was no space for the others in the dwelling, still occupied by the purchaser and his flock, so the boys, "Buck" and "Ben," and their father slept in an outbuilding on the premises, rigging up temporary living quarters.

The farm had been stripped of almost everything that could be used or sold, but one thing the greedy soldiers had overlooked—a quantity of leaf tobacco. The only commodity visible that could be converted into money or bartered for supplies, before this could be disposed of to advantage it must be put into form for smoking. On the premises was a log barn, sixteen

LOG BARN THAT WAS THE DUKES' FIRST FACTORY

DURHAM PLANT THAT MADE CIGARETTES BY MILLIONS

LOG BARN TO FACTORIES

by eighteen feet. Here the Dukes set up their first "factory." Having no machinery, father, children and all hands worked at the task. Beaten with flails, the pulverized leaf was sifted and packed in bags. There was nothing fine or fancy about the manufacture or packing, but it was sound, honest tobacco that made a good smoke, and the amateur manufacturers, creating a brand of their own, boldly labeled their bags "Pro Bono Publico"—For the Public Good.

Selling it was the next problem. Loading the "Pro Bono" into a covered wagon, the Dukes set forth on their first business trip. No millionaire could have been prouder of his Rolls-Royce than they were of this ramshackle old wagon in which they journeyed by day and slept at night, their itinerant home and store.

Drawn by the blind mules Mr. Duke had brought back from the army, the wagon carried, besides the smoking tobacco, duly packed and labeled, two barrels of flour. Attached at the rear was a "victual box," with a frying pan, tin plates and cup, a side of bacon, one bushel of meal and some sweet potatoes; for the travelers had to camp where they could, and cook their own meals. Blankets, water buckets, and fodder and corn for the mules completed the outfit.

Heading for the southern part of the State, where tobacco was scarce and in demand, making their way through the country, they traveled from place to place, selling at the cross-road stores, on farms and in villages. Proving good salesmen, the amateur merchants did well along the route. When buyers could not pay cash, things that could be used or sold were taken in barter. At any rate, the adventurers drove a trade, and better still, were gaining friends and customers.

When meal time came, the frying pan was gotten

out, pones of corn-bread made, bacon and sweet potatoes fried and, with appetites sharpened by life in the open air, they enjoyed every mouthful.

The tobacco being readily sold, with the money received a quantity of bacon was bought. Exchanging the barrels of flour for two hundred pounds of cotton, which were sold at Raleigh, Mr. Duke brought home as a present for the children what was a rare luxury to them—a bag of brown sugar. Hardly tasting sugar for months, the only substitute they had was molasses or sorghum, known as "long sweetening," and scarce enough at that.

Pouring the sugar into a bucket, placed in the middle of the room, the children, spoons in hand and poised for the attack, were invited to "go to it." Gathered around the bucket, sitting flat on the floor, they pitched into the sugary mass ravenously. "Buck" ate more than his share, so much, in fact, that it "lasted him for life." Caring nothing for sweets in later years, he traced his aversion to the overdose of sugar when his father brought back the "treat."

This initial trip proved so successful that Mr. Duke and his sons decided to go into tobacco manufacturing as a business. "Buck," then eight years old, "going on nine," was as deeply interested in the enterprise as were his older brothers. Though hardly waist-high beside his father, he was taking an active part in the work on the farm and in the barn where they beat out their tobacco. So was Ben, two years older. Growing up together, these lads were more than brothers. Lifelong partners, they were bound in close association by ties that were never broken.

Mary, the only daughter, who later became the wife of Robert E. Lyon, was but twelve years of age when they returned from Alamance. But, having learned a

LOG BARN TO FACTORIES

lot about cooking and household affairs at Granny Roney's, she insisted on doing her share, and soon became the recognized housekeeper, succeeding so well that father and brothers left home matters in her hands and gave their undivided attention to the farm and factory.

Brodie Duke, the eldest son, returned from the war like his father, ragged and penniless. Visiting his Uncle William, he found that relative in the depths, "terribly mournful."

"Well," said Brodie, "what are you worrying about?"

"We're ruined," his uncle told him. "Haven't a thing left. The Yankees have driven off the stock, carried off all the stuff fit for anything on the place, and the land hasn't been worked in two years."

Seeing a raw-boned horse some soldier had discarded and a decrepit army mule grazing in the tall grass, Brodie inquired:

"How about that horse and mule out there?"

"Oh, shucks," Uncle William said. "Those old bags-o'-bones couldn't do any work."

Hunting around, Brodie found enough bits of harness to piece together. Under the barn shelter was a battered wagon the Yankees had failed to commandeer. Not much of a vehicle; but, hitching the bony animals to the battered "carryall," they had at least a team. Providing for the younger children was task enough for his father. Brodie, being old enough to shift for himself, proposed to join forces with his uncle in farming the land, dividing the crops. That arrangement was satisfactory to both and they went into partnership "on shares."

Getting decent clothes was a problem. The tattered Confederate uniform Brodie wore, ingrained with dirt, was fast falling to pieces. There was no money to buy another. Finding in a closet a suit that had belonged to a cousin killed in the war, Brodie scrubbed and pressed the coat and trousers, burned the remnants of his old uniform and donned his first presentable outfit since leaving the army.

Late in planting, they raised a fair crop, sufficient to buy another team and wagon; but scant surplus was left. Six barrels of corn and three of flour was the total Brodie reaped for the season's work. Seeing no prospect of making money farming, he joined his father and brothers in manufacturing tobacco.

Deciding a real factory was necessary, they proceeded to put up one. Twenty by thirty feet in size, that was also built of logs, but afforded better facilities. This was soon outgrown, and an abandoned house which had been used as a stable was utilized. As trade increased, a more impressive and convenient structure was erected, a frame house designed for and adapted to manufacture. The new building compared favorably with the tobacco factories which were operated on many farms in that part of the Carolinas and which, before the war, made mostly plug tobacco, before the industry was concentrated in cities and towns. Negro boys with hickory sticks "beat out" the leaf, which was packed in home-made bags. Later crude machinery was installed, and packages and product made more attractive.

Prospering from the beginning, the Dukes in 1866 manufactured 15,000 pounds. Revenue taxes were high, following the war, but tobacco brought thirty to forty cents a pound, yielding a substantial profit. By 1872, selling 125,000 pounds a year, they had become factors in the local industry, and the junior member of the family was "cutting his eye-teeth," learning the trade.

LOG BARN TO FACTORIES

Born and reared in the country, he had been familiar with farm work from his earliest remembrance. Riding horses and driving oxen when hardly tall enough to reach to a mule's back, he liked nothing better than "riding to mill," carrying a bag of corn or wheat and bringing back the meal or flour. Waiting while the miller ground the grain gave the boy undisturbed hours when he could lie on the grass, and meditate on what he would do when he grew to manhood.

Water fascinated him. Watching the stream pour over the big wooden wheel, he often longed for a mill of his own, with the water flowing by unceasingly. This youthful ambition was vividly recalled nearly half a century later when he was developing waterpower on a scale that was unthought of in his boyhood.

Older residents recall seeing "Buck" Duke, when a mere lad, driving into town in a cart drawn by a yearling ox, bringing in tobacco and taking back goods and supplies. "He took to trade like a duck to water," his former townsmen will tell you, and even then was entrusted with business transactions. Full of ideas, he was constantly seeking new and better ways of manufacturing and merchandising.

Tobacco was one thing with which he was thoroughly familiar. Planting, "priming" and "suckering" the growing plants, spending days picking off and killing the green worms that were the crop's worst enemy, he had held the long sticks while the laborers cut and slit the plants and placed them, heads down, on the sticks on which they were hauled to the barns. Gathering tobacco, when the broad leaves turned from green to yellow with a touch of brown, was a busy time, in which the help of every man, woman and child, white and colored, on the place was needed.

Plastered with mud to fill every "chink," the log

JAMES B. DUKE

barns were made as nearly air-tight as possible. The barns filled, packed to the roof, tier on tier, the plants hanging downward from the rows of sticks resting on the rafters, pine wood, cord length, was packed into the "flues" beneath and set afire with lightwood knots. Once kindled the fires must be kept burning day and night until the "curing" was completed. If the blaze was once permitted to die down, the tobacco was ruined. Piling in wood, keeping up the fires, was one of a farmer boy's duties, until the leaves turned to the yellow and brown of "bright" tobacco, and the expert curer in charge decided that the plants had the proper feel and color.

Stripping and tying were the next processes, stripping the leaves from the brown stalks, and tying them together in small bundles—something in which every one, from the oldest to the youngest, could join—work for rainy days when the leaf was moist and pliable enough to handle.

On the farm and in the factory "Buck" Duke learned the numerous details of raising and handling tobacco, from burning the "plant beds" and sowing the seed, in the spring, to the time the leaf was cured and the finished product ground into "smoking" or pressed into "plugs."

With few associates, even among the neighbors, having no holiday but Sunday, when the whole family attended church, and no time to play as other boys did, work was his pleasure as well as occupation. Thoughtful and reserved, with few friends or amusements, he grew up disciplined, self-reliant, with an independence and initiative which were to serve him well in after years.

Traveling from town to town in the covered wagon, camping out in the woods or at the edge of villages, when permitted to accompany father and brothers on their selling expeditions, gave him the keenest pleasure. It was on one of these trips that he met Walter Page. As the itinerant merchants parked near Morris Station, the mules unhitched and camp arranged for the night, students from a neighboring school gathered around the wagon. Among them, Col. F. A. Olds, of Raleigh, who was in the group, recalls, was Page and it was there that they scraped acquaintance. Who would have imagined that one of these youngsters sitting around the camp-fire would become the largest tobacco manufacturer of his day and another the American Ambassador to England?

Buck and Ben, between times in factory and field, went to school in Durham, driving into town with their books and slates. Attending the Academy, taught by Dr. Morgan Closs, a man of parts and learning who left his impress on his pupils, the Dukes recalled him with sincere affection. Both were bright pupils, and Buck could "out-figure any one in his class." In fact, it was a common saying that, when problems were given out, he could "get the answer before the teacher could." Ben, his brother, and others might excel in reading, writing or history, but when it came to "figuring out" anything, Buck had no equal.

Wishing both his boys to go to college, Mr. Duke, after they had attended several sessions at the Academy, sent them and their sister to the excellent school at New Garden, in Guilford County, conducted by the Quakers, now Guilford College. Ben and Mary enjoyed their studies, but the boarding school life did not appeal to Buck. Caring little for books, impatient under the slow routine of instruction, he felt that he was not "getting anywhere." Learning lessons was not difficult, keeping up with classes was easy, but he could not "see the use of it." Longing to get back to the farm and factory, where there was always something doing and he was a factor in affairs, he left New Garden when the term was hardly half over.

Presenting in after years an imposing building, a Memorial Hall, to Guilford College, which had grown to full collegiate rank, the Dukes looked back with pleasant recollections to the days spent in its groves and class-rooms. But Buck never would admit that a college education would have been of great advantage to him.

"That is all right for preachers and lawyers," he said, "but what use would an education be to me? My father wanted me to go to school, and I did go to this Quaker School near Greensboro for about three months. Elwood Cox [now a leading High Point banker] was there at the time. I went home and told my father that I wanted a share in the business. He didn't give it to me then, but finally he did."

Education that fitted for commerce, however, was another matter. Eager to learn bookkeeping, how to estimate costs and profits, and carry on the varied details of running a store or factory, he was determined to take a business course and finally his father consented for him to go to the Eastman Business College at Poughkeepsie, N. Y.

Passing through New York, on his first trip North, he caught a glimpse of the metropolis. It appealed to his imagination. Here was a larger world, with boundless possibilities. His vision no longer bounded by the towns in the Carolinas, he was reaching out toward greater things.

He absorbed everything available in business methods and procedure at Eastman, studying day and night, and could hardly be induced to engage in play or recreation. Caring nothing for the amusements that most boys crave, he regarded them as a waste of time, not half so interesting as getting on with his work. He was there, he said, for business, not pleasure.

Passing the rest of his class, the young "Tar Heel" made a record, completing the course in less time than any other student who had been there. His instructors knew they had trained an exceptionally bright pupil, but must have been surprised a few years later when they saw the stripling from a Carolina farm becoming one of New York's leading business men. Not forgetting his tutors or the days spent at Poughkeepsie, Mr. Duke, when he organized the American Tobacco Company, gave the man who signed his diploma a responsible position in the big concern, making a former teacher one of his auditors.

Some men are born for business, and Duke was one of them. Asked, at the height of his career, the secret of his success, he said:

"I have succeeded in business not because I have more natural ability than those who have not succeeded, but because I have applied myself harder and stuck to it longer. I know plenty of people who have failed to succeed in anything who have more brains than I had, but they lacked application and determination.

"I had confidence in myself. I said to myself, 'If John D. Rockefeller can do what he is doing in oil, why should not I do it in tobacco?' I resolved from the time I was a mere boy to do a big business. I loved business better than anything else. I worked from early morning until late at night. I was sorry to have to leave off at night and glad when morning came so I could get at it again. Any young man can succeed

JAMES B. DUKE

if he is willing to apply himself. Superior brains are not necessary."

When only fourteen he was taking a large part in the family's affairs, and was made manager of the factory. But his ambition was to be one of the owners. A few years later, at eighteen years of age, his mind was made up. Failing to get a share in the family's enterprise, he would strike out for himself. Having pondered the matter thoroughly, he put the case squarely up to his father.

Mr. Duke was surprised when his youngest son came to him one day and said:

"Father, I want you to emancipate me."

"What do you mean?" he inquired.

"I want to go into business for myself."

"What do you intend to do?" his father asked. Buck told him. There was no further argument.

"All right," said Mr. Duke. "Go and write a check to yourself for a thousand dollars, so you will have some capital to start on."

Holding the check in his hand a moment, thinking, Mr. Duke then tore it up.

"No, Buck," he said. "I'll not sign this. I've thought of a better way. I've decided to take you and Bennie into partnership with me."

There was no need of any formal partnership or articles of agreement. Buck was satisfied. It was more than he had hoped for. His father's word was better than any bond or legal document drawn up by clever lawyers. Thus was born a firm which was to make some stir in the world—"W. Duke and Sons."

CHAPTER FOUR

The Rise of "Golden Belt" Tobacco

Though meager in population, Durham was growing into a manufacturing center. The coming of Johnston's and Sherman's armies, regarded at the time as an unmitigated calamity, had proved to be the luckiest thing that ever happened for that section.

Factories had been raided, some stores burned, farmhouses rifled and barns stripped, but the soldiers, Yankee and Confederate, had "taken a liking" to the local tobacco. Bearing away all they could carry, on arriving home they let neighbors sample it, and when supplies were exhausted, sent back for more. Among the thousands of troops camped thereabouts were men from almost every state. They spread the fame of Durham tobacco far and wide, blazing the way for a big industry in the tiny hamlet.

Ten years before the town had been only a depot, the railroad having reached there in 1854. Making it even a stopping-place was unintentional. The station was to have been located at Prattsburg, two miles west, where there was a store, cotton gin and blacksmith shop, as well as a tavern and grog-shop. But William Pratt, fearing the locomotives would frighten the farmers' horses and drive away his customers, demanded an exorbitant price for the right of way. Dr. Bartlett Durham offered to donate four acres on his place, the railroad builders made a detour around Pratt's land, located the station on the doctor's property, and gave it his name, first Durhamville, later shortened to Durham's.

Two stores were established, one by James W. Cheek, the other by M. A. Angier, father of Mrs. Benjamin N. Duke. Soon another store was erected

JAMES B. DUKE

near by as well as two barrooms and a carpenter shop, in which was the post-office.

In 1858 Robert F. Morris and his son began manufacturing tobacco, the town's first industrial enterprise. There were a score or so of residences in the village before 1861, two churches, a log school house and an academy, as Dr. W. K. Boyd records in his history, "The Story of Durham"; but the war put a stop to construction there, as in most parts of the South, and in 1865 the place had fewer than a hundred inhabitants. But the one tobacco factory was still running, operated by John Ruffin Green, who had bought the interests of the former proprietors.

War seems, somehow, to stimulate tremendously the use of tobacco. Nearly every soldier carried a pipe or plug in his knapsack, taking a puff or chew whenever there was opportunity. The weed was in great demand in the army. Soldiers going to the front, University students passing to and from Chapel Hill, stopped at Durham to fill their pouches, and Green did a flourishing business.

Then calamity overtook him. Johnston's Confederates as they retreated captured a plentiful supply of his tobacco. Sherman's troops, who followed, raided the factory and swept it clean.

Ruin stared Green in the face. But in a few months the ex-soldiers and others began to write back for "smokes." Trade revived with a rush, and the plant had to be enlarged. The raiders had been his best advertisers. Other factories, like that of the Dukes', sprang up in the town and on farms near by. Consumers began to demand "Durham" tobacco. Manufacturers at other points, taking advantage of this popularity, began to label their products "Spanish Flavored," Green's variety, and "Durham" mixture.

"GOLDEN BELT" TOBACCO

Seeking a distinctive brand which rivals could not use, Green finally adopted the Durham Bull. Inspired by two things, a massive bull owned by a neighbor, and the picture on Coleman's mustard, manufactured in Durham, England, the sign of the bull, painted on sheet-iron and mounted in front of the factory, then widely advertised, became one of the best known of trade-marks.

Under the management of William T. Blackwell, who became Green's partner in 1867, and Julian S. Carr, who with James R. Day entered the firm after Green's death, this became the largest smoking tobacco factory in existence. Blackwell had bought Green's share from his estate for only $2,000.

Extensive as were the Blackwell and other local enterprises, another firm was coming into the field, which, small and modest at the start, was eventually to tower so far above them that finally the big Bull factory became merely a unit in their enterprises.

Brodie Duke, not satisfied with the outlook on the farm, left his father and brothers in 1869, bought a small two-room building on Main Street, and began manufacturing on his own account. Grinding tobacco on the lower floor, keeping supplies in the upper story, he slept and lived in the factory, cooking his own meals for a while, later having a colored servant come in to cook for him, clean the rooms and keep the place tidy. "Semper Idem," the title used originally for his product, was soon succeeded by another brand which was to become universally known—"Duke of Durham."

Five years later Washington Duke and the other sons, James and Benjamin, moved to Durham. Joining forces with Brodie, they bought a lot on Main Street, and built a factory for their joint use. Three stories high with a floorage of forty by seventy feet, this was a sizeable plant, fifteen "hands" being employed. The building stood on part of the site where the Dukes later erected their huge plant, now occupied by the Liggett and Myers Company, which produces "Chesterfield" cigarettes by the million.

Operating side by side, the two firms were separate concerns. A partition divided the building, Brodie occupying one portion, his father and brothers the other. When more room was required another building was put up for Brodie. Manufacturing different brands, each having his own customers, they coöperated closely, sold goods for each other, and made money.

"Buck" Duke, though a mere stripling, took a leading part in the enterprise. Attending the "breaks," as the sales in the warehouses were known, buying the raw material for the factory, he was soon regarded as one of the best judges of leaf and shrewdest buyers in the town. That was saying a good deal, for Durham had become an important market, the leaf was sold at auction and competition was fierce. To compete with the clever traders who gathered at these sales a buyer had to know his business thoroughly. But the youthful trader reveled in the daily battles of wit and trade, and held his own with the best of them.

Talking with the farmers who brought their tobacco to market, he was eager to get their views, constantly asking what they thought of crops and prices and how they were "getting along."

Mornings he spent in buying tobacco, afternoons working with the hired hands in the factory, at night he planned means of attracting customers; thus learning the details of buying, manufacturing, packing, shipping and advertising. Then he turned to salesmanship.

"GOLDEN BELT" TOBACCO

Fond of "trading," feeling sure of his ability to sell goods, he was determined to "have a try" at it. Sent out in 1875, his first trip was so successful that from that time forth, going on the road at every opportunity, he traveled throughout the South and West. Soon dealers in a dozen States knew and liked "young Duke," as they called him, and he won a host of friends and customers.

Before reaching voting age he was in general charge of the business, directing the buying and manufacturing as well as selling, though, "when I was away on the road," he explained, "one of my brothers, father or somebody else looked after those things."

Though the firm was prospering and tobacco salesmen as a rule were known as liberal spenders, Duke practiced the most rigid personal economy. Calling on customers as long as the stores were open, he traveled at night on freight trains and by day in coaches to save the expense of a bed at a hotel or a berth in a sleeping car. Such large sales were made that more money was needed to buy raw material and manufacture goods. Unwilling to borrow, even with the prospect of larger profits, the problem was finally solved by selling a fractional part of the business to a partner at a price that put them in possession of the needed funds.

This was brought about in 1878, when the firm of W. Duke, Sons and Company was formed. Gerald Watts, of Baltimore, impressed with the enterprise of the Dukes, sought the agency for their tobacco in Maryland. He was also seeking a business opening for his son, and convinced that the Duke concern offered an excellent opportunity, proposed an investment and partnership. Having kept the ownership up to that time strictly in the family, the Dukes were impressed with the possibilities of expansion. They were

JAMES B. DUKE

making substantial profits, but were far from rich. Every dollar that could be raised was being put into the business, which was growing rapidly. With additional capital, a great deal more could be accomplished.

The Baltimore capitalist's offer was accepted and a partnership formed with $70,000 capital, the firm consisting of the four Dukes and George W. Watts, each putting in an equal share. Though James had worked like a Trojan, saving every dollar, all he could raise was $3,000. But they had no idea of leaving him out of the company. He was too important a factor. His father loaned him $11,000 to make up his share, and he held an equal part with the others. Two years later Richard H. Wright, who manufactured the "Orange of Durham" brand, bought Washington Duke's interest and was taken into the firm.

Each of the partners was put in charge of some particular part of the enterprise, James Duke taking charge of manufacture, running the factory; Benjamin conducting the correspondence and business of the office, Mr. Watts being the treasurer, Mr. Wright head of the sales department. Making a strong combination, they began to cut a wide swath.

Tobacco is almost the oldest of American products. Columbus, discovering it in use among the natives, was amazed at the sight of men walking around with burning firebrands in their mouths, blowing clouds of smoke from their lips.

When Amadas and Barlowe sailed into the waters of what is now North Carolina, in 1584, they found the Indians smoking, using tobacco not only in ceremonials, puffing pipes of peace, but much as men do now, for the soothing effects and the indefinable pleasure it affords them. It was their patron, Sir Walter Raleigh, who introduced tobacco at Queen Elizabeth's court

"GOLDEN BELT" TOBACCO

and popularized its use in England. Tobacco is closely linked with the history of the earliest English settlements, with Raleigh's first colonists who landed on Roanoke Island, but disheartened, were carried back to Great Britain by Sir Francis Drake; and their successors, the "Lost Colony of Roanoke."

Following the permanent settlement at Jamestown tobacco culture became an important industry. In 1613 the leaf was already being raised in commercial quantities in Virginia, and became the colony's most valuable product. Adopted officially as the standard of value, notes issued against the leaf stored in warehouses were used as cash, and were for years the principal currency.

Captain John Smith related that tobacco culture paid six times as much as the same labor expended in growing wheat. The "gentlemen adventurers" naturally turned to raising tobacco. Acreage and yield increased enormously, with consequent overproduction.

From 54 cents a pound in 1620, when 55,000 pounds were produced, the market went down to six cents in 1639, when a "bumper" crop of 1,500,000 pounds was gathered. Suffering and hardship followed, discouraging the colonists, who blamed almost everything but themselves for their condition, denouncing tobacco growing as a failure—and that was almost three centuries before a "trust" was thought of.

Before the Revolution the prosperity of nearly half the Southern States depended on tobacco. By 1790, when Washington was President and the new republic was getting on its feet, the yearly crop had reached 120,000,000 pounds. Lower in price than it had been during the hard times of 1639, the poorer grades bringing only three to four cents a pound, the crop was made profitable by culture on a large scale.

Cotton is generally looked upon as the principal

source of the South's wealth, and so it has been for more than a century. But cotton culture was extremely limited in colonial days. Enough was raised to supply the spinning wheels and hand-looms which made coarse cloths for dwellers on the plantations. But so long as the lint had to be picked off the seed by hand, the process, even with slave labor, was slow and costly. It was not until Eli Whitney invented the cotton gin and the power loom was devised that real manufacture began, and cotton cultivation became general. Up to the beginning of the Nineteenth Century tobacco, not cotton, was the principal "money crop" of the South, and had been so during the entire colonial period.

In the half-century between 1790 and 1840 the industry made slow progress. The French Revolution, the long Napoleonic wars and our own War of 1812, with subsequent embargoes and conflicts at sea, interrupted commerce. High import duties followed, tariffs and taxes were imposed, and there was small increase in tobacco exports for many years.

Tobacco culture was general in North Carolina from its first settlement, but in the forties Virginia and Kentucky were still producing 60 per cent of the total crop. Virginia in 1849 raised nearly five times as much as North Carolina, producing 56,803,227 pounds to the latter's 11,984,786. The principal markets and factories being in Virginia, most of the Carolina product was sold there. Practically the entire crop was dark leaf, "sun cured," of which other States produced a better grade.

In 1852 came a discovery which brought about a radical change. Two farmers in Caswell County, N. C., not far from Durham, Eli and Elisha Slade, "curing" by chance some tobacco by fire, found that, instead of the dark brown color resulting from ex-

"GOLDEN BELT" TOBACCO

posure to sun and air, the product was a bright yellow leaf. This resulted, it appeared, from curing by artificial heat. Barns were built with sheet-iron covered firing flues beneath, and "flue curing" became a widespread practice.

The flue-cured product bringing high prices, farmers strove to produce the new grade. But experience proved that by no means all tobacco would cure with this attractive color. It was confined in fact to almost a new type of the weed, grown only in sandy, siliceous soil. The region in which Caswell and Durham were located proving particularly adapted to its culture, production soon spread to the adjoining counties.

Brighter in color than that produced elsewhere, the leaf was called "bright" tobacco, and the region in which it was produced the "Bright Tobacco Belt." Later a more idealistic title was adopted, "The Golden Belt"—not inappropriate, for the yellow leaf brought a flood of gold to growers and manufacturers.

Farmers began to shred and press this tobacco, for smoking and chewing. Loading wagons with the smokers, plugs and twists, they peddled the product through the country. First the crude work of manufacture was done in barns, granaries or prize-houses, where tobacco had been prized into hogsheads in the days when the leaf was packed into these huge barrels, through which were run axles, and pulled by horses the cumbersome cylinders were "rolled" to Petersburg or Richmond. Small factories were built on the farms, and a considerable industry developed. It was in this way that the Dukes, like many others, began manufacturing.

With the establishment of factories in the towns came a demand for more leaf than near-by farms could supply. To induce growers further away to bring in

JAMES B. DUKE

their crops, warehouses were built, at which the loads of leaf were sold at auction. Competition was keen between the rival buyers, bidding was brisk, good prices were paid, and Durham became the largest market south of Virginia.

Even more potent was the energy with which its manufacturers prosecuted their efforts for trade. Seeking customers everywhere, they sold their goods throughout the United States, and exported to Europe. Distributing lithographed posters and window cards by thousands, painting signs on fences, barns and billboards, they spent large sums also for advertising in newspapers and magazines. Premiums and prizes ranging from mantel clocks to razors were offered to dealers and consumers. Sign painters were sent throughout America and finally to Europe and Asia, painting advertisements in every available spot.

Vastly effective, this exploitation made Durham "the town renowned the world around." Its tobaccos were sold in almost every land. James Russell Lowell introduced this favorite smoke to his friends in England. Thomas Carlyle used it. When Anne Thackeray called on Lord Tennyson, she found the poet laureate peacefully smoking "Bull Durham." Blackwell and Carr had led the way, but it was the Dukes with their cigarettes who finally "taught the world to smoke Southern tobacco."

CHAPTER FIVE

Making Cigarettes by the Million

NOT content with "playing second fiddle" to any one, James Duke sought a field in which his firm would not be overshadowed. Hundreds of factories were making smoking tobacco, one so firmly established that rivaling it seemed hopeless.

"My company is up against a stone wall," he remarked. "It can't compete with Bull Durham. Something has to be done and that quick. I am going into the cigarette business."

The Dukes, however, did not plunge into the venture without due consideration. Making a survey of trade conditions, the partners studied the matter from every standpoint, but finally "J. B." was permitted to try out his plan.

Cigarettes, almost unknown in this country before the Civil War, were just coming into general use. Russians and Turks had smoked them for generations. French and British soldiers acquired the habit when serving in the Crimea in 1856. After the Crimean War they carried home the paper-covered tubes, which became favorites in England, and from there the custom spread to America.

Introduced here in 1867, their manufacture was begun in a small way. But in 1869 only 1,751,495 were made in the United States, not enough to keep a modern factory busy half a day. By 1880 they had become an important part of the industry, revenue tax being paid on 408,708,366 that year, but the trade was yet in its infancy.

"Bright" tobacco, raised in North Carolina, was found particularly adapted to cigarettes. But not until 1881 was cigarette manufacture begun in Durham, both

JAMES B. DUKE

the Dukes and the "Bull" factory concluding to go into it at about the same time.

Local workers being unfamiliar with cigarette manufacture, the labor had to be imported, the first rollers, both in England and America, coming from Russia, where cigarette making was a government monopoly, its secrets closely guarded.

When the Dukes entered this field only a few firms in America, mainly in New York and Virginia, were making cigarettes on a large scale. Foremen and expert workers had to be drawn from them. Two brothers, Jewish workmen from Russia, who learned their trade in Kovno and had worked in London and New York, were the first makers brought to Durham— J. M. Seigel, who took charge of this department for the Dukes, and David, employed in the "Bull" factory.

Making cigarettes by hand, as were all these early cigarettes, required hundreds of trained "rollers." Even with the use of negro labor it was a costly process. Not long after the Duke firm began manufacture, however, developments occurred which revolutionized the industry.

Most important was the introduction of machinery. Inventors, realizing the demand, had been at work along this line for several years. James Bonsack, a young Virginian, finally succeeded in devising a machine which fed in the tobacco and paper in continuous rolls, pasting, cutting the tubes into proper length, and performing the entire operation. An expert hand roller might make 2,000 or 2,500 cigarettes a day. Here was a mechanism that could turn them out at the rate of 100,000 daily. A wonderful invention, it was erratic, still to be perfected.

Any one investing in the contrivances was taking a

CIGARETTES BY MILLIONS

chance. Leased to manufacturers on royalty, the machines had been placed in several plants, but failed to meet requirements. Mechanics and tobacco experts seriously doubted whether they could ever be made to work satisfactorily. There was, moreover, a distinct prejudice against machine-made cigarettes.

Recognizing fully the hazards as well as the possibilities in mechanical production, the Dukes decided to make the experiment. Two of the Bonsack machines were ordered, and installed in their plant. Overseeing every detail of installation, Buck Duke regarded them as his "babies," and no mother ever watched over her infants more carefully than he did over those initial machines.

As the devices had made no marked progress elsewhere, and the Dukes were willing to install a considerable number if they proved successful, the inventor granted them a lower royalty than was being charged other companies, an advantage worth considering. But numerous difficulties were to be overcome.

Marvelous pieces of mechanism, it was irritating and discouraging to find that minor imperfections were preventing the success of a device on which so much depended.

As he watched the machines being installed, "J. B.," impressed by one of the mechanics who seemed to him unusually bright and capable, turned to his brother Ben and said, "We must keep with us that young Irishman." The young Irishman, William T. O'Brien, proved to be a mechanical genius, and became one of their mainstays.

Studying the machines from every angle, Mr. Duke asked countless questions and figured out how they could be improved. Working with O'Brien, often far into the night, defects, one by one, were remedied and

JAMES B. DUKE

improvements made. At one time only a little rubber band, to which the tobacco stuck now and then, clogging the mechanism, stood in the way of success, but this required days to overcome. At last they had a machine which worked perfectly. The problem of quantity production was solved.

The Dukes had no monopoly of the invention, however. Allen and Ginter, of Richmond, had installed a few Bonsack machines, but feared their practicability, and did not until 1887 place them throughout the Richmond factory. The Kinney Tobacco Company also later used the Bonsack invention. Goodwin and Company had a second device, the Emory, which they owned, and Kimball and Company had another, the Allison machine. But the Bonsacks proved the most successful, and the Dukes were first to use them in numbers.

Cigarettes had been poorly packed. Some were sold in boxes, which were expensive; but for the most part they were put up in flimsy paper packs, easily crushed. A proper package was needed, attractive in appearance, protecting cigarettes from breakage or crushing, and so devised that they could be readily extracted by the smoker. There being nothing in existence meeting these requirements, Mr. Duke himself invented it. The result was the familiar sliding box, which later came into general use.

Composed of two pieces of pasteboard, one, pasted together, constituting the cover; the other, folded, forming the inner portion, the sliding box, millions of them were used annually, and bore on the inside slip Duke's name and signature.

Machines were designed which would at a single blow stamp out the pasteboard shapes, and the Dukes installed their own printing and box-making machinery,

CIGARETTES BY MILLIONS

and all the operations of cutting, printing and completing the package were performed automatically in their plant.

Marketing then became the problem. The Bonsack machines turned out cigarettes more rapidly than they could be sold, the first year there was a large overproduction, and warehouses were piled with surplus stock.

Use of the machines had reduced the cost of manufacture from eighty cents to thirty cents a thousand. Turning out better made, better packed cigarettes at less cost than other manufacturers, the Dukes could produce them in unlimited quantities. The one thing necessary was to sell them.

With a daring out of all proportion to their financial means or backing, they decided upon a selling campaign that would cover Europe and the Orient, as well as America. In charge of the campaign in this country, covering the principal cities as thoroughly as he had the local territory, James Duke began an intensive drive for new customers, eventually selling more cigarettes in three months than some competitors had disposed of in as many years.

Sent abroad to introduce the firm's products in other lands, Mr. Wright made a trip around the globe, traveling from one country to another for nineteen months, familiarizing dealers and wholesalers with the new brands and contracting for their sale. Going to London and Glasgow, he sold tobacconists in England, Scotland and Ireland. Antwerp, Brussels and Rotterdam were visited; Paris, Berlin, Bremen and Hamburg, establishing agencies in Germany, France, Belgium and Holland. Denmark, Norway and Sweden were invaded, stocking the dealers in Copenhagen, Christiania and Stockholm, and he made a trip to St.

JAMES B. DUKE

Petersburg, entering Russia, the home of the cigarette.

Penetrating into Africa and Asia, Australia and the isles of the sea, he visited Cape Town, Durban, Mauritius, Bombay, Delhi, Benares, Madras, Ceylon, Singapore and Java, returning by Sydney, Melbourne and New Zealand. After a year and a half abroad, Mr. Wright, succeeding far beyond expectations, returned to find that even more had been accomplished in this country.

In connection with the sales drive the firm carried on an extensive advertising campaign that familiarized the public with their brands and made their largest competitors "sit up and take notice." But advertising alone was not depended upon to market their products. They backed it up by salesmanship that extended from the factory door clear through to the consumer.

Making a move that won thousands of customers at one stroke, Duke captured the lion's share of the trade while his competitors were doubtfully considering what action to take.

Following the Civil War, the United States Government had imposed a heavy internal revenue tax on all kinds of tobacco. As the nation recovered from the ravages of war and governmental receipts from other sources increased, a point was reached where revenue taxes could be reduced. This reduction was being discussed in Congress at the very time the Dukes had gone into machine production and were seeking some means of disposing of their surplus.

Congress voted finally, in March, 1883, to reduce the tax on cigarettes. Smokers, of course, expected some reduction in the selling price, but not more than a cent or two on the package, if that. Cigarettes were then selling at ten cents, the universal price for the less expensive grades. Deciding that the moment had ar-

CIGARETTES BY MILLIONS

rived to make a bold play for trade, Duke cut the price in half, to five cents a package. Not waiting until the new taxes went into effect, he announced that orders from jobbers would be filled immediately at the lower prices, if three-fourths of the goods ordered were to be delivered after the reduced tax was in force.

The Duke cigarettes suddenly became the cheapest in the market. Orders poured in from every part of the country. No question now as to disposing of the surplus; that was quickly absorbed. The problem was to enlarge manufacturing facilities quickly enough to take care of the increased business. Competitors were distanced. With low manufacturing costs, better packing, large advertising and lower prices, the Dukes were in the strongest possible position.

The wooden factory in which they had operated for years being too small for their needs, work was begun on the large brick structure, known for a generation as the "Duke Factory," which was completed in 1884, and enlarged from time to time, eventually reached a capacity of ten million cigarettes a day.

What a close shave they had in getting started in cigarette manufacture, how near they came to failure and how that one stroke carried the undertaking through to success was revealed by Mr. Duke long afterwards.

"We commenced in 1881 and did not do very much," he said, "because the Government at that time was agitating the reduction of the tax from $1.75 a thousand to fifty cents. They did not get the bill through Congress until March, 1883, reducing the tax to fifty cents a thousand, which took effect the first of May.

"During the agitation of the tax our brands, of course, were not in public favor. Dealers would not buy to any extent and take the chance of losing the

JAMES B. DUKE

difference in tax, provided it should be reduced. So we had a pretty hard struggle those two years. We had accumulated quite some cigarettes on hand and were ready to close our factory and did close it. As soon as Congress passed the law reducing the tax to fifty cents, I saw then that there was a chance to sell ten cigarettes for five cents, and we immediately reduced the price."

Making the reduction two months before the tax went into effect entailed considerable loss. But the move gave a large immediate market for the surplus, started the factory going again, and put the business on a firm footing. In the next nine months they sold 30,000,000 cigarettes, which was merely the start. Orders came in rapidly, larger buildings were erected, and in two years the $70,000 capitalization was increased to $250,000.

This period also marked two important changes. James Duke in 1884 established his factory in New York, and Washington Duke, who had been out of the business for several years, in 1885 reëntered the firm, buying back the interest he had sold to Mr. Wright, who left Durham to go with the Lone Jack Cigarette Company in Lynchburg, Va. The Duke firm was incorporated as a joint stock company, and father and sons were together again in business as they had been in the beginning.

CHAPTER SIX

The Youngest Duke Invades New York

MEASURED by local standards, the Dukes were on the high road to success. But this did not satisfy the junior member of the firm, who had a vision of national commerce and world trade. New York was the commercial center of the country. He determined to plant the Duke banner there.

Older firms, with larger capital—Kinney Brothers, Goodwin and Company, W. S. Kimball and Company, Allen and Ginter—still dominated the cigarette industry. Close proximity to the long-established trade of the larger cities gave them a distinct advantage. Duke decided to fight these competitors on their own ground.

Leaving his partners in charge of the home office, in the spring of 1884 he moved to New York. This seemed a hazardous venture. The firm was earning handsome profits, but most of its available funds were needed to run the Durham plant.

Only twenty-seven years old when he launched his New York enterprise, Duke had less than $100,000 capital at his command. To enter into competition with the large and wealthy firms that were his opponents was like a young David going up against commercial Goliaths.

Beginning in the most modest way, setting up his establishment in a region of low rents on the crowded East Side, he first opened a small factory at No. 6 Rivington Street, near the Bowery, enlarging his quarters as the output increased. Among the brands produced were "Cameo," "Cross Cut" and "Duke's Best."

Days he spent in the factory, superintending every part of the manufacturing, from the leaf to the fin-

JAMES B. DUKE

ished product. Nights were devoted to visiting tobacco stores, meeting the dealers.

"Getting acquainted" was quite as important here, setting up in a new location, as it had been in starting out to drum up trade in North Carolina. And he made friends in the tobacco shops of New York in very much the same way he had in the country stores and towns down South. Talking with proprietors and clerks, he not only won new customers, but learned what appealed most to dealers and consumers, what would and would not sell. Probably no one in the industry knew so many dealers personally, or was more familiar with all the ins and outs of the trade. Wooden Indians were then the standard signs, standing in front of nearly every tobacco shop. Mr. Duke, his friends remarked, knew more of these Indians and their owners than any other man in New York.

Putting into the business every dollar at his command, he sought the cheapest decent living quarters that could be found, taking a room in Harlem. That proved too far away; too much time was lost in getting to and from work. So he rented a room nearer the factory, taking his meals at restaurants on the Bowery.

Keeping down personal expenses and the cost of manufacture to the lowest practicable point, Duke was lavish in expenditures for advertising and exploiting his goods. By intensive sales methods he gained, within a few months, a foothold in the city, his brands being placed in hundreds of stores where larger competitors, with infinitely more capital and prestige, had been supreme. Within a year he was winning his way steadily in New York and the Northern markets. Smokers liked his cigarettes, which were selling rapidly, and the little factory was kept busy. By the end

THE RISING YOUNG TOBACCO MAGNATE

INVADES NEW YORK

of the second year the New York branch began to pay.

But this necessitated drawing heavily on the home office for funds. His wealthy competitors could command almost unlimited amounts, but Duke, with his slender capital and small plant, had no such standing with the banks—a handicap that must be overcome.

Going to a bank president, met in the course of business, he told of his broad plans and narrow means. Surprised at the young manufacturer's ambitions, but more impressed with his simple integrity and truthfulness, the banker agreed to extend the needed credit. Duke, however, considered this a reserve to be used only in case of necessity, and carried through this campaign successfully without borrowing the money he might have had. But he almost "scraped the bottom of the barrel," as Southerners say, moving from a room costing three dollars to one that could be rented for two dollars a week.

Having turned the corner financially in cigarette manufacture, and seeing a big future for a combination smoking and chewing tobacco sold at a low price, he put on the market "Honest Long Cut," which, quickly introduced in the principal cities, had a considerable sale.

Widespread advertising was needed to "put over" this novelty, however, involving large sums of money much of which had to be borrowed. D. C. Patterson, now president of the Imperial Tobacco Company of Canada (Limited), who labored in close association with Mr. Duke during that period, relates how he built up his credit, to be used in case of emergency.

"About this time, while maintaining a fair bank balance," Mr. Patterson recalls, "Mr. Duke began to negotiate with the financial house of Goldman, Sachs & Co., for small loans of $10,000 or so, at thirty to sixty days. These notes were always paid a day in advance. I don't think one of them ever came due without Mr. Duke making inquiry and cautioning me not to overlook payment. It was not long before representatives from Goldman, Sachs & Co. and Ward & Co. called on us regularly, soliciting W. Duke Sons & Company's paper, and we kept discounting notes and piling up funds in the bank.

"I asked Mr. Duke why he was borrowing at six per cent when he had a big balance in the bank drawing no interest. He smiled and said: 'It's all right; you will know some day.' Of course I did know later what, at that time, I was unable to comprehend, that his purpose was to establish a credit for the firm's paper on the money market."

The wisdom of this foresight was soon disclosed. Sales of the new brand had become "spotty." Total volume had decreased, but there was sufficient demand to indicate that it had merit. Then Duke marshaled his resources, consisting principally of absolute faith in himself and an established credit, and launched a huge publicity campaign.

G. Houghtaling & Co., at that time the largest sign painters and bill posters in the United States, decorated the country from Maine to California, north of the Mason and Dixon Line, with bill posters and signboards advertising "Honest Long Cut." Under the stimulus of this and other forms of advertising, costing more than $750,000 annually, that brand alone reached a sale of over 500,000 pounds a month.

Next, Duke began to popularize his cigarettes by putting photographs of stage celebrities in each package. Then coupons were placed in the packages, entitling the holder, for a given number, to a crayon picture of some historical notable. The list ranged from

INVADES NEW YORK

Christopher Columbus to George Washington, appealing to all nationalities. Later pictures of baseball players, sovereigns and rulers, flags of all nations were placed in cigarette packs. Boys began to make collections of "cigarette pictures," to trade and preserve them, and the craze extended to every town and village.

Duke became one of the country's largest advertisers, setting the pace for big business in other lines as well as his own. In the use of large space in newspapers, magazines, theatre programs, on bill-boards and everywhere signs and arguments catch the public eye, he was a pioneer, backing his faith with his money.

At times his partners were alarmed by the vast sums poured out for publicity. But he demonstrated that national advertising on a large scale not only could be made to pay, but was one of the best investments for any firm that had something to sell that the public wanted. He created what experts now call "consumer demand." Smokers and chewers walked into stores by thousands, calling for his brands by name. Familiar with them, they would take nothing else.

From this extensive exploitation the firm reaped rich returns. Factories and plants had to be enlarged continually, to keep pace with sales. In a few years the Dukes occupied a commanding position in the North and West as they had in the South, and held a large part of the national trade.

Expenditures, however, had run into millions of dollars, at times approaching if not exceeding the entire amount invested in bricks, mortar and machinery. But it was this enterprise that made their products known in every city and hamlet, making their brands and good-will more valuable than their factories.

During these six years, pouring out money in extending his business, Mr. Duke was spending less on himself, working harder and devoting more attention to details than was many a clerk drawing weekly wages.

His mode of living was simplicity itself. He had a modest room on Gramercy Park at $10 a week just before the consummation of negotiations which gave the Duke concern $7,500,000 interest in the newly-formed American Tobacco Company. That was more than he had previously paid for such accommodation. Not mean or "close" in any sense of the word, economy was a cardinal principle with him, one which he continually preached to employees, telling them that whatever salary a man received he should save half of it. "Walk while you are young so that you can ride when you are old," was one of his mottoes.

Making a practice of being at his office in time to see the factory hands arrive in the morning, he made repeated excursions through the work-rooms, examining the stock on the work benches. Employees believed he had the uncanny faculty of picking the only faulty package out of a lot containing thousands otherwise perfect. Sending for a carton of goods already packed, he would open it on his desk and examine each package. If a stamp or label pasted on crooked was discovered, the superintendent was sent for. Needless to say, the whole working force was kept on its toes.

He personally selected his advertising matter, and when show-cards, calendars or posters were submitted the office staff would be called in and each one asked which he or she preferred and why. Keeping an ear close to the ground in estimating popular taste, he catered to the wants of the masses rather than the select few.

His hobby in the office was a book in which was recorded, independently of the sales ledger, "Sales by

INVADES NEW YORK

Brands by Towns." Poring over this for hours he would study the increase or decrease in sales in various sections of the country, and in case of a decrease would send an inquiry at once to the salesman in that territory, and strengthen the weak spots by increased effort and advertising.

A watchful eye was kept on credits, especially the weak accounts, and he had many, his chief accountant recalls, for he based credit largely on character and enterprise. An energetic peddler whose trade reached into nooks and corners overlooked by the jobber was considered a more important distributor than the big jobber with a Bradstreet's rating. If there was an occasional loss, which seldom occurred, it was good advertising. Goods well advertised were sure to reach the larger buyers through one jobber or another, he pointed out, but the peddler does introductory work, placing the products most easily procurable in advance of the introduction by the regular jobber of opposition brands.

No detail escaped his scrutiny and constructive criticism. Certificates for dealers packed in each 500-package carton, having a cash value of fifty cents each, had to be signed as a safeguard against fraud. Five girls were assigned the task, and after a week four of them averaged some three thousand signatures each per day. The fifth, Maggie McConichie, did scarcely more than half that number. Too long a name to write, Mr. Duke decided. "One name is as good as another," he told her; "change your signature to A. B. Cox." Thenceforth "Miss Cox" doubled her capacity, thereby saving half her wages and having the satisfaction of excelling in her work.

Keeping in touch with the trade was a cardinal point. Even after the business ran into millions, Duke spent

JAMES B. DUKE

many of his evenings in visiting retail tobacco shops. Making some purchase, he would sit on a shipping case, if no chair was available, listening to customers' comments, asking questions between sales until the storekeepers not infrequently were provoked. Then he would ask the dealer if he would not like some showcards to decorate his store. These would be sent up next day, and the merchant was almost invariably flattered by discovering that he had talked with Duke, "the tobacco man," and was thereafter free with information.

Another method he had of gauging the relative demand for different brands was by counting the empty cigarette packages on the streets. This habit of watching the sidewalks as he walked along disclosed at least one superstition of his. He picked up every pin that pointed toward him, and the under lapel of his coat was sometimes padded with "lucky" pins.

Not believing in vacations, the proprietor took none himself in that busy period and held that no one really interested in his occupation should need a vacation; that the pleasure he got out of his work was all the recreation needed.

After the formation of the American Tobacco Company, when the talent represented by the five companies was recruited into the service of the one corporation, he did not relax, as he might have done, but became engrossed in the task of coördinating the several units.

Devotion of his wealth to the good of others was in his thoughts even at that early period. Asked what he intended doing with his money, for he was a bachelor and already had more than one man could possibly need, he replied:

"I am going to give a good part of what I make to

INVADES NEW YORK

the Lord, but I can make better interest for Him by keeping it while I live."

"This was not said in any spirit of irreverence," Mr. Patterson states, "but was in accord with his wise judgment in conserving rather than dissipating the resources necessary for the accomplishment of greater aims, which he then had in mind, and which have since been realized in a practical way for the increasing benefit of future generations.

"In this connection, I have often heard Mr. Duke say that he would do something for the 'poor old nigger,' for whom, as a race, he seemed to have a great sympathy. Behind all this ambition and tireless energy was a fixed purpose, and who can doubt that through that purpose the guiding hand of Providence was working to this noble end."

Having a rugged constitution, never tiring of work, his deep interest in it seemed to have a regenerating effect. His retentive memory was sometimes disconcerting to those who did not recall details which he remembered vividly, to the last date and figure. Thoughtful, believing every man should think for himself, he frequently remarked that he did his best thinking after going to bed. He loved to have his little joke with associates whose only reason for their politics was the section of their birth.

" 'Why are you a Democrat?' he would ask," one of them recalls. "The best answer I could give was that I was born that way. Laughing heartily, he would say: 'You are a Democrat because your father was. That's no reason at all; you ought to think for yourself.' "

Having a strong family attachment, being particularly devoted to his father and brother, he had few social friends outside of business and never encouraged

JAMES B. DUKE

his employees to make such acquaintances, believing it a waste of time and a distraction that hindered one's success.

Dignified and serious in manner, cordial and friendly toward employees, high and low, he was intensely interested in their welfare, and they valued nothing so much as his approval. Without urging or pushing workmen or aids, laboring harder than they did, and always "on the job," the example of his own industry and their confidence in his judgment and sincerity drew from them the best they had to give, and this was given in a spirit that wages or salary alone could not compensate.

"Is it fair?" was his yardstick in dealings with others, workmen as well as business men. One evidence of this was the fact that during his régime there was not a strike in the Duke factories, and few labor troubles occurred in any of his large establishments.

Going straight to the point when he had anything to say, his decisions were based on deliberate, logical reasoning. Never a reader, he was at the same time an earnest student, but his study was men and affairs, not books. A keen observer, quick to remedy mistakes, he was not slow to profit by experience and observation.

"By industry, thrift and self-denial while maintaining the highest standard of business ethics, he built his own character, shaped his own ideals," says one who was at his side during the years of struggle in New York, "and out of this process came the man of vision, who overcoming all obstacles, succeeded in reaching the top, was acknowledged leader of his peers and has, to his everlasting credit, left a legacy to others in character building that is not second in importance to his wonderful gifts to charity."

His promptness in selecting assistants was thoroughly

INVADES NEW YORK

characteristic. "On one of his visits to Durham, in the spring of 1885," Mr. Patterson relates, "Mr. Duke sent for me and offered me a position in his New York office. In answer to his question, I told him I would like to go to New York. He told me what my salary would be at the start, and said:

"After that everything will depend upon yourself. I have only one instruction to give you—don't ask me to raise your salary. I always know what my people are worth to me, and I pay them what they are worth without being asked."

Leaving on time, at three days' notice, Mr. Patterson, like many others whom Mr. Duke took into his employ, was put in the way that led to steady promotion, with continually increasing pay, and remaining with the Dukes and allied interests, won a high position in the tobacco trade.

Generous to those who rendered loyal service, Mr. Duke gave credit for everything of value accomplished, as well as financial rewards. Eager to have others prosper with him, this feeling extended to dealers, agents and customers, as well as stockholders and employees.

When the gift of millions to education and philanthropy was announced and praise of his generosity filled the newspapers early in 1925, a former employee in his first New York factory, signing himself modestly "One of the Hands," wrote from Brooklyn this letter to the New York *Evening Post*:

"When I read your account of James B. (Buck) Duke's phenomenal rise from poverty to riches, I thought that a few words appended to that tale would not go amiss.

"When James B. Duke opened a cigarette factory at No. 6 Rivington Street near the Bowery, thirty-five or thirty-six years ago, I was one of the many to be employed by him. He, a few years later, moved to a larger factory at 28th

JAMES B. DUKE

Street and First Avenue, where, within a short time, he had four machines installed and had men from the South to operate them. The output increased to such an extent that he sought and obtained larger quarters at 39th Street and First Avenue, where he installed eighteen or twenty more machines and where he remained up to the merging of the Kinney Tobacco Company and Duke Tobacco Company into the American Tobacco.

"During all these years, I, as well as the rest of his employees, found 'Buck' Duke (as we always termed him) one of the most kindly, affable men we have ever met. Considerate in all ways, his employees' interests were his, and his kindly word and genial smile were the factors which kept the Rivington Street hands with him until years later when a fire wiped out the plant at 39th Street and First Avenue."

Six years after landing in New York the Carolinian had become the largest factor in the cigarette industry. In 1890, just before the formation of the tobacco combine, a book of sketches of leading firms stated:

"The Dukes have enlarged their facilities from time to time until at the present writing they have the largest cigarette and smoking tobacco establishment in the world, and are doing a business that amounts to about $4,500,000 per annum. In addition to their mammoth tobacco works at Durham, they have a branch factory in New York, in which they employ over five hundred hands. They have also in Durham, ware and prize houses which combined would cover five acres of land."

Internal revenue taxes, the barometer of tobacco manufacture, indicated strikingly their progress. From $90,000 in 1883 these taxes paid by the Dukes increased by 1888 to $517,783, and in 1889, just before the American Tobacco Company was organized, reached a round $600,000. Their output had increased to 940,000,000 cigarettes annually, nearly half of the country's total production.

CHAPTER SEVEN

Founding the American Tobacco Company

Success was won only after a long and desperate fight. Finding that the young Southerner was cutting deeply into their trade, distancing them in their own territory, the "Big Four" retaliated. A "tobacco war" ensued that was memorable.

Money was poured out like water, not only in advertising but in giving premiums to consumers, paying bonuses to dealers and in various other ways. Every scheme that could be devised or influence exercised was brought to bear. Five firms—Allen and Ginter, W. S. Kimball and Co., Goodwin and Company, the Kinney Brothers and the Dukes—were the chief contestants, but there were many smaller concerns reaching out for a share of the trade.

"The manufacturers divided their energies," as the New York *Herald Tribune* expressed it, "between pushing their own businesses and cutting each other's throats. Never was there keener, more bitter or more incessant trade rivalry. In one year the Duke firm spent $800,000 in advertising and made net profits of less than half that sum."

Such large amounts were expended that few made any profit at all, and some lost heavily. Out to defeat the audacious invader at any cost, older manufacturers were smashing away vigorously, almost blindly—too exasperated to quit, but wondering when the contest would ever end. Though the attacks were centered on him, Duke, working day and night, directing his forces, devising new moves and checkmating those of opponents, thrived on opposition.

But, detesting waste in any form, incessant warfare seemed foolish to him, "bad business." Why should

JAMES B. DUKE

manufacturers spend time and money fighting each other? Why couldn't they get together, operate in harmony and make larger profits? That this was the logical way out Duke sensed long before, but the time was not ripe for it. Declining to admit defeat, opponents refused to give in, and the "war" went on.

As late as 1887, when some of the largest manufacturers were preparing for their annual dinner, one of them asked in jest if Duke should be bidden to the feast.

"We don't consider him a manufacturer of cigarettes; he will be broke before the year is out," was the reply.

Hearing of the incident Duke laconically replied, "I don't talk, I work."

In a year's time they had offered to buy him out. But his answer, as an associate expressed it, was like that of the Helvetians to Cæsar, "We are accustomed to ask, not to give, hostages."

In another year these manufacturers had agreed to sell their businesses, plants and trade-marks to a company formed on lines laid down by Duke, on terms proposed by him, and of which company he was to be the president. Receiving more than was paid to any other manufacturer save one, he was paid exactly as much as that one was allotted.

With their power, capital and prestige, the older firms had been unable to oust the newcomer. Studying the demands of dealers and customers closely, operating his factory economically, he was still earning a profit when they were losing heavily. But the contest could not continue indefinitely. It was too costly to all concerned.

Combination being the sensible solution, how to bring it about was the question. Through an advertising

AMERICAN TOBACCO CO.

agency which served the various interests, Duke learned of the concern he was giving his competitors. Redoubling his efforts, he increased advertising, pushed sales and forced the fighting.

Soon this brought results. Overtures came from one of his leading rivals, the Kinney Tobacco Company, and through an intermediary negotiations were begun in 1889. Shortly afterward the other companies were brought into the conference.

Consolidation, however, was no easy matter—bringing together vigorous competitors, reconciling conflicting claims and interests, apportioning stock and determining the amounts each was to receive.

Behind the scenes some hard battles were fought. Most difficult to convince was the firm of Allen and Ginter, of Richmond, long the largest factor in the cigarette business and the Dukes' strongest rival.

Taking up the matter with Lewis Ginter, head of the Virginia concern, Mr. Duke explained the plans and suggested his entering the merger. Here was upstart young Durham talking to rich and well-established old Richmond. Mr. Ginter heard him through, and smiled.

"Listen, Duke," Ginter said, "you couldn't buy us out to save your neck. You haven't enough money and you couldn't borrow enough. It's a hopeless proposition."

"I make $400,000 out of my business every year," Duke answered. "I'll spend every cent of it on advertising my goods as long as it is necessary. But I'll bring you into line."

Nearly a year longer the contest continued, but Ginter was at last won over, and the combine was completed.

It was in the "tobacco war" that Mr. Duke first in-

JAMES B. DUKE

troduced the coupon system, now so widely used by the chain tobacco stores. Sending out armies of signpainters, the names of his products were blazoned on walls, barns and billboards, and newspapers and magazines were enlisted in the greatest burst of advertising known in the industry.

Against this, Allen and Ginter, as the New York *Sun* described it, "stuck to tradition, putting in each package of cigarettes a bright picture of a lady in tights. It was a spectacular fight—a battle of tights and paint brushes—but Duke won in the end. Nobody else had then the courage to give battle and the trust was formed."

The story has been told that, when the representatives met to form the merger they agreed to lay their cards on the table, present the complete figures of their business, and the firm which had lost least would be chosen head of the consolidation. When the figures were exhibited, only one showed no loss at all, but a substantial profit. That was Duke and, consequently, he was elected president.

As a matter of fact, that story was apocryphal. There was no such casual agreement, but the result was much the same as if there had been. Investigation of the various firms' affairs demonstrated that, in sales, economical production and marketing, the Dukes were in the lead. James Duke had originated the combination. He was recognized as the ablest, most energetic and successful of them all, and was unanimously elected president.

As a compliment to Major Ginter, regarded as the dean of the manufacturers, the corporation was originally organized in Richmond, being granted a charter by the Legislature, but that action was violently at-

AMERICAN TOBACCO CO.

tacked as legislation encouraging a trust, and the application for a Virginia charter was withdrawn.

As this was the beginning of the various combinations which revolutionized manufacture and marked the rise of Mr. Duke to a commanding position in the industry, it is worth some study in detail.

Organized under the laws of New Jersey, then more liberal to corporations than those of other States, the American Tobacco Company was chartered on January 31, 1890. Five concerns were in the consolidation, the company acquiring the entire plants, good-will and business of Allen and Ginter, Richmond; W. Duke, Sons and Co., New York and Durham; the Kinney Tobacco Co., New York and Virginia; W. S. Kimball and Co., Rochester, N. Y. and Oxford, N. C., and Goodwin and Co., New York.

The capital stock was $25,000,000, consisting of authorized issues of $10,000,000 eight per cent noncumulative preferred, and $15,000,000 common stock. Par value of the preferred shares was $100, and of the common $50. Of this the Dukes received $7,500,000, Allen and Ginter the same amount, the Kinney Company $5,000,000 and the other two firms $2,500,000 each.

Lewis Ginter and John Pope, of Richmond; George Arents and James B. Duke, of New York; Benjamin N. Duke and George W. Watts, of Durham, N. C.; Francis S. Kinney, of Butler, N. J.; William H. Butler and Charles G. Emery, of Brooklyn, N. Y.; and William S. Kimball, of Rochester, N. Y., were the directors, the officers being: James B. Duke, President; John Pope, First Vice President; William S. Kimball, Second Vice President; William H. Butler, Secretary; Charles G. Emery, Treasurer, and Stephen Little, Comptroller.

JAMES B. DUKE

When in September, 1890, the preferred shares were listed on the New York Stock Exchange, the application, signed by the Farmers' Loan and Trust Co., W. D. Searls, vice-president, stated:

"The company is organized for the purpose of curing leaf tobacco, to buy, manufacture and sell tobacco in all its forms, and to establish factories, agencies and depots for the sale and distribution thereof, and to do all things incidental to the business of trading and manufacturing aforesaid, etc., with power to carry on its business in all the other States and Territories of the United States, and in Canada, Great Britain and all other foreign countries."

The corporation, it was announced, "has purchased and is the owner of all real estate, cigarette and tobacco factories, storage warehouses, leaf-curing houses, machinery, fixtures, patents, trade-marks, brands, good will, etc.," of the five firms included; the assets consisting of real estate, factories, patents, brands, good will, etc., $22,365,353; leaf tobacco and raw material, $2,634,647; total, $25,000,000, and cash and cash assets of $1,825,000.

There were no mortgages, liens or liabilities except the ordinary current liabilities incurred in carrying on its business, which did not exceed $100,000. The entire issue of common stock, $15,000,000, and $5,000,000, half of the total issue of preferred stock, were deposited with the Farmers' Loan and Trust Co., to be held in trust for the owners until September, 1891.

Giving his own account of how the American Tobacco Company was formed, Mr. Duke said one of the principal reasons was to "get an organization."

"My father was a very old man and had practically retired from business," he said. "Mr. Watts and my

AMERICAN TOBACCO CO.

brother, B. N. Duke, were in bad health, my brother Brodie L. Duke had nothing at all to do with the business; so that practically left the management in my hands. I had not had the time really to build up an organization to help me, except to do the clerical work or what I directed to be done.

"I thought in selling our business to the American Tobacco Company in connection with other manufacturers we would get a good organization of people who would be of assistance in conducting the business, and then besides I expected to make a profit out of it, because you can handle to better advantage a large business than a small one."

Buying leaf tobacco cheaper was not in his mind, Mr. Duke said. In fact he believed the prices the farmers received averaged more than before, as the company bought direct at the warehouse auctions, eliminating the speculators who had been buying and selling to manufacturers. Cutting out the speculators' profits, he thought, meant more money for the farmer.

One of the greatest economies was in cutting down advertising and selling costs. The Dukes' advertising expenses, he pointed out, were about twenty per cent of their sales. "In other words," he explained, "we spent about $800,000 in 1899 and did a business of between $4,000,000 and $4,500,000." Other companies were spending similar amounts.

Prices of cigarettes to consumers remained the same, five cents a pack. Rates to dealers, which had varied, were in some instances reduced, the manufacturers' price being fixed at $3.80 a thousand, with a rebate of 30 cents to the jobber.

Cigarettes made of Southern "bright" tobacco constituted ninety per cent of the output. Too narrow a dependence, Duke thought. Public taste was fickle; if

JAMES B. DUKE

it changed they might be left in the lurch. Selling one specialty was uneconomical. His company ought to be able to carry a full line to supply all classes of consumers.

That was his object, Mr. Duke said, in buying various factories later. "We wished to manufacture a full variety to make every style of tobacco the public wanted."

Pursuing this policy, other plants were acquired from time to time. In April, 1891, the factories of Marburg Brothers and Gail and Ax of Baltimore, were brought into the combine. Three months later the stockholders voted to increase the common stock issue from $15,000,000 to $21,000,000 and the preferred from $10,000,000 to $14,000,000, making the total authorized capitalization $35,000,000.

From its inception the company earned substantial profits. After paying eight per cent on the preferred and twelve per cent on the common stock in 1891, there was a surplus of $1,291,995, which two years later was increased to $5,333,062. The net earnings in 1894 were $5,069,416, and the total surplus, $7,198,290.

For some years no additional plants were purchased, but going successfully through the panic of 1893 and the succeeding period of depression, when so many firms succumbed, the company demonstrated its earning capacity and the soundness of its structure. A large surplus had been accumulated, and the corporation was in a strong financial as well as commercial position. Mr. Duke's confidence in his plan had been abundantly justified.

Competition, however, was still active. Far from having a monopoly, the combine had to fight for business in not a few lines and sections.

Attacked from the time of its organization as a

AMERICAN TOBACCO CO.

"trust," the American Tobacco Co. differed, in many respects, from others so designated. Henry O. Havemeyer's dictum, "The protective tariff is the mother of trusts," did not apply to the tobacco combine, which in no sense depended on the tariff and, in fact, derived very little benefit from it. Neither did it depend on discriminative railroad rates as had the Standard Oil Company in its early days, or on exclusive contracts. In fact, in characteristics and methods, it differed widely from many other combines.

Though exercising a potent influence, the company could not control the prices of either the raw product or the manufactured article. Any one with sufficient capital was free to set up cigarette or smoking tobacco machinery and begin manufacturing tobacco. Cigarettes were the only products in which the corporation was supreme, and there were many independent manufacturers in that field.

Economy and efficiency in manufacture and marketing; the possession of well established brands which had been made popular through extensive advertising; aggressive business methods and superlative salesmanship were mainly responsible for the company's progress.

Mr. Duke himself never did consider that mere combination was the basis of its success. He had brought the leading firms together to end costly and foolish rivalry and reduce the cost of doing business. That seemed to be, and probably was, the best thing to be done at the time. But when, twenty-one years later, the combine was ordered dissolved, and many stockholders feared ruin and destruction of their interests, of all those concerned the least disturbed was the man who had formed the consolidation and directed it. He had no fears for the future. The company he had

JAMES B. DUKE

built up did not depend for its existence on any arrangement, however strong. His business could get along, combined or alone. Years afterward he remarked:

"I don't know that the combine was really of much advantage to us after all. We were doing well as we were; we were beating the other fellows in manufacturing and selling anyway. I believe we would, in time, have put them out of the running and gotten practically all the business if there never had been any combination."

Not until 1895 did the American Tobacco Company begin to reach out aggressively after other branches of the trade. In May of that year the common stock was listed on the New York Exchange. The statement then issued was very similar to that made when the preferred was listed five years before. Dividends of ten per cent had been paid in 1890 and twelve per cent each year thereafter. With such a record the stock, of course, had a high rating on the Exchange.

Steps were taken soon afterwards to acquire the extensive interests of P. Lorillard and Co., large producers of snuff and plug tobacco. At the same time there were reports of negotiations for various other concerns.

The company was assailed from all sides. Suits were brought in New York and Illinois to prevent the corporation from doing business in those States. Proceedings were instituted in New Jersey to nullify its charter.

A second tobacco contest ensued, this time a determined struggle between the American and the independent cigarette and plug manufacturers.

Under attack from so many quarters, political, legal and commercial, the newspapers reported that the com-

AMERICAN TOBACCO CO.

bine was "fighting for its life." It was a critical time. One emergency after another arose, but Duke met them as they came. Keeping his own counsel, seldom revealing his plans, when he had anything to say he said it in few words, stating exactly what he meant. To those used to the careful phrases and vague statements with which many corporations concealed their operations, his frank, direct announcements came as something of a shock. With him to decide was to act, and his actions at times surprised his own stockholders as well as competitors.

Holders of American Tobacco common who had depended on a steady yield were amazed when, in December, 1895, its president announced that the usual quarterly dividend on the common stock, which in due course was expected in February, would be omitted. Tobacco stocks broke sharply on the exchange. The bears made a vigorous drive on the securities. Many of those who were speculating on narrow margins lost heavily. Mr. Duke and the company were severely criticized, opponents charging that the insiders were depressing the stock in order to "clean out the little fellows" and buy in the outstanding shares at their own figures.

That was far from the truth. Two months in advance Mr. Duke announced that the dividend would be passed and stated his reasons as follows:

To the Stockholders of the American Tobacco Company:

The usual quarterly dividend of 2 per cent on the preferred stock of this company will be paid in February, but no dividend will be paid at that time on its common stock.

From the earnings of the company during the ten months of the current year it is estimated that the earnings of the year will permit the addition of over one and a quarter mil-

JAMES B. DUKE

lion dollars ($1,250,000) to surplus, after paying 8 per cent on the preferred stock and 9 per cent on the common stock.

Yet, on account of the increasing volume of the company's business and the acquisition during the year of new plants and businesses, the company requires more cash working capital than heretofore.

Therefore, in the judgment of its management, it is to the interest of the stockholders, and proper for the prudent prosecution of its growing business, that the sum necessary to pay further dividends on its common stock for this year be retained and applied to working capital.

Thus the business of the company can be properly cared for and extended without departing from its consistent policy of not borrowing money and its assets kept as they now are, the free and unencumbered property of its stockholders.

Very respectfully,

THE AMERICAN TOBACCO COMPANY.

December 6, 1895.

Various explanations and speculations regarding this action were published. "A large holder of tobacco" was quoted as saying: "The tobacco war became virulent only last summer. Up to that time the company's sales were larger than ever before. Clearly, in the last six months the war has resulted in enormous losses." But that was incorrect. The combine's earnings had been reduced, but it was still making substantial profits.

The treasurer's annual report, which appeared early in 1896, showed that the company's funds had been used in a broad expansion. During the year it had purchased three New York concerns, Hall's "Between the Acts" Cigarette Company, H. Ellis and Company, and the Consolidated Cigarette Company, and the James G. Butler Tobacco Company of St. Louis.

Behind these purchases were some interesting moves. Anti-cigarette agitation was at its height. Long-haired

MRS. JAMES B. DUKE

AMERICAN TOBACCO CO.

men and short-haired women were uttering solemn warnings against their baleful effect. Listening to their lurid accounts one would have thought the boy who hid behind the barn to sneak a smoke was taking his life in his hands. Tobacconists were warned not to sell to boys, and several States passed laws prohibiting the sale of cigarettes. Some of these remained on the statute books until the present year, Kansas being last to remove the ban.

This furor over the mildest form of using tobacco seems rather absurd to-day when the use of these "smokes" is almost universal. But it was serious then when the very existence of the "fags" was threatened. Curiously enough, the opposition was directed almost wholly at the paper-covered cigarette. Those made entirely of tobacco escaped criticism.

If conditions changed, Duke was determined to be ready to meet them. Within a few months he bought three of the leading makers of all-tobacco cigarettes and was prepared to turn them out in quantity.

"We thought from the way legislation was going all over the country that the paper cigarette was going to be knocked out," Mr. Duke explained, "and we wanted to be prepared with an organization of people, machinery and brands to go ahead with the all-tobacco cigarette to take the place of the paper ones."

Herman Ellis' plant was bought to bring him into the organization, said Mr. Duke; Hall's to get the popular "Between the Acts" brand, the Consolidated to acquire valuable machinery they owned. There was a definite object behind each purchase made.

The effects of the "tobacco war" were reflected in the earnings, which had declined to $3,971,521 as compared with $5,069,416 for the previous year. Profits had decreased more than a million dollars, but the

JAMES B. DUKE

losses of competitors were much larger in proportion. Eight per cent had been paid on the preferred and nine per cent on the common stock. The surplus, invested mainly in plants, had increased $1,402,000 during the year, making the total $8,600,871.

Two months after the dividend was passed the tobacco combine, in the phrase of Wall Street, "cut a melon." On April 1, 1896, the company announced that it would pay a common stock dividend of two per cent in cash, and twenty per cent in scrip. The scrip, redeemable in common stock, at the option of the company, bore six per cent interest payable out of net earnings after payment of the dividend on preferred. Dissatisfaction on the part of some preferred stockholders resulted. One of them, a Mr. Hull, brought suit to enjoin payment of the scrip dividend, but the move was unsuccessful. His suit was set aside and the scrip distributed.

In the meantime the legal attacks were renewed. The suits in the New Jersey courts continued for months. On May 7, 1896, Mr. Duke and all the directors of the American Tobacco Co. were indicted, charged with violating the anti-trust laws. That had no marked effect on the combine's operations, however. Mr. Duke felt confident that the company was not violating the law, but was thoroughly justified in acquiring plants engaged in every variety of tobacco manufacture, so as to round out the business.

In January, 1897, the three per cent quarterly cash dividends on the common stock were resumed. In March the New Jersey suit against the company was dismissed. A month later, at the April period, two per cent was paid on the common stock. At the same time it was announced that the "secret factor agreement," which was one of the things complained of in the anti-trust suits, had been abandoned.

CHAPTER EIGHT

A Wall Street Battle in Which the Loser Won

No new companies were acquired for nearly two years after the "cigarette war" ended and the New Jersey suits were dismissed. But the most aggressive individual in the industry had not been resting on his oars.

Bringing to his support men of large means, Duke had taken into the management prominent figures in the financial world. Oliver H. Payne, of the Standard Oil Co., had acquired a considerable amount of stock, bringing the tobacco interests in close touch with the Rockefeller group. John G. Moore, Grant B. Schley and others had made substantial investments in its securities. With annual earnings of $4,179,460, a surplus of $7,447,849, and fresh capital at its command, the combine was well prepared to branch out into wider fields.

But Duke had a strenuous struggle, with determined opposition from without and within, before his dominance was incontestably established.

Earning millions, with larger dividends in prospect, American Tobacco was a tempting prize. Many of the industrial combinations were organized by bankers, who reaped their profits by watering stocks and piling up securities as high as the traffic would bear. This one had been formed to end costly competition and enforce economies. Its stock was represented by plants, properties and brands worth in earning capacity if not in tangible values what had been paid for them. Organizing and conducting the corporation as a commercial enterprise, paying dividends on every share issued, Duke boasted that there was "not a dollar of water in the whole concern."

Capitalists saw in the company unusual opportuni-

JAMES B. DUKE

ties if they could gain control. Duke had his own ideas about financing. Certain financiers and at least one of his own officials considered him "bull-headed" on that point. If they could once gain a majority of the stock, as principal owners they could dictate the company's policy.

The task was not so difficult as might seem. There was only $35,000,000 of stock outstanding,—$14,000,000 preferred, $21,000,000 common. Holding a considerable proportion of the shares, the Dukes had by no means a majority. Others owned large blocks; the shares were listed on the Exchange where any one might buy. The annual stockholders' meeting was near, when those who held a majority could elect directors and officers.

The plans of his opponents were well laid. Duke was no speculator. Busy with his factories and sales forces, he paid scant attention to what was going on in the stock market.

Working under cover, engaging James R. Keene, the shrewdest manipulator in Wall Street, to "turn the trick," they quietly lined up large blocks, then made a drive for control. Not until everything was ready to spring the trap, did they come out into the open. With millions at his command, Keene bid in every share that was offered, and believed he had sufficient stock in hand to assure success.

The manipulators were jubilant. Duke had been caught napping, his opponents said: Wall Street had taken him into camp. Keene felt so sure of this that he told Duke his reign was ended.

But they were sadly mistaken. "J. B." might be defeated, but had no thought of surrender. Payne was the chief financier behind the move, had furnished, it was understood, most of the money for Keene's opera-

A WALL STREET BATTLE

tions. As his advisers debated what should be done to meet the situation, Duke ended the conference by saying: "I'll tell you what I'm going to do; I'm going to see Colonel Payne."

Though Payne had bought a large amount of Tobacco stock, Duke had never met him personally. A broker friend offered to arrange an appointment, but Payne at first refused, saying he "had no business with Duke." Finally he consented to see him, Duke went to his office and they discussed the matter frankly.

One of the directors, who had been brought into the company through the purchase of his factory and disagreed with its president on many points, had, it appeared, enlisted Payne and other capitalists in the scheme. They planned to place him in charge of the corporation's finances, ousting George Arents, the treasurer. Mr. Duke was to remain operating head of the company, it was explained.

Duke would not consent to any such arrangement. While the fight was made ostensibly against the treasurer, Duke realized that it was really aimed at him. Whether his opponents had, as they claimed, a majority of the stock, or not, they had enough to hamper him seriously.

"If you fellows want to do this," said Duke, "you won't have to turn me out; I'll quit. If Arents goes, I'll go, too, and my crowd will go with me."

"What will you do?" Payne asked.

"I'll sell every share of my stock and start another company."

"If you leave, I'm going to sell my stock, too," Payne said. He had misunderstood the situation, and Duke had won him over in twenty minutes.

The tables were turned. The hand that had built up the big tobacco structure might as easily tear it down.

JAMES B. DUKE

With a powerful rival, headed by the most resourceful man in the industry, the combine's supremacy would be in danger. The stock in which the schemers had invested millions might be worth about as much as ticker tape.

Coming to terms, his former opponents assured Duke that he would be left in full control. He would accept no dictation; wished it plainly understood that in the conduct of the company's affairs he should be absolutely unhampered, as he had been—and this was agreed to.

Payne and Schley voted with him in the stockholders' meeting. The very men who had fought him in Wall Street became his strong supporters. That was the only effort ever made by stockholders or financiers to unhorse Mr. Duke or dispute his domination. Through the various commercial and financial deals in after years, the numerous arrangements which involved the larger part of the entire tobacco trade, he was the acknowledged leader and directing force.

The air being full of rumors of mergers, changes and deals in the industry in 1898, there were, as is usual under such conditions, wide fluctuations in securities. American Tobacco shares rose to dizzy heights, then declined.

Early in September the price of the common stock broke suddenly. In three or four days there was a fall of thirty points. Not knowing what was going on behind the scenes, the public could see no reason for this sharp drop, save that the stock had been driven so high that the bears found it an easy target. Timorous investors sold out, fearful that the expected mergers would not be put through. Yet at that very time Duke and his associates were putting into effect plans which

A WALL STREET BATTLE

resulted in far larger profits, with a corresponding increase in value of the securities.

Complaints were numerous, however, of manipulation by insiders. Speculators who had lost in the decline and some newspapers were severe in their criticisms. *The Commercial and Financial Chronicle*, for example, said in an editorial:

"Politics, the industrials and the wheat market appear to have occupied chief attention the current week. Perhaps we ought to put, in place of industrials, American Tobacco stock, though following, as the break in Tobacco has, the decline in Sugar Refining, a tumble such as it has made (about 30 points in a few days) in a measure weakens confidence in the entire class of issues to which it belongs, and has been an unsettling influence to the whole Stock Exchange list.

"We do not suppose the general public has suffered to any great extent in this latest bout. The reasonable presumption is that it must have been a very small and a very gullible crowd that would have followed the speculation up to the dizzy heights the stock was made to climb, and that the week's antics are a result of a struggle between insiders, instead of the usual attempt at bleeding the inexhaustible army of innocents forever vainly groping through Wall Street after a short road to wealth, but as a rule finding that all roads from that center lead to bankruptcy."

But Duke was not responsible either for the rapid rise or the sudden fall.

Not many days later, on October 1st, the plans for the plug tobacco combine were announced. Half a dozen or more leading companies were to be consolidated in a new corporation, the Continental Tobacco Company, to which would also be turned over the plug business and plants of the American Tobacco Company.

Five years previous an attempt had been made by others to combine the principal manufacturers of chewing tobacco, but the effort failed, and fiercer competition ensued. The American Company, which upon entering this field had made only three per cent of the plug tobacco production, was, by 1898, producing double that proportion.

In April the Duke interests were reported to be negotiating for two important St. Louis concerns, the Brown and Drummond companies. A month later the American stockholders voted $3,100,000 additional common stock for "acquiring new enterprises." But the St. Louis deal was not carried through at that time.

Reports were current all that summer that plans were on foot for a plug merger. But this came to pass only after months of negotiation. Though Duke was the most important factor and eventually became its head, he did not originate the proposed consolidation.

Telling how this was brought about, in his testimony years later in the anti-trust cases, Mr. Duke said that his company had bought a few concerns manufacturing plug, smoking, snuff and other products. He had advocated engaging more extensively in plug manufacture, which was opposed by the Ginter and other interests but was finally agreed to. Purchase of the National works stirred up Drummond and other manufacturers and severe price-cutting ensued. "Toddy," the Drummond's cheap brand, was cut to 14 cents; the American retaliated by reducing "Battle Axe" to 13; Sorg, Liggett and Myers and others put out cheap brands, and there was a lively contest for customers. Duke spent large amounts in advertising and pushing "Battle Axe" and other brands, which had an enormous sale. But the game was costly and not very profitable.

Sometime in 1898, Mr. Duke recalled, Frank Ray and a Mr. Hughes called at his offices, saying they had

DORIS DUKE, JAMES DUKE'S ONLY CHILD

A WALL STREET BATTLE

options on several plug factories and wanted to sell them. But Duke declined to buy.

"After several visits," he said, "they proposed to buy out our plug business and named a price which I told them I would accept. They went along and hadn't succeeded in financing it or getting in the crowd they wanted, and we didn't pay much attention to them, either one way or the other.

"In the meantime Brown in St. Louis had gotten out a plug tobacco under a formula that seemed to sweep the country. We tried to have it duplicated, couldn't do it, and finally bought Brown's brand, together with the formula. While we were closing that trade, the Drummond people wanted to sell their business. They offered it at what I considered a cheap price. I advised our people that we ought to buy it, and we did."

Ray had, meanwhile, organized an underwriting syndicate to furnish funds to float the merger and wished Drummond included. "I told them no, I thought that was off, we didn't want to go into the thing," Mr. Duke said. Finally they proposed to include both that and the Brown concern, as well as the plug business of the American, and Duke and his associates agreed to enter the combination.

Duke had no desire to be president of the plug combine. "I didn't want it and the reason I became president was this," he said. "Mr. Ray, Harry Drummond and Pierre Lorillard were candidates for the presidency of the Continental. I expected to be a director, but I didn't expect to hold any official position because I had the American Tobacco Co. to look after. It seemed to be quite a contest between these people, and Colonel Payne and Mr. Terrell came to me and asked me to accept the presidency of the Continental Tobacco Company.

JAMES B. DUKE

"At first I declined, then they said we had a large interest in the concern, they did not believe these fellows would ever be able to organize and run the thing, did not know how it would get along, and thought we would lose a lot unless I took the presidency. I considered it a while and finally decided to do it, and I did."

Once the preliminaries were settled, Duke and his associates moved swiftly. The Drummond Company was bought on October 11th. Six other large concerns were acquired and when the Continental Tobacco Company was incorporated, under the laws of New Jersey, in December, 1898, its broad scope was revealed. With a total authorized capital of $75,000,000, divided equally into common and preferred stock, there was an immediate issue of $30,000,000 each, leaving $15,000,000 in the treasury to be issued later.

In addition to the plug business of the American Tobacco and Drummond companies, the new corporation had acquired the business and plants of P. Lorillard & Co., Jersey City, N. J.; the P. J. Sorg Tobacco Co., Middletown, Ohio; John Finzer and Brothers, Louisville, Ky.; Daniel Scotten and Co., Detroit; the Henry Weissinger Co., Louisville, and P. H. Mayo and Brothers, Richmond, Va. The Brown factory, previously bought, was included in the plants turned over by the American. The combined annual output was estimated at more than 105,000,000 pounds.

Separate corporations, the Continental and American tobacco companies were operated in close accord. Though others had prompted the plug merger, Duke was at its head and in cities where independent tobacco manufacture had figured extensively there was no little bitterness at the prospect that the "trust" would obtain control of the local plants, reducing their impor-

A WALL STREET BATTLE

tance in the industry. This was particularly true of St. Louis, which had taken a leading place in the manufacture of plug.

Expressing the feeling against the combine, the St. Louis *Globe-Democrat* estimated that the Drummond plant, bought by the American Company for $3,500,000, could be replaced, with modern appliances, for $450,000 to $500,000, and that $3,000,000 had been paid for the "good-will, trade-mark, etc." "The *et cetera* in this case," that newspaper concluded, "is said to represent the trust's desire to acquire the plant and shut off the competition which was hurting it. Only the Liggett and Myers concern now remains as a thorn in the flesh of the trust, and interesting developments cannot long be postponed."

Similar comments were made in other quarters. Opponents of the merger raised the objection that too high a price had been paid for the various companies. But, knowing the potential as well as immediate worth of the concerns, Duke felt sure of his ground. More than factories and securities he was buying brands whose popularity had been established, companies whose earning capacity had been demonstrated and could easily be increased. The outcome confirmed his judgment. From the first the Continental was successful.

One concern, the largest in plug manufacture, Liggett and Myers, remained outside the combination. Wall Street had expected that, in some way, that firm would be brought into camp, but the owners absolutely refused to sell or enter the merger. Speculators made much of the failure to acquire the big St. Louis plant, which had an annual output of 27,000,000 pounds, and used this argument to depress stocks.

Duke's next move was to bring into line the Union Tobacco Company, in which Thomas F. Ryan and other

JAMES B. DUKE

financiers were interested. Desiring its owners more than the company, in acquiring this corporation he brought into alliance with him not only Ryan but also William C. Whitney, P. A. B. Widener, Anthony N. Brady and other leading capitalists.

Voting on March 28, 1899, to increase the common stock from $21,000,000 to $56,000,000, the stockholders of the American Tobacco Co. amended the charter so as to increase the number of directors to fifteen. The new directors chosen were Ryan, Brady, and Widener. With powerful connections, commanding almost unlimited capital, their experience and advice as well as their money were of the utmost value.

Declaring a 100-per-cent stock dividend, to be taken out of surplus, in addition to the usual two per cent quarterly dividend, the directors cut one of the largest "melons," in the language of Wall Street, on record up to that time. With immense earning capacity, the combine was revealed as one of the most profitable, as well as one of the largest corporations in America. To pay the stock dividend $21,000,000 additional common stock was issued, the remainder of the new issue authorized, $14,000,000, being intended, according to reports, to acquire the Union Tobacco Company and for other purposes.

A separate corporation, though closely affiliated with the Continental, the R. J. Reynolds Tobacco Company, was chartered in New Jersey with $5,000,000 authorized capital, bringing into the alliance one of the largest factories and ablest tobacco manufacturers in the South.

The Continental, in applying for admission of its stock to quotation in the unlisted department of the New York Exchange, set forth that of the authorized capital of $75,000,000 there was outstanding $31,145,000 preferred and $31,146,500 common stock.

A WALL STREET BATTLE

Duke was president; Harrison I. Drummond, Frank F. Ray and Oren Scotten, vice-presidents; P. Lorillard, Jr., treasurer and D. A. Keller, secretary, and the other directors were Herbert L. Terrell, Marks Leopold, Robert B. Dula, Oliver H. Payne, Basil Doerhoefer, Joseph B. Hughes, J. B. Cobb, Thomas Atkinson, Grant B. Schley and Paul Brown.

Increasing both common and preferred stocks from $37,500,000 to $50,000,000 each, on May 1, 1899, announcement was made that Liggett and Myers had been acquired by the Continental, the price paid being estimated by outsiders at approximately $12,500,000.

Employing three thousand workmen, Moses C. Wetmore, president of Liggett and Myers, stated that during the previous five years the company had made average profits of over $900,000 annually, and that there were on its books approximately one million pounds of unfilled orders for tobacco. "I received at the rate of $15,000,000 ($1,366 per $100) for my stock," Mr. Wetmore admitted.

Three other plants were acquired within the next few weeks—the Gradel and Strotz Tobacco Company; August Beck and Company, Chicago, and the Buchanan and Lyall Tobacco Company.

The last big rival had been brought into line. The Plug Combine was practically complete.

The earning power of the American Tobacco Company was shown clearly in the report for 1898. With net earnings of $4,957,804, there was a surplus, from all sources, of $22,557,689, including the proceeds from the sale of the plug business to the Continental, which yielded $11,700,000. A 100 per cent stock dividend was issued, deducted from the surplus.

The American, in May, 1899, listed $12,500,000 of additional common stock to acquire the entire capital

JAMES B. DUKE

stock of the Union Tobacco Company. Subscribers to the Union syndicate, when that was dissolved in July, received for each $100 they had actually paid in $170 par in American Tobacco common stock, a total of 91,800 shares of $50 each, equal, at par, to $4,590,000.

Another object which Mr. Duke had long had in mind, and had before attempted without success, was attained. Through the Union corporation he brought into his combination his earliest and most powerful rival, Blackwell's Durham Tobacco Co., whose factory had been the largest establishment in his home town, and whose hold on the smoking tobacco trade had caused the Dukes to turn to the manufacture of cigarettes. At last the "Bull Durham" brand, which had seemed so formidable to him twenty years before, had fallen into his hands.

CHAPTER NINE

Many Companies in One, with Duke in Full Control

IT was a remarkable group of men Duke gathered around him—Ryan, Payne, Widener, Whitney, Brady, R. J. Reynolds, Pierre Lorillard, Jr., Benjamin N. Duke, J. B. Cobb, C. C. and Robert B. Dula, Percival S. Hill, W. W. Fuller, George W. Watts, Grant Schley, Charles E. G. Halliwell, F. H. Ray, Harrison Drummond, W. R. Harris and many others—capitalists, manufacturers and master salesmen who understood production, marketing and finance.

In charge of each activity, buying the raw product, manufacturing, shipping, selling, advertising—the thousand and one operations involved in these varied enterprises—were experts, some with the older companies from the beginning, others youngsters Duke had developed, his "boys" whom he had given a chance and who had more than "made good."

With buyers in the principal markets abroad—Turkey, Greece, Egypt, India, Sumatra, Cuba, Jamaica, the Orient and the West Indies—as well as America; salesmen in almost every country and leading city, he had created and directed one of the largest and most effective industrial machines of modern times.

Concerning a similar organization, the Standard Oil group, William H. Vanderbilt, in testifying before the Hepburn Congressional Committee, in 1879, said:

"I never came in contact with any class of men as smart and able as they are in their business, and I think that a great deal of their advantage is to be attributed to that. They never could have got in the position they are in now without a good deal of ability, and one man would hardly have been able to do it. It is a combination of men. I don't believe that by

JAMES B. DUKE

any legislative enactment or anything else, through any of the States, or all of the States, you can keep such men down."

What Mr. Vanderbilt thought of the Rockefellers and their partners, who organized and ran the first big industrial merger, was as true of Duke and his associates. They would have succeeded in any line they entered, with or without any "trust." Mr. Duke himself regarded the organization he had built up, the men of ability and talent enlisted, as more important and effective than plants, capital or corporation.

The Continental placed firmly on its feet, the Union company absorbed; cigarette, plug and smoking tobacco largely in their hands, Duke and his allies began to reach out for other branches of the industry.

Early in 1900 the American Snuff Company was formed, with $25,000,000 capital, acquiring the leading snuff producers—the Atlantic Snuff Co., Philadelphia; George W. Helme Co., Helmetta, N. J.; the Southern Snuff Co., Memphis, Tenn.; Bruton & Condon, Nashville, Tenn.; and the Stewart Ralph Snuff Co., Clarksville, Tenn.; the snuff business of the American Tobacco Company, which owned plants at Baltimore and Helmetta, N. J.; of the Continental, which owned the Bowers plant at Changewater, N. J.; of the Lorillard factory in Jersey City; W. E. Garret & Sons, Inc., and the Stewart Ralph Snuff Co., Philadelphia; and the Dental Snuff Co., Lynchburg, Va. These factories were producing some 15,000,000 pounds of snuff annually.

Cigar manufacture was next. On January 11, 1901, the American Cigar Company was organized, capitalized at $10,000,000. This was beginning on a small scale in a big field, but behind it was an idea, that of making cigars by machinery. Nearly twenty years be-

MANY COMPANIES IN ONE

fore the Dukes had won supremacy by introducing machine manufacture of cigarettes. The same thing might be done in cigars. Attractive in theory, the scheme did not work so well in practice, but at the time seemed to offer large possibilities. Devices for the purpose had been invented, and the International Cigar Machinery Co. was incorporated, with $10,000,000 capital, acquiring the patents.

Cuba, with its famous Vuelta Abajo and other tobaccos, was the home of the cigar, the leading brands were made in Havana, and one of the first steps was to gain a foothold there. Negotiations were begun for the Havana Commercial Company, a $20,000,000 concern comprising factories producing 100,000,000 cigars annually. More than a year elapsed before this deal was completed, but in the meantime numerous other Cuban factories were purchased.

Mr. Duke was given practically a free hand in carrying out his expansion program when, in April, 1901, the stockholders of both the American and Continental approved amendments to their articles of incorporation permitting the directors, by a two-thirds vote, to guarantee the principal or interest, or both, of securities issued by allied companies. Deals involving large sums could be quickly made, factories acquired or new corporations established under this sweeping authority —a flexible means of financing which at the same time assured control by the parent companies.

This broad power was first used the following month when the American Cigar Co. secured control of the Havana-American Cigar Co. by issuing $4,000,000 of four per cent notes, guaranteed by the American and Continental. That deal brought in ten large Havana factories. Later the Havana Commercial Co., the Henry Clay-Bock, the Cabanas and other concerns were

JAMES B. DUKE

acquired. The Havana Tobacco Co., capitalized at $35,000,000, was organized, and the Duke alliance became a leading factor in the Cuban industry.

Customers who puffed fragrant Havanas and could pay the price for their Carolina Perfectos, Henry Clays and Corona Coronas were given a wide range of choice. El Principe de Gales and other favorites were extensively advertised, and sales rapidly increased. But the vast majority of smokers could not afford such expensive brands, and Mr. Duke and his aids devoted time and attention to them.

"What is the greatest need of America?" an earnest and anxious inquirer asked Thomas R. Marshall, in the midst of World War problems. "I can't tell you that," drawled the Vice President, as he took a half-smoked stump from his mouth; "but one of the greatest is a good five-cent cigar."

That was one need Mr. Duke sought to supply—the best cigar that could be sold for a nickel, as well as the better quality for a dime. "Cubanolas" and various other brands were put on the market and sold by the million. Even the lowly "two-fer"—two for a nickel—was not neglected, and the rough and ready cheroot and the humble stogie, furnishing a long and lasting smoke for a penny or two, were extensively cultivated.

Cheroot and stogie factories had been picked up from time to time, the first bought being P. Whitlock, Richmond, Va., manufacturers of "Old Virginia" cheroots. Stogie plants in Pittsburgh and elsewhere were brought together, and the American Stogie Company formed, capitalized at $11,976,000, which soon bought the United States Cigar Company, owning numerous plants that turned out 280,000,000 stogies a year. The combined factories had an annual production of 700,000,000 stogies.

MANY COMPANIES IN ONE

Realizing his ambition, Duke was at last manufacturing every variety of tobacco. The various groups operated in close accord, under his direction; but having them in separate corporations was a rather cumbersome arrangement. Some means of bringing them together in a definite organization was needed.

On June 5, 1901, a holding corporation, the Consolidated Tobacco Company, was incorporated under the laws of New Jersey, the entire authorized capital of $30,000,000 being immediately paid in, in cash. Mr. Duke was, of course, the head of it, and the stock was owned by the interests allied with him in the American and Continental.

William C. Whitney, the brilliant lawyer who had been Secretary of the Navy in President Cleveland's cabinet, was one of Mr. Duke's chief advisers in the formation of the Consolidated, and the conferences were held and the articles of incorporation and other legal documents perfected at his residence.

"The leading consideration in the organization of the Consolidated Tobacco Co.," the officials announced, "is the importance of concentrating the control of the American and Continental companies so as to insure their harmonious operation. Each of the old concerns owns thirty-five per cent of the stock of the American Cigar Company, and their amalgamation will prevent the latter company from passing to outside interests."

Issuing four per cent fifty-year bonds sufficient to cover the outstanding common stock of the older companies, the Consolidated offered to exchange these bonds on the basis of $200 for each $100 of American and $100 for $100 par value of Continental common. As the American had $54,500,000 common stock outstanding and the Continental $48,884,600, a total of $157,884,600 was involved.

JAMES B. DUKE

Kuhn, Loeb and Co. and Thomas F. Ryan formed a syndicate to provide $25,000,000 in cash and facilitate the transfer. Stockholders who were to receive more than $70,000,000 of the new bonds agreed not to sell until the syndicate operations were completed. Mr. Duke and the largest holders announced that they would keep the bonds for investment. So the largest financial transaction in the tobacco trade, up to that time, was readily accomplished and control concentrated in a single corporation.

From time to time the constituent companies acquired plants here and there which were advantageous to them. On November 1, 1901, the American Cigar Company bought the Brown Brothers Company, of Detroit, whose annual output was about 40,000,000 cigars. Three weeks later the American Tobacco Company purchased outright the entire properties of D. H. McAlpin and Company, of New York, its most important rival in the East.

In the meantime Mr. Duke had bought Ogden's in Liverpool, and was making a strong bid for the British trade, which eventually resulted in an alliance covering all the most important foreign markets.

The combine's position had not been acquired without strong opposition. Each new consolidation or purchase was followed by a fresh outcry. In articles under glaring headlines and editorials, newspapers pointed out the dangers. Politicians never tired of denouncing the concern as a huge monopoly. When tobacco crops were large and prices went down, as occurred during this period, the farmers blamed Duke and the "trust."

Owning nearly all the most popular brands, the combine, opponents pointed out, could easily establish its own stores, and put out of business the thousands of small tobacco shops scattered through every city and

MANY COMPANIES IN ONE

town. Retailers in leading cities organized, "for mutual protection," the Independent Cigar Stores Company. A few independent concerns were still manufacturing cigarettes. There were numerous cigar factories, producing in the aggregate far more than the Duke companies. Many dealers produced their own cigars, making them in their shops.

The combine's widely advertised brands had to be kept in stock to meet demands of customers, but hundreds of retailers were giving preference to "non-trust" goods. Finding a ready market, new cigarette factories were beginning to spring up.

The United Cigar Stores Company, organized not long before, began opening stores in various cities. There was bitter rivalry, and another tobacco "war" ensued, this time in the retail trade. Competition was keen, with price cutting and retaliation, until the fall of 1903, when a settlement was reached and the controversy ended.

Out of this grew the systems of chain stores which now dot the country. The "United," with its thousands of stores and agencies, stretching from coast to coast, selling to more than a million customers a day, is one of the best known of American enterprises. Its origin and growth is worth recounting.

On a visit to New York, George J. Whelan, of Syracuse, seeking a smoke, found there was no tobacco shop near. He was surprised. Here in the largest city a man had to walk blocks to find a place where he could buy cigars or cigarettes. The stores, when he found them, were usually ill-kept and uninviting.

"There ought to be a cigar shop on every corner of busy streets," Whelan thought, "and they ought to be much more attractive in appearance than those dingy little places with battered wooden Indians outside and

JAMES B. DUKE

show windows heaped with cigars, cigarettes and cans of tobacco."

That gave him an idea. He was a cigar dealer himself, the youngest of seven brothers who had entered the business in Syracuse twenty years before. They had succeeded there. Here was a wider field, with infinitely larger possibilities. Why not come to New York, and establish a chain of tobacco shops?

Returning "up-state," he tried to raise capital, but met with little encouragement. At last a friend advanced him a small amount. Whelan came to New York and, in 1901, opened his first store at No. 84 Nassau Street. It was a tiny shop, but the floor was clean, the shelves orderly, and the goods attractively displayed. Moreover, the familiar sign that had marked tobacco stores for centuries was missing. That marked the passing of the Wooden Indian.

The first day's receipts amounted to only $3.47, but the idea of having a chain of stores appealed to dealers, some began to operate with Whelan, his brothers and others joined in, and the enterprise was started.

Whelan made efforts to interest the American Tobacco officials, but they were at first not very favorable to the project. He had been active in the "Admiral" cigarette concern, formed to compete with the combine. Mr. Duke was prejudiced against him, and did not like the idea of opening chain stores, fearing it would "upset all these little retailers," as he expressed it, would cut prices and demoralize trade as the Gluckstein stores had in England.

Mr. Cobb, president of the American Cigar Co., reported that Whelan was going to open stores anyway. "Of course we wouldn't prevent it and couldn't if we tried," Mr. Duke said. As he was leaving for England, he told his vice-president, Mr. Hill, to watch the

MANY COMPANIES IN ONE

Whelan operations, as "if they were going to do anything great in that line we should have some control of it." Before Duke returned, Hill had acquired virtual control of the United Cigar Stores.

"When I got back," Mr. Duke said, "I saw Whelan, and he told me of his plans. I advised him against slaughtering prices, and he said that wasn't his idea, but to go ahead and build up a business." There was a chance of making a great deal of money in the retail trade, Whelan felt sure. But Duke thought they would find difficulty in organizing the system so as to handle it on a profitable basis. He "didn't think much of it," and stated frankly that his interests would not stay in the concern unless it made money.

But he backed Whelan, gave him a free hand, and the "United" rapidly won its way. One thing he told Mr. Whelan, however, was that he would fail unless he kept goods customers asked for, no matter by whom they were made, and he must supply the goods of other manufacturers as well as those of the American Tobacco Co.

Capital was made available for the United, stores were opened at first by scores, then by hundreds. Strategic locations were selected, desirable corners and stands that the older dealers never thought any tobacconist could afford.

New methods of merchandising, display and advertising were put into effect. Clerks were trained in the art of serving customers. In a few years a remarkably efficient organization was developed, under which the business has grown continually until annual sales now amount to nearly $85,000,000 and the company has assets of more than $92,000,000.

The United formed the final link in the chain of enterprises which bound together the tobacco trade of the

JAMES B. DUKE

United States. Pursuing the policy of having at his command everything necessary for production, Mr. Duke had assured a plentiful supply of the commodities required in tobacco manufacture. Licorice, largely used as a flavoring material, was supplied by the MacAndrews and Forbes Company. Tin foil, extensively utilized in packing tobacco products, was assured through purchase of the Conley Foil Company. Partial ownership in the Mengel Box Company provided an adequate supply of boxes. The same applied to other lines.

The Consolidated Company, through which a majority of the American, Continental and other stocks were held, paid a cash dividend of twenty per cent to stockholders in January, 1903, out of profits for the previous year. The net earnings for 1902 were $13,291,460, and there was a surplus, after payment of interest on the four per cent bonds, of $6,915,206. The twenty per cent dividend required $16,000,000. Immediately after that was disbursed, the capital of the Consolidated was increased to $40,000,000, the new shares being sold to the stockholders at par.

In 1904 the Consolidated, American and Continental were all merged into one under the original name, the American Tobacco Company, bonds, preferred and common stock of the new corporation being issued in exchange for their securities.

When this was effected, the new corporation had outstanding some $125,000,000 of funded debt, created principally through exchange of stock for merged companies; $78,000,000 preferred and $40,000,000 common stock. With a surplus of $26,000,000 its total assets aggregated $274,000,000.

But that told only half the story. The company and allied interests controlled numerous other concerns, in

MANY COMPANIES IN ONE

nearly every line of tobacco handling and manufacture, with large capital and securities, the aggregate approaching that of the parent organization.

Beginning in 1890 with five companies and eight plants, the combination had in fourteen years acquired 150 manufactories, and had grown from a $25,000,000 corporation to a mammoth aggregation, controlling a capitalization, in parent and allied companies, of $502,-000,000, according to the estimate of John Moody, the financial expert and editor of *Moody's Manual*. Wall Street authorities estimated the market value of the securities controlled at approximately $470,000,000.

Analyzing the tobacco combine, and pointing out the difference between that and other industrial combinations, Mr. Moody in his book, "The Truth About the Trusts," published in 1904, said:

"The development of the Tobacco Trust from a modest consolidation, in 1890, of Eastern tobacco and cigarette manufacturers, to a world-combination of every form of tobacco production and distribution, is a phenomenon of absorbing interest. To-day the tobacco combine makes its influence felt in every clime, and dominates the tobacco industry in all its branches on both sides of the Atlantic. It grows the raw tobacco, transports it, converts it into its various uses in the shape of cigars and cigarettes, chewing tobacco, snuff, and so forth, and distributes it to the four quarters of the globe.

"The element of monopoly is comparatively light in the Tobacco Trust and its stability and success up to the present time have been due quite largely to the fact that its promoters have from the beginning recognized this lack of a strong monopoly element and have seen that they would inevitably be forced to do one of two things: either to progressively absorb all competition as rapidly as it might spring up, until they finally controlled the tobacco production of the world, or else succumb to open competition from all comers, and operate entirely on the basis of low-cost production and non-inflated capitalization.

"The latter course, however, while more conservative, was the least inviting, particularly as the combine had started with a watered capitalization; and therefore the resolve was doubtless made early in the history of the Trust to progressively reach out and control the entire industry, buying in competitors as rapidly as they might spring up and become formidable. That this policy, so bold and venturesome, has, up to the present day, succeeded so well, is a living testimonial to the genius of the remarkable group of men who stand at the head of this wonderful aggregation of consolidated industry. The Tobacco Trust to-day stands out a shining example of the adherence to an ambitious, bold, aggressive policy in modern finance, which, up to the present time, appears to have reaped marked success. Like the Copper Trust, it began its work with no monopoly, but with the hope of gradually acquiring one; but unlike the ill-fated copper combine, it has never yet 'fallen down' in its program. By steady, progressive steps, now covering a period of fourteen years, it has gradually taken unto itself all that is important or profitable in the tobacco and its allied industries."

But Mr. Duke himself, explaining how the combine had been developed, declared:

"I never bought any business with the idea of eliminating competition. It was always with the idea of an investment, except probably in the one case of the Union Tobacco Company, and in that case we had an idea of getting in with ourselves a lot of rich financial people to help finance our properties."

The Consolidated corporation, he explained, was formed to provide working capital for the American and Continental, and served its purpose. After the Supreme Court's decision in the Northern Securities case, which made doubtful the legality of all holding corporations, the directors decided that the Consoli-

MANY COMPANIES IN ONE

dated should not be continued as a holding company, and that all three concerns should be merged into one corporation, with direct ownership of the properties. That was done in the American Tobacco Company.

The simpler form of organization was easier for the public and investors to understand, Mr. Duke pointed out; permitted more effective handling of the business, "put our securities on a better basis, and I think helped everybody connected with it."

CHAPTER TEN
British and Americans in a World-Wide Alliance

FOREIGN trade had been a prime consideration with the Dukes from the beginning. Sending representatives through Europe and Asia, to South Africa, India, Java, Australia and New Zealand, they had built up a flourishing business in those countries, as well as in China and Japan. Following the formation of the American Tobacco Company, this custom had been considerably extended. Yet the aggregate was small in comparison with the domestic sales.

When the tobacco interests of America were firmly welded together, Mr. Duke's mind naturally turned to other countries. There were boundless possibilities in Europe and the Orient, but British manufacturers were cutting into his trade in China and elsewhere. Duke decided to compete with them on their own ground.

Tobacco being one of the few commodities protected by high tariff in free-trade England, the trade was jealously guarded. The American Company maintained a depot in London and was doing well there, but made-in-England goods had first call in the British market. The only way to get a firm foothold was to gain control of some established British firm manufacturing well-known British brands.

Beginning his campaign in the fall of 1901, Duke invaded England as calmly and assuredly as if he had been going across the river to New Jersey to buy a local factory. Reaching his London office, he looked over the products of the chief English manufacturers, learned their comparative positions, size of their factories, output, capital and the popularity of the various brands. "In two days," he said, "I decided that I wanted control either of Player's or Ogden's."

WORLD-WIDE ALLIANCE

Going to Player's at Nottingham, stating precisely what was contemplated, he asked what they would sell for, lock, stock and barrel. They named too high a price. Proceeding next to Ogden's at Liverpool, he made them an offer which the managers were willing to accept. Within a few days the directors approved the deal, subject, however, to the sanction of the stockholders. Acquiring the entire capital stock of Ogden's, £200,000 (approximately $1,000,000), and the £60,000 ($300,000) of its 4½ per cent debenture bonds, he took possession.

His object, as Mr. Duke emphasized, was not to form a trust in England or control the British industry, but merely to obtain a share of the business and prevent them from cutting in on his foreign trade. The Britishers, however, would not have it so. Sounding the alarm, they pictured him as a powerful invader, threatening to capture their factories and interests.

"They showed up at Ogden's the day the stockholders met and tried to queer my deal by offering to pay a higher price," Mr. Duke related. "But the Ogden directors stood by their agreement, and we bought the business."

Led by W. D. and H. O. Wills and others, the principal British manufacturers organized the Imperial Tobacco Company of Great Britain and Ireland, to fight Duke and his allies.

It was a battle royal. The Americans began to extend the scope of Ogden's, and were prepared to acquire other concerns as opportunity offered, not only in England but on the Continent. Going into Germany in December, the Jasmatzi cigarette works in Dresden were bought and overtures made for an interest in the plants of Kyriazi Brothers of Berlin. At the same time

JAMES B. DUKE

there were rumors that their field of operations would be extended into Russia.

With £15,000,000 ($75,000,000) capital, the Imperial Tobacco Company was striving energetically to line up every British manufacturer and dealer who could be induced to join in the attempt to drive the Americans from the field. Having scored an important victory in enlisting the coöperation of the Salmon and Gluckstein interests, the largest tobacco chain stores in the Empire, operating more than two hundred stores in London alone, the Imperial, considering the time opportune to shut out the Americans, played its trump card. This was no less than an attempt to start a boycott that would close the doors of British tobacco stores against the Duke products—those made in England as well as goods of American manufacture.

Springing a novel proposition on the British retailers, the Imperial offered a large bonus to all who would agree not to handle or display any goods but theirs for a term of years. Dealers were given only a few days in which to sign.

So sudden and unexpected was the stroke, offering such a decided advantage to the dealers, that its promoters thought the *coup* could not fail. Duke and the principal owners of Ogden's were across the Atlantic, three thousand miles away. Taking them by surprise, the plan was to have the British dealers' exclusive contracts signed, sealed and delivered before the American rivals could checkmate the move.

Quick decision was required. Duke did not hesitate an instant. When news of the Imperial's proposition was cabled to New York, he called his advisers in conference to consider what steps should be taken to meet the situation. Deciding on immediate action, he pro-

WORLD-WIDE ALLIANCE

posed a plan which, though tremendously costly, would completely knock out the Imperial scheme.

That was to give the entire profits of Ogden's, some $200,000 a year, to its customers and in addition to give them in cash as a bonus approximately $1,000,000 annually for four years, if they would purchase and sell Ogden's goods. No strings were tied to the offer; no demand made that the Imperial products be excluded. In fact, it was plainly stated that dealers were not asked to boycott the goods of any manufacturer. That was the stroke that won the battle.

The circular in which this was announced, bold, clear, straightforward, was written by Mr. Duke himself and is so characteristic of the man and his methods that it is given below in full:

"Commencing April 2, 1902, we will for the next four years distribute to such of our customers in the United Kingdom as purchase direct from us our entire net profits on the goods sold by us in the United Kingdom. In addition to the above, we will, commencing April 2, 1902, for the next four years distribute to such of our consumers in the United Kingdom as purchase direct from us the sum of £200,000 per year. The distribution of net profits will be made as soon after April 2, 1903, and annually thereafter, as the accounts can be audited and will be in proportion to the purchases made during the year. The distribution of the £200,000 per year will be made every three months, the first distribution to take place as soon after July 2, 1902, as accounts can be audited, and will be in proportion to the purchases during the three months' period. To participate in this offer, we do not ask you to boycott the goods of any other manufacturer."

Cabling his proposition to London, Mr. Duke ordered it sent out immediately to the entire trade.

JAMES B. DUKE

Next morning the offer was telegraphed to seven thousand retailers throughout the British Isles. Many dealers had resented the demand of the Imperial that they bind themselves, with hardly time for consideration, in a hard-and-fast agreement to handle only Imperial goods. When the Ogden's offer was received, there was instant reaction.

Thousands flatly refused to sign the Imperial agreement. Others ignored it. Duke's proposition had freed them from galling restrictions. There was such resentment against the British combine that one large London house issued a statement that, as the Imperial Tobacco Company was really competing with the retailers, it would not in future sell the Imperial's brands.

The victory was decisive, but by no means complete. Duke had effectually prevented the boycott of Ogden's, but the Imperial, which comprised most of the leading manufacturers and brands, still held the bulk of the trade. Sailing for England, Mr. Duke pushed energetically the business of Ogden's. A widespread contest ensued, prosecuted vigorously by all concerned, involving price cutting, as well as large bonuses and considerable losses on both sides.

Carrying the war into the United States, the British manufacturers announced the purchase of an American headquarters in Richmond, Va., proposing to erect a large factory there and enter into direct competition with the Americans. A few months previous the Imperial had purchased Mardon, Son & Hall, Limited, of Bristol, and were planning to acquire other large concerns.

Having won a place in Great Britain, Duke was getting his share of the trade, but at heavy cost. The game was not worth the candle.

Why should the British and Americans keep fight-

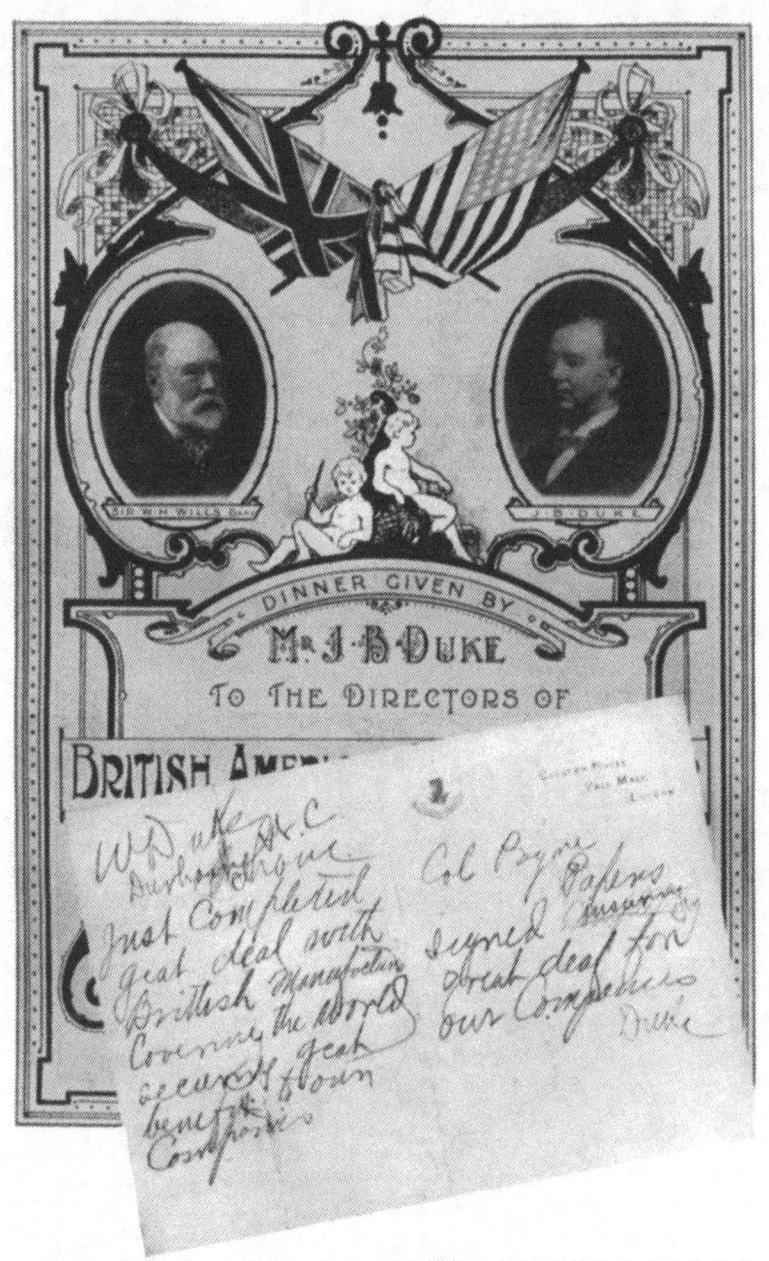

BRITISH-AMERICAN BANQUET MENU—CABLES SENT BY DUKE

WORLD-WIDE ALLIANCE

ing each other, wasting money and energy? He felt about this very much as he had concerning the New York, Richmond and Durham cigarette makers when they were slashing at each other before the American Tobacco Company was formed. Conditions were different, it was true. Trade in many lands was involved. But there must be some way in which they could work together harmoniously and profitably.

Determined not to be boycotted, Duke was prepared to defend his rights as long as necessary, but was willing to treat at any time fair terms were offered.

The initial overtures came from the owners of the Imperial. Mr. Wills, whose uncle, Sir William Henry Wills, later Lord Winterstoke, was head of the leading tobacco firm in England and largely interested in the Imperial, in June, 1902, wrote a private letter to Thomas F. Ryan, inviting him to England, intimating that they would like to take up negotiations to settle the differences between the Ogden and Imperial interests.

"I hesitated about going, and made up my mind not to go," Mr. Ryan said. "I didn't know anything about the business and told them if they wanted to talk to anybody, they would have to talk to Mr. Duke and Mr. Fuller. I answered the letter, they finally cabled and in response to that cable I sailed in August. I met Lord Winterstoke and had a great many meetings with him."

Lord Winterstoke had the officers of the Imperial to lunch and dinner with Mr. Ryan, and they got acquainted. After two or three meetings, Mr. Ryan said, he had not the slightest idea anything would be done. But Mr. Duke had agreed to come to London, if there was any real business. The British investors seemed anxious to make some kind of arrangement,

JAMES B. DUKE

and Ryan, some ten days after he arrived, cabled for Duke, who sailed at once.

After Mr. Duke arrived the negotiations became definite, Mr. Ryan recalled. As they began to work out the plans Duke cabled to New York for his attorney, and further conferences were held. The purpose was, of course, to arrive at an understanding that would bring about harmonious relations between the Imperial and American interests. Finally this was accomplished, along lines worked out by Mr. Duke, the terms agreed upon and two contracts carrying them into effect were executed on September 27, 1902.

The Consolidated Tobacco Company, the Duke-Ryan corporation, acquired the British rights in America, the Imperial bought the American rights in England, and together they formed a corporation to handle the remaining trade.

Transferring the business of Ogden's to the Imperial, a joint stock corporation was formed, the British-American Tobacco Company, Limited, with a capital of £6,000,000 (approximately $30,000,000) to represent the tobacco interests of both countries in the Orient and other parts of the world outside their own territories.

Mr. Ryan, who had returned to America before the negotiations were concluded, announced that "the Consolidated Tobacco Co. will now pursue its business in the American field, including not only the United States, but Cuba, Porto Rico, the Hawaiian Islands, and the Philippines. The Imperial Company will carry on the business in the United Kingdom of Great Britain and Ireland, including Scotland and Wales. In the new British-American Tobacco Company, Limited, the Imperial Company has one-third of the stock,

WORLD-WIDE ALLIANCE

and the Consolidated Tobacco Company two-thirds. The British-American Tobacco Company will carry on the entire business in all foreign countries, including India, Canada and Australia."

That marked the end of the conflict. The result was entirely satisfactory to Mr. Duke. In the negotiations with the British manufacturers and financiers, his fairness, ability and consideration were so evident that he won not only their respect but esteem. Former rivals became his warm friends. The very men who had fought him so vigorously voted to place him in control of the corporation which was to represent them in foreign lands—a tribute to the man, as well as the manufacturer and merchant.

Mr. Duke announced this achievement in five or six lines. Scratching a few words on a sheet of Carlton Hotel note-paper, he handed two messages to his secretary, M. E. Finch, for transmission by cable to America. One was to Oliver H. Payne, the Standard Oil millionaire and early partner of John D. Rockefeller, who had been for years one of Mr. Duke's chief backers and associates. This read:

"COL. PAYNE:
"Papers signed insuring great deal for our companies.
"DUKE."

He started to write "completing" as the third word, then scratched that out and changed it to "insuring."

The other cablegram was to his father, Washington Duke:

"W. DUKE,
Durham, N. C.
"I have just completed a great deal with British manufacturers, covering the world, securing great benefit to our companies."

JAMES B. DUKE

"This cablegram sent immediately after the closing of the deal," Mr. Finch commented, "was characteristic of Mr. Duke's great affection for his father, who, as you recall, was a very old man at that time."

The tobacco treaty was not to go uncelebrated. On the evening of October 7, 1902, Mr. Duke gave an elaborate banquet to the directors of the British-American Tobacco Company. The scene was the "Charles II" dining room of the Carlton Hotel. Around the table were gathered leaders of the tobacco industry in Europe and America. On Mr. Duke's right sat Sir William Henry Wills; on his left, William C. Whitney. Next to Sir W. H. Wills was Mr. Fuller, the Dukes' attorney and counselor. The other guests included Charles Edward Lambert, Harry Payne Whitney, James Inskip, John Dana Player, William Nelson Mitchell, John MacConnal, Percy Callaghan, Walter Butler, H. W. Gunn, Percy Handle Walter, William Goodacre Player, William Barker Ogden, John Blackwell Cobb, Henry Herbert Wills, Ernst F. Gutschow, Hugo Von R. Cunliffe-Owen, Thomas Ogden, Thomas Gracey, Morton Easley Finch, Percy Ogden, William Plender, Harold Arbuthnot, Joseph Hood, William Rees Harris, Robert Henry Walter, and George Alfred Wills.

London, accustomed as it is to elaborate social functions, was impressed. The newspapers spoke of the significance of the occasion which marked the bringing together of industrial leaders of Great Britain and America, and the partition of the tobacco trade.

Illustrated journals reproduced the elaborate menu, which bore on its front the crossed flags of the two countries and photographs of Sir William Henry Wills and Mr. Duke, and the legend, "In Union There is

Strength." Under the heading "A Millionaire's Dinner Party," the *Illustrated London Mail* said:

"Mr. J. B. Duke, one of the heads of the British-American Tobacco Company, Limited, recently gave a dinner at the Carlton Hotel, London, to celebrate the great amalgamation. His guests, as will be seen from our second illustration, taken from the fourth page of the Menu, constituted a remarkable gathering, including as they did thirty members of the most prominent Tobacco Houses in England and America. The Menu, the cover of which we reproduce by permission of Messrs. Waterlow Brothers and Layton, was beautifully designed, and printed in gold and bound with white silk. After the dinner several of the American guests ordered them in hundreds to send to their friends 'across the way.'"

Picturing the scope of Mr. Duke's accomplishment and the significance of the arrangement which this banquet celebrated, Mr. Fuller wrote afterwards:

"To fortify his trade and protect his foreign markets he went across the waters to attack in their own citadels the British manufacturers who were menacing his trade in the East, and to cause them to withdraw from the fields he had discovered and the markets he had made.

"Those who understood the genius of the British merchant, whose vessels sailed every sea and who acknowledged no limits save those of the planet, can surmise what this meant. Tobacco was one of the very few commodities protected by a tax in a free-trade country, the trade in which they were asked to divide with a foreigner. It seemed to ask them to desert their traditions as well as to yield their profits. Duke accomplished his purpose, and with so little friction and with so much equity that it was not a nine days' wonder.

"At a dinner given in honor of the consummation

JAMES B. DUKE

of the negotiations, which began shortly after Duke reached England, during Mr. William C. Whitney's reply to a toast in praise of his own patriotic work in rebuilding our navy, the great Secretary laid his hand on Mr. Duke's shoulder and said:

"'It is such marvelous merchants as this man who make a great navy necessary to carry and protect a trade which seems to know no bounds.'

"This tribute to successful effort was praise indeed, but his keenest satisfaction from this international triumph came to him in the knowledge that he had gotten an almost unlimited and more lasting market for the tobacco made by his own people on their small farms.

"If he had dreamed dreams, they had all come true, and if delight in conquering was his ruling passion, it was likely to waste away now for want of other equal fields. What he did was to set himself at once to the more thorough organizing and development of the spheres of trade he had brought within his ever extending lines."

Mr. Duke's own arrangements for this elaborate banquet were very simple. Turning to his associates, he said with a smile: "Fuller, you take charge of the grub; Cobb, you get the wines." Never relishing "putting on frills," he desired everything about this occasion done in the best of style. It was, and he thoroughly enjoyed it.

Having consolidated the tobacco interests of America and made the British his allies, Duke, with redoubled energy, set about seeking larger foreign trade. Unusual enterprise had already won for him the leading position in China and Japan. After his cigarettes were introduced in Japan, that country imposed a heavy import duty, threatening exclusion of the American

WORLD-WIDE ALLIANCE

product. Building a chain of factories, Duke began manufacturing cigarettes there, and within a few years was making and selling three billion cigarettes annually in the Flowery Kingdom. Japan raising very little tobacco, the heavy duty was on the manufactured, not the raw product. American tobacco used in the Japanese factories eventually furnished a market for 10,000,000 pounds of Southern leaf. An even larger custom was built up in China, and the trade extended throughout the Far East.

Before establishing factories and spending several million dollars in Japan, Mr. Duke sought some assurance of the safety of his investment, in case the Japanese Government should decide to take over the properties and make tobacco manufacture a government monopoly. Calling on John Hay, Secretary of State, Mr. Fuller discussed the matter. Mr. Hay cabled the American minister in Tokio, and received a favorable reply. But on one important point the Japanese proved decidedly elusive. That was in regard to payment for brands and good will, more valuable than the factories. State Department representatives could not pin them down on that point. At last Mr. Hay said, "I've gone as far as diplomacy will permit. I suggest you see the President."

Mr. Duke and his attorney went to Washington, and Secretary Hay accompanied them to the White House. Received cordially by the President, Mr. Roosevelt said he knew about the matter, and remarked:

"It is all perfectly straight, now they are trying to wriggle out of it. We will make them do it."

Diplomacy, however, failed to bring this about, but Duke found a means of accomplishing it through his own representatives. Japan did, in a few years, create a tobacco monopoly, a possibility Duke had foreseen,

JAMES B. DUKE

taking over his interests. But he secured payment for the brands and good will, as well as the physical properties.

Establishing factories and depots at strategic points in China and other Oriental countries, salesmen were sent far into the interior, penetrating at times to remote regions where white men had never gone before. Camel and pony caravans were organized, carrying goods hundreds of miles over untraveled routes. In regions where there was hardly a road, salesmen were carried in chairs by native bearers.

Making friends of the local dealers, treating them liberally, the goods were introduced and a steady custom created. In myriads of tiny shops, thatched stores and bamboo huts the Duke products were sold, and their colored lithographs and displays, printed in the native language, were the most familiar signs.

Tobacco had been raised in China since 1660, millions of pounds were produced, but it was strong and bitter stuff, smoked only in tiny pipes. American tobacco, mild and sweet, in cigarette form, caught the Chinese fancy. Many years ago, as William G. Shepherd recounts in a recent article in *Collier's*, "cartons of cigarettes were sent from America to Chinese firms to distribute. Customers took to them immediately.

"Then the American tobacco men got an idea—'cigarette pictures,' a picture to a package. China took the idea without a halt. Pictures of Chinese statesmen, going back to heroes of over two thousand years ago, led in popularity. Next came a series of pictures showing the birds of China. These pictures were drawn by the best Chinese artists, and it became a vogue to attempt to secure the entire series.

"To-day the Chinese smoke 40,000,000,000 cigarettes a year, as against America's 90,000,000,000, and

WORLD-WIDE ALLIANCE

American tobacco advertisements appear constantly in all the Chinese magazines and newspapers."

The methods originated by Duke, pursued first by his firm and later by the American Tobacco Company, were continued and extended by the British-American, after that company came into existence. Distributing the product in some countries through local subsidiary companies, in others by direct depots or agencies, the company's policy was to send out the most capable representatives and salesmen that could be found. Not confined to Britons or Americans, these included men of various nationalities. Managers were encouraged to employ as much local and native talent as could be used. Thus the various branches were firmly rooted as local institutions.

Catering to the tastes of different nationalities, devoting as careful attention to the vendor in India or the Chinaman in his bamboo shack as to the dealers in European cities, this corporation is truly international.

Not long ago a college president, returning to America after spending years in the Far East, replied:

"There are three great agencies in China, the missionaries, the British-American Tobacco Company, and the Standard Oil Company, with one accord—'Let there be light.'"

All through the Orient the tobacco company is regarded not only as a commercial pioneer, blazing the way in trade, but as a distinct civilizing influence. Fair dealing and considerate treatment have led the native merchants to consider the tobacco men their friends and partners. The factories and depots in cities and ports are local enterprises, by no means foreign to those who work in or deal with them.

This is due to the high character of the representatives, as well as to the general policy of the company.

JAMES B. DUKE

Many of them, living abroad for decades, have become thoroughly identified with local interests. Experts in their line, they are outstanding individuals who would measure up well in any community.

One of the men Mr. Duke chose to direct his enterprises in Japan, and who continued there until the Japanese made tobacco manufacture a government monopoly, was Captain E. J. Parrish, who in the early days had been the Dukes' local rival, selling his "Pride of Durham" smoking tobacco in competition with them. Experienced in every branch of the trade, as manufacturer, buyer and warehouseman, he was an example of the able, energetic emissaries who built up the trade in other countries.

Long before the British-American was organized men were sent to Java, Sumatra, the Straits Settlements, the Philippine Islands, Siam and Burma as well as to China and Japan. Among these was James A. Thomas, whose special field was China. Meeting him in the elevator at the New York office as he was preparing to leave on a trip extending from Calcutta to Shanghai, Mr. Duke, noticing in his hand a formidable typewritten document, asked what it was. Informed that it was from the Export Department, embodying the instructions his representative was to follow on arrival in India, he tore up the forty page memorandum, threw the pieces in the waste basket, and said:

"The last man I sent out to India had a list of instructions, but he did not do anything. If you are starting for India with so many instructions, I think you had better not go.

"You will make some mistakes in India," he remarked. "I make them every day; but don't make the same mistake twice."

One of the things to be settled on this trip was the

WORLD-WIDE ALLIANCE

case of a retail dealer in Java who had copyrighted one of the Duke brands then owned by the American Tobacco Company, and from whom, after six years of correspondence, the company could get no satisfaction. Getting out his files, which began with his first order in 1884, showing a number of letters signed by James B. Duke, stating how his firm appreciated the interest he was taking in their goods, and inviting him if he should ever come to the United States to call upon them, the dealer said he had copyrighted the brand solely in the interest of W. Duke Sons and Co., who were friends of his. Told that Mr. Duke was president of the American Tobacco Company, he gave up his rights and made the transfer there and then, refusing any pay for it. To reward his friendliness and confidence, his wife was presented with a silver tea set, which this Javanese family treasured as having been sent to them by their American friend.

Chinese tobacco dealers, seeing Mr. Duke's photograph in the company's office in China, asked who he was. Looking at the picture earnestly, concluding that he had a "good face," they were certain he was a "good man," and felt like sending him a present. Deciding to have two lions, each weighing a thousand pounds, carved out of granite, they placed the order in Ningpo, and took up a collection among the Chinese tobacco dealers. Hundreds contributed, the contributions varying from one copper to a dollar. The total cost was about $1,000. The lions, carefully packed for shipment, were sent to Mr. Duke's place at Somerville, N. J., with a book containing the names of the contributors, in Chinese and in English. It was their voluntary contribution to the ornamentation of his home.

Having, as a rule, a high sense of business honor,

JAMES B. DUKE

the Chinese become warm supporters once one gains their confidence, and Mr. Duke had that to a marked degree. Mourned in China, as in America, his Oriental customers felt that in his death they had lost a valued friend.

One of the foremost of Chinese merchants, Mr. Cheang Park Chew, generally known as Mr. Wing Tai, of Shanghai, wrote to Mr. George G. Allen, of the British-American Company in New York, sending a check for $1,000, stating that he presumed a monument would be erected to Mr. Duke, and he wished to make a contribution toward it. Owing so much to Mr. Duke, the Chinese merchant explained, and considering him so largely responsible for his success, he wished to pay this tribute to his memory.

Translations from the vernacular press in China were frequently received containing complimentary remarks about this manufacturer whom the Chinese had never met and knew only through selling his tobacco.

Mr. Duke's grasp of conditions in other countries and his promptness in deciding how to deal with them often surprised his foreign representatives.

Deciding to produce a cigarette in China that could be sold for a copper a package, Mr. Duke, explaining that he had an urgent engagement and was in a hurry, asked the manager of his Chinese business to go along in the car with him. Discussing the details as the automobile sped through the streets, as they parted, he said:

"You put out that cigarette in China immediately, and don't stop unless you receive a letter or a cablegram from me to do so."

In this brief ride his representative had been instructed to buy land, build a new factory and buy

WORLD-WIDE ALLIANCE

twenty million pounds of tobacco for this cigarette, putting it on the market in the way they had agreed upon.

Arriving in China the following month, ten days later he received a cablegram from Mr. Duke inquiring whether the land and tobacco had been bought and the factory was under construction. The work was already under way. Introduction of this cigarette in China increased the sale of all the better grades for which the tobacco was grown in the Carolinas and Virginia. It was Mr. Duke's own idea that gave the Chinese that important factor in the trade, "five cigarettes in a package for a copper."

Southern leaf was selling at low prices. India and China, with their vast populations, were growing enormous quantities of tobacco, and had done so for centuries. It seemed almost futile to undertake introduction there of American-grown tobacco. But Duke decided to go on with the proposition in the big way he had outlined.

After they had estimated how much tobacco would be necessary to carry his plan into effect, Mr. Thomas asked: "Mr. Duke, how long will it take you to double the price of tobacco in the two Carolinas and Virginia and add $15 an acre to the value of the land which grows this tobacco?" Thinking a moment, he replied: "It would take about twenty years." As a matter of fact, the price was doubled in little more than half that time.

Speaking of China, Mr. Duke inquired the distance between two towns. Told it was approximately a thousand miles, he said, "Go and build a railroad there and create a wage for the people, and you will be helping the whole country." He often spoke about

JAMES B. DUKE

harnessing the Upper Yangtze River, and what could be done with its water power.

In constructing factories and other buildings abroad, he impressed upon his managers that he did not want any "fancy work" put on them. Durability and success in the undertaking were the most important points.

The British-American Tobacco Co., founded and conducted on this sound basis, stands to-day as one of the most efficient organizations of the kind in existence. Doing an immense business in the Orient, with factories and agencies in China, India, Australia, New Zealand, the Straits Settlements, in Egypt and other parts of Africa; its agents stationed at the producing centers of Greece and Turkey, the company's trade lines extend across Europe, through Switzerland, Holland, Belgium, Denmark and Finland. With large establishments in Canada, Mexico, the West Indies, and Panama, in Brazil, Argentina, Venezuela and Chile, it is also the largest distributor of tobacco products, outside of the United States, in North and South America.

In Shanghai are two factories which turn out 20,000,000 cigarettes a day—two billion a month. There are other plants in Hang-Kow, Tientsin, Tsing-Tau, and at Mukden and Harbin, in Manchuria. All these are in one country, China, but this gives some idea of the international corporation's immense output and sale.

After the dissolution of the American Tobacco Company, Mr. Duke for several years devoted the major part of his attention to the British-American, becoming Chairman of the Board. From the beginning he had, in a general way, supervised its operations. But the British stockholders wished him to take a more active part in its management, to have the whole organization under his personal direction.

WORLD-WIDE ALLIANCE

The opportunity came when the American combine was dissolved. Each of the succeeding companies had been placed in the hands of competent executives who had been his aides and associates. Managing any one of these smaller concerns did not appeal to the man who had been at the head of them all. Greater opportunities were presented in the foreign trade. The British-American Company offered attractive inducements, and he accepted.

The corporation's main offices being in London, necessarily spending much of his time in England, Mr. Duke set up an establishment there, as well as in New York. This led to the impression in some quarters that he had taken up his permanent residence in England. Some newspapers violently attacked him, reporting that he had "deserted America" and transferred his allegiance to Great Britain. A few went so far as to state that he had become a British subject.

Nothing was farther from the truth. The thought of renouncing American citizenship had never entered his mind. Abroad when the World War broke out, caught, like thousands of Americans, in the war zone, Mr. Duke had difficulty in arranging his affairs and getting passage to America. This gave fresh currency to the reports of his change in allegiance, which were published in the North Carolina as well as the New York newspapers. Further, they alleged that the tobacco magnate had left America in order to avoid paying income tax. Paying no attention to such publications, Mr. Duke had never taken the trouble to enter a denial.

Resenting the injustice which was creating a false impression among his own home people, one of his former partners, George W. Watts, wrote to the newspapers, explaining the entire matter, and making public

JAMES B. DUKE

a letter which Mr. Duke himself had written him. Mr. Watts in his statement said:

"Many of the papers of North and South Carolina have apparently taken delight in censuring Mr. J. B. Duke upon an unfounded and untrue statement that he had become a citizen of Great Britain. It seems very strange to me that these papers would not first investigate the truthfulness of such slanderous rumors before publishing and giving approval to them.

"Upon the dissolution of the American Tobacco Company by the United States courts, Mr. Duke found nothing attractive in managing or directing any of the smaller companies into which the American Tobacco Company had been subdivided. His whole life having been devoted to the tobacco business, and being recognized as a leader in this line, his services were eagerly sought. The British-American Tobacco Company (whose market is the world) having made him a satisfactory proposition, he accepted the chairmanship of its board, which is equivalent to its management. This requires Mr. Duke to spend six months in each year abroad.

"Mr. Duke while being one of the most progressive and vigorous men the South has produced, is also one of the most modest, so never makes reply to any newspaper articles reflecting upon him or his business. But I, as his friend and associate with him in business for over thirty-six years, feel that this is an injustice and should be corrected. I am therefore enclosing a letter just received from him.

"Yours very truly,
"GEORGE W. WATTS.
"Durham, Sept. 26, 1914."

The letter from Mr. Duke to which he referred, which was written on September 22nd, is as follows:

"GEORGE W. WATTS, ESQUIRE,
   "Durham, N. C.

"My Dear George: I have been told of the articles charging me with having become a British subject, but press of matters

WORLD-WIDE ALLIANCE

excluded them from mind until recalled by your letter of the 16th, which is now before me. While these articles are entirely unfounded, as you and my other friends know full well, I did not take notice of them—because that has not been my custom. The fact is that I am now a citizen of the United States. I do not contemplate and have never contemplated becoming a British subject.

"So far as the income tax is concerned, I am always ready to bear my part of any taxes deemed necessary. You know how I have labored to build up and advance the business and commerce of the United States at home and abroad, and of my abiding faith and interest in this endeavor. To mention no other reason, I have too much at stake in this respect and too much hope in the future of American business and commerce to ever cease to be a citizen of the United States. The result is that as soon as I could, after war was declared, I hurried home because my first interest was here, and have since been giving my whole time to the situation, which demands the best of all of us.

"I sincerely regret missing you when you were here last week and shall look forward with pleasure to your promised visit at an early date.

"Sincerely yours,
"J. B. DUKE."

CHAPTER ELEVEN

Dissolving the Combine—Setting Up New Companies

RUNNING a single concern, even one as large as the British-American, must have seemed almost like a rest to Mr. Duke after handling so many varied and often conflicting interests.

For years he had been under constant fire—investigated, prosecuted, hounded by newspapers and politicians, charged with maintaining a monopoly and finally ordered by the courts to dismember the immense combination he had brought together. Taking apart its numerous elements, he had reconstructed old companies, established new ones, and put the tobacco industry on a competitive basis. But this had been a long and painful process. Carrying out the court's orders to the letter, efficiently and conscientiously, he always felt that the prosecution was unjust and uncalled for, and nothing would convince him that he or his company had been guilty of anything that was not in accord with sound commercial and legal principles.

Many able financiers and economic authorities believed that the huge aggregations of capital which dominated finance and industry could not be divided without causing enormous losses and upsetting the business of the country. "You can't unscramble eggs," said J. Pierpont Morgan, who regarded it as almost a hopeless undertaking.

The task was one of the utmost difficulty, especially in the case of industrial corporations such as the tobacco combine.

But when the United States Supreme Court ordered the American Tobacco Company dissolved, Mr. Duke went about ending the big corporation as energetically as he had in creating it—and with the same confidence.

DISSOLVING THE COMBINE

How the properties and securities could be divided without injury to investors or the industry neither legal nor financial experts could tell. Mr. Duke, however, was sure this could be done somehow—and he found the way. Here was one "trust" that was successfully dissolved.

The Federal litigation against the tobacco interests covered a period of nearly five years. Having won the Northern Securities decision and its case against the packers, the Roosevelt administration turned its guns on Standard Oil and American Tobacco.

A grand jury investigation was begun and subpœnas issued for officers of the American Tobacco Company, directing them to produce papers and documentary evidence. When these were refused the officials summoned were adjudged in contempt of court. In June, 1906, indictments were returned against the MacAndrews and Forbes Company and the J. S. Young Company, charging them with combining and conspiring to regulate the trade in licorice paste, largely used in the manufacture of tobacco. On January 10, 1907, the case was decided against them on two counts and fines of $10,000 and $8,000 respectively imposed.

Just six months later the major prosecution, against the parent corporation, was instituted. On July 10, 1907, the Department of Justice filed, in the United States Circuit Court in New York, a bill in equity against the American Tobacco Company and others, charging that they were maintaining a combination in restraint of trade and commerce in the manufacture and sale of tobacco.

Eminent counsel were employed on both sides, and months devoted to the taking of testimony. Officers, directors, heads of departments, nearly every one concerned with the corporation, its subsidiaries and com-

JAMES B. DUKE

petitors, independents and trust magnates alike testified in the course of the proceedings. The printed record, volume after volume, covered thousands of pages.

Mr. Duke was ill at his home at Eighty-second Street and Fifth Avenue. He was unable to appear in court, so his bed-chamber was turned into a courtroom. James C. MacReynolds, of Tennessee, later Attorney General in President Wilson's administration and now a Justice of the United States Supreme Court, was the special representative of the Department of Justice. Judge Lacombe had appointed U. S. Commissioner James A. Shields special examiner to take testimony. W. W. Fuller, general counsel; Junius Parker, assistant general counsel; DeLancey Nicoll and Judge William M. Wallace represented the American Tobacco Company. They gathered in Mr. Duke's room on February 25, 1908, and for three days he was testifying, under direct examination.

Giving a detailed account of how the American Tobacco Company and allied corporations had been formed, Mr. Duke explained how and why the numerous companies and factories had been acquired, reviewed the various deals and arrangements entered into, and gave a comprehensive history of the company and its operations.

He was so frank in his testimony, covering the ground so thoroughly, that he was not submitted to cross-examination by the Government's attorney, Mr. MacReynolds, who contented himself with a question here and there to clear up some point about which he was uncertain.

His principal object in going into the American Tobacco Company, Mr. Duke reiterated, was to get a better organization. W. Duke, Sons & Co. were al-

DISSOLVING THE COMBINE

ready the leading cigarette manufacturers, turning out nearly half of the country's total production, and he regarded the $7,500,000 they received for their property as only a fair value. The five firms acquired were sold directly to the corporation, which had not, he declared, raised prices to consumers or attempted to depress prices of the raw product.

Factories in other branches—plug, snuff, cheroots, cigars, makers of various specialties—had been acquired later because he wished his company to have a complete line, manufacturing every variety of tobacco. In some instances they bought a company to get a popular brand; in others to bring in some particularly capable man.

Going into the various consolidations—the Continental, American Snuff Co., Consolidated, American Cheroot Co., American Cigar Co.,—he told how they were brought about and why each was formed. To make a success of any particular line, he said, required men who knew that specialty; the business could often be handled better separately than together with other lines. That was the main reason for forming most of the subsidiary companies.

"We decided we could not properly go into the cigar business," he said, for example, "unless we had a cigar organization, people that understood that business." The same thing applied to other branches.

The prosecution made much of the fact that the American Tobacco Co. had bought or acquired a large stock interest in various concerns which were still being run under their own names. Mr. Duke admitted as much, but said that old established firms like Blackwell's Durham Tobacco Co., S. Anargyros, and Spaulding and Merrick were kept as separate organizations because they could be more efficiently conducted that way.

One of the charges was that the company had bought up a number of firms—The Penn, Wells-Whitehead, R. A. Patterson Tobacco Co. and others—and kept secret the fact of its ownership, producing the impression that these were independent competitors.

"I was always opposed to that from my standpoint," Mr. Duke said. "I thought it was foolishness; but to the man who is going to run a business I say, here, go ahead and run it any way you like, so you make profits; that is all I care. I thought it was foolish to run a business secretly. I would rather not do business than to have to do it that way."

He wanted the various concerns to compete with each other, however; the more the better, as it increased trade. "I think that one of the mistakes the American Tobacco Company made in the beginning was that we didn't keep a separate organization for all of the principal businesses we bought."

An example of how that worked was the R. J. Reynolds Company, which manufactured "Prince Albert" smoking tobacco and various brands of plug. The Continental bought two-thirds of the stock, regarding this as a good investment. But Mr. Duke would not consider the purchase unless Mr. Reynolds would retain a large interest, remain in charge of the business and run it. "Mr. R. J. Reynolds is a very able tobacco merchant," he said. The Continental had no organization to manufacture or which understood how to make his goods. Mr. Reynolds continued in charge, and the business increased enormously, selling within a few years several times as much of his product as before.

Mr. Duke resented the charge that he had set out

DISSOLVING THE COMBINE

to create or had created a monopoly. He did not buy out concerns to get rid of competition, he declared, but as investments.

"We don't gain anything by getting rid of competition," he said. "If we started to buy them with that idea they would start to build them faster than we could buy them.

"We want the competitors to go on. I think we make more money that way than if we had a monopoly. I know it is the case in the cigarette business, because when we had so nearly all of it, it was cut in half in four or five years, and as soon as we had competitors we built it up again."

He felt the same way about the raw product. Competition in buying leaf tobacco was better for all concerned.

"The farmer has got to have a good price for his tobacco, or he won't grow it," he remarked. "We are just as much interested in the farmer as we are in the consumer."

A man could go into manufacture and make money as easily as he ever could, if he had a brand that pleased consumers, was Mr. Duke's opinion. Going into business independently, he would have as good, probably a slightly better chance to succeed, because of the prejudice against big concerns.

The Government representatives, however, held and produced quantities of evidence, including statistics covering almost the entire industry, designed to show that the American Tobacco Company had created a virtual monopoly in certain lines and controlled most of the trade, domestic and foreign. The prosecution contended that the Sherman law prohibited any act or acquisition in restraint of trade; that the acquirement of any competing concern was a violation of the statute. There had been dozens of such purchases, many mergers and various deals of that character. The Government attorneys demanded not only the conviction of the defendants, but the appointment of receivers and dissolution of the company.

On November 7, 1908, the case was decided against the defendants, with a few exceptions, the Imperial Tobacco Company, the United Cigar Company and one or two others. Judges Lacombe, Coxe and Noyes presented the majority opinion of the court, Judge Ward dissenting.

"The record in this case," said Judge Lacombe, "does not indicate that there has been any increase in the price of tobacco products to the consumer. There is an absence of persuasive evidence that by unfair competition or improper practices independent dealers have been dragooned into giving up their individual enterprises and selling out to the principal defendant.

"During the existence of the American Tobacco Company new enterprises have been started, some with small capital, in competition with it and have thriven.

"The price of leaf tobacco—the raw material—except for one brief period of abnormal conditions, has steadily increased until it has nearly doubled, while at the same time 150,000 additional acres have been devoted to tobacco crops and the consumption of the leaf has greatly increased.

"Through the enterprise of defendants, and at large expense, new markets have been opened or developed in India, China and elsewhere."

"But all this is immaterial," the court held. The Sherman anti-trust act, as construed by the Supreme Court, prohibited every contract or combination in restraint of competition. "Each one of these purchases

DISSOLVING THE COMBINE

of existing concerns, complained of in the petition, was a contract and combination in restraint of competition when it was entered into, and that is sufficient to bring it within the ban of this drastic statute."

The result was a blow to the combine and endangered its existence. But the charges of unfair practices had not been sustained, as Mr. Duke pointed out in an open letter to the stockholders; the violations of law were largely technical, and the court had seen no necessity for the appointment of receivers. The decision was not satisfactory to either side, and both appealed.

The case was twice argued in the United States Supreme Court, first in January, 1910, then a year later. DeLancey Nicoll, of New York, and John G. Johnson, of Philadelphia, appeared for the American Tobacco Company when the case was first argued. It was reargued in January, 1911, by Mr. Nicoll, Mr. Johnson and Junius Parker, who continued the argument on behalf of the company when the Philadelphia lawyer was taken ill, after speaking for ten minutes, and had to leave the court-room. Attorney General Wickersham and Mr. MacReynolds prepared the briefs and argued the case for the prosecution.

The Supreme Court, on May 29, 1911, handed down a sweeping decision against the defendants, holding that the tobacco combination "in and of itself, as well as each and all of the elements composing it, whether corporate or individual, whether considered collectively or separately" was "in restraint of trade and an attempt to monopolize, and a monopolization within the first and second sections of the Anti-Trust Act." The American Tobacco Company was ordered dissolved, the constituent elements to be separated so that competition would be restored.

The principles of law involved had been announced

previously in the Standard Oil decision, but that was so largely a holding company that the court concluded that disintegration could be sufficiently effected by getting rid of stocks and subsidiary companies.

In the case of the American Tobacco Company, however, there were found to be not only holdings by corporations of stock in subsidiary companies, but it was declared also that the company itself had, by direct ownership of plants, brands and physical properties, so large a proportion of certain lines of the tobacco business, and certain of its subsidiaries, like the American Snuff Company, had also so large a proportion of other lines, that a mere disposition of stock would not be sufficient.

The Supreme Court, therefore, remanded the case to the Circuit Court of Appeals in New York with directions that it should "hear the parties by evidence or otherwise as it may deem proper, for the purpose of ascertaining and determining upon some plan or method of dissolving the combination, and of re-creating out of the elements now composing it a new condition which shall be honestly in harmony with, and not repugnant to the law, but without unnecessary injury to the public or the rights of property." If no practicable plan was devised within six months which would bring about this condition, the court was authorized to appoint receivers for the properties.

The responsibility of devising some plan by which the court's decree could be made effective, and the interests of all concerned protected, was placed squarely upon the company's officials. In this they had able legal advisers—Mr. Fuller, general counsel of the company; Mr. Parker, assistant general counsel; DeLancey Nicoll, who had represented the corporation in the case; and Lewis Cass Ledyard, who was in close

DISSOLVING THE COMBINE

touch with the financiers and stockholders' committees. With Attorney General Wickersham and Special Assistant MacReynolds, they arranged a series of conferences, during the summer and fall, with the judges of the Circuit Court.

Attending every one of these conferences, Mr. Duke studied carefully the points discussed. The problems were intricate and seemed to be almost insoluble. First, the public interest had to be considered, and arrangements made so that no manufacturer should have a monopoly or preponderance of trade in any class of tobacco properties. Second, the rights of investors, holders of millions of dollars of securities which had varying priority, had to be considered. No one company was to be left in a monopolistic position respecting the purchase, manufacture or sale of any type or grade of tobacco. Securities might be distributed, physical properties allotted, but trademarks and brands were indivisible. The most popular of these, widely advertised, covering large output, were of enormous value. How they could be placed with separate concerns, competing in manufacture, was difficult to determine.

He was aided by statisticians, auditors and lawyers, but Mr. Duke had to be relied upon to work out these problems, so far as the division of properties, brands, factories, securities and business were concerned. Before the first conference he had prepared figures and charts, showing the proposed distribution of stocks, formation of new companies, conveyances to them, and what the result would be with respect to distribution of brands, competition, and leaf tobacco requirements by territory, type and grade. So complete, fair and comprehensive was this proposal that any amendment made to carry out the public requirements was only trivial. This was, in all essentials, the plan adopted and under

JAMES B. DUKE

which the major portion of the tobacco industry has been conducted ever since.

The American Tobacco Co. was to be continued, handling its full share of the business and two new corporations were to be organized, bearing well-known names—the Liggett and Myers Company and the P. Lorillard Company. To the former was allotted the following plants and their brands: Liggett and Myers, St. Louis; Spaulding and Merrick, Chicago; Allen and Ginter, Richmond (this not including the "Sweet Caporal" brand, which was manufactured partly in New York); the American Tobacco Company's smoking tobacco factory in Chicago and its Catlin branch in St. Louis; Nall and Williams, Louisville; the John Bollman Co., San Francisco; the Pinkerton Co., Toledo, Ohio; W. R. Irby, New Orleans; two "little-cigar" factories in Baltimore and Philadelphia, making principally "Recruits," and the Duke-Durham branch of the American Tobacco Co., at Durham, N. C., manufacturing "Piedmont" and "American Beauty" cigarettes, and "Duke's Mixture."

The Lorillard Company, in addition to the Lorillard properties, was allotted S. Anargyros, manufacturing Turkish cigarettes; the Luhrman and Wilburn Tobacco Co.; plants in Philadelphia, Wilmington, Brooklyn, Baltimore and Danville, Va., manufacturing little cigars, principally the brand known as "Between the Acts," and the Federal Cigar Co., with its brands and properties.

To handle the snuff trade, two corporations were organized, the George W. Helme Co. and the Weyman-Bruton Co., the assets of the American Snuff Company being divided between them. The R. J. Reynolds Co., which has since, through its production of the "Camel" brand, become the largest of cigarette manufacturers,

DISSOLVING THE COMBINE

was released from any control by the American Tobacco Company, and so were other prominent concerns in which the company held considerable amounts of stock. The American Stogie Co. was dissolved. The licorice and tin-foil interests were divided between two companies. The American Tobacco Company, whose existence was continued, disposed of its stock in the United Cigar Company, the British-American and various other corporations.

Extensive competition was assured. Furthermore, the work was done so fairly and efficiently that all the resulting companies were able to operate successfully as independent concerns.

The most difficult question, after this general plan was presented, was the distribution of securities. The American Tobacco Company had outstanding over $100,000,000 of bonds not secured by mortgage but by a trust indenture which declared that about half of the six per cent bonds had a prior claim and approximately half of the four per cent bonds a secondary claim; both being prior in right to the six per cent preferred stock, then about $78,000,000, and the $40,000,000 common stock. How could properties of immense value which constituted the security for these bonds be transferred to independent companies?

The bonds were not callable and did not mature for thirty years. The preferred stock was not callable. Suggestion was made that the American Tobacco Company receive into its treasury the purchase prices of properties transferred to Liggett and Myers and Lorillard, principally in bonds of those companies. The Attorney General was unwilling that this be done, conceiving that it would leave the American Company undue financial power.

Many conferences were held, Mr. Duke consulting

JAMES B. DUKE

his legal and financial advisers, but they offered no solution. His family being at Newport for the summer, Mr. Duke usually spent Saturdays and Sundays with them. Returning from Newport one Monday morning in September, he called his counsel together, and presented a practical plan that met all requirements. This was that the Liggett and Myers and Lorillard companies acquire the tangible properties at book value, and good will at a value based on the comparative earnings of the brands. The total amounted to $115,000,000.

To meet the Government's objections to receiving cash or holding securities to such a large amount, Mr. Duke proposed that the purchasing companies issue bonds of substantially the same classes as those of his company, secured by similar indentures, that these be exchanged for American Tobacco bonds and a certain proportion of preferred stocks, and that American bonds and stock of this amount be canceled. Thus the company could receive full value for the properties, using the major portion to retire its bonds and reduce its preferred stock. To induce holders of the American bonds to make the exchange the new companies' bonds were to bear a slightly higher rate of interest.

The two newly-organized companies were to issue 7 per cent bonds to an amount equal to exactly half of the American 6 per cent bonds outstanding, $26,441,325; 5 per cent bonds for half of its four per cents, $25,677,050; 7 per cent preferred stock for one-third of the American's preferred, $26,229,700; and the remainder of the purchase price, $35,651,925, in common stock.

This proved acceptable to the Government's representatives. The question then was, how could the

DISSOLVING THE COMBINE

holders be induced to present their stocks and bonds for cancellation? An offer much above the market would be required, as Mr. Duke realized, to attract them.

Fortunately committees of representative bankers, advised by noted lawyers, had been organized to look after the interests of the many bond-holders and stockholders. Joseph H. Choate was the adviser of one of these committees, Judge Morgan J. O'Brien and Adrian Larkin of the others. Finally it was agreed that the holders presenting 6 per cent American bonds would be paid $120 in cash for each $100 face value of half of their holdings and the holders of four per cents $96 in cash for half the bonds surrendered, provided they took the other half in the new bonds.

As the market price of the "fours" was not over 80 and the six per cents were selling around 104, this plan afforded considerable profits. The proposals had to be kept strictly confidential in order to prevent extensive speculation. Those on the inside or any one having advance information could have gone into Wall Street, bought large blocks of the bonds, before the bond-holders learned of the proposition, and made millions in a few hours. But those who had their money invested in these bonds and stocks were given the fullest protection. Neither Mr. Duke nor his advisers took any advantage of their knowledge concerning the plans. Practically all the bond-holders accepted the offer, and the financial problem was solved.

Not relaxing his efforts until the various companies were established on a firm footing, able to compete on equal terms, when they were placed in the hands of men competent to run them Mr. Duke retired from active management of or connection with American companies and turned his attention to other enterprises,

JAMES B. DUKE

principally the British-American Tobacco Company, becoming Chairman of its Board when W. R. Harris retired in 1912.

Nothing could more thoroughly demonstrate the skill and foresight displayed in this allocation and readjustment of the tobacco interests than has the record of the resulting corporations. Through some sixteen years of independent operation, their individual business and earnings have continually increased, mounting to figures that hardly seemed possible when the "trust" was dissolved. Liggett and Myers, the Reynolds, American Tobacco and Lorillard companies, United Cigar and various others are among the leading American corporations.

Consumers' tastes have changed. "Camels," "Chesterfields," "Lucky Strikes" and other brands have supplanted "Duke of Durham," "Cameos" and "Cross Cuts." A few of the old favorites, "Sweet Caporals," "Richmond Straight Cuts," "Virginia Brights" and "Piedmonts," have a steady sale, but many of the brands popular forty years ago have vanished, and new ones have taken their places. Yet the structures erected by Mr. Duke remain, growing constantly. The organizations he set up, guided largely by men trained by him or brought to his association, are still the largest factors in the trade.

CHAPTER TWELVE
Jobs for Men and Men for Jobs

PROVIDING opportunities for others is quite as important as getting ahead yourself, Mr. Duke held. Contending that only a few men can "create jobs," establish enterprises that employ large numbers, he considered it incumbent upon them to recognize ability, reward faithfulness and stimulate ambition. Regarding this as largely responsible for his own success, he did not see how any large undertaking could succeed without it.

His astuteness in selecting aids and associates was proverbial. Yet his conclusion, after long experience, was: "The greatest difficulty is not to find jobs for men, but men for jobs."

Merit was his test in filling responsible positions. Nothing else counted. Now and then some one who had been successful in another line or establishment was employed, but promotion from within was the rule.

"I doubt if he, personally, ever hired half a dozen men after he got well started," one of his associates remarked. "He built up men by placing responsibility upon them. But they had to 'make good.' Not bothering them with detail, he 'let them make their own mistakes,' as he expressed it. But woe to him who made the same mistake twice."

"I never find fault with any man who does his best, no matter how poor that is," he would say, recognizing that some have more ability than others. Employees were made to feel that there was no position which they could not attain; but they must rise by their own efforts, and only those who proved their competence were chosen for important posts.

One official who, beginning as a clerk, had become

JAMES B. DUKE

head of one of the largest of the Duke enterprises was asked how he had risen when so many who set forth with him had fallen by the wayside.

"When I came into the New York headquarters, knowing I had to begin at the bottom, and saw a hundred clerks in that one office alone, I wondered," he said, "if I had to make my way through all that force, where I was going to land." But the large majority, he soon found, were doing only what was assigned them, not looking beyond the minor places they held. Offering to help in anything there was to do, remaining over hours, laboring nights and holidays without extra pay, he was told by fellow clerks, "You are working yourself to death; and it is not appreciated." But his capability as well as willingness to tackle hard propositions had been demonstrated, the office manager had begun to rely on him, and when a higher position was open, he was the one selected.

Being in the Export Department, he was fascinated with its possibilities. Studying figures, reports and correspondence, talking with the representatives returning from China and India, he learned a lot about the foreign trade. One reason so few men rose to the top, he discovered, was that the large majority, familiar enough with the branches in which they were employed, never did get a knowledge of the business as a whole. That broad perspective, Mr. Duke held, was essential in conducting a trade where the whole world was open to them.

"Merchant ability," sought in his chiefs of corporations and sales departments, included what he said most men failed to acquire—the proprietorship viewpoint. Another requisite was a thorough knowledge of the business "from the ground up." Many of those around him had been "raised in tobacco." Some, like himself, had come from farms and worked in tobacco fields. Others had begun in the factory, and a large proportion had worked in warehouses and prizeries, buying and handling the leaf.

Employees, salesmen, managers were drawn from various walks of life, but each one must "know his job." Experts were demanded in every line. J. B. Cobb, who was vice president of the American Tobacco Co. and president of the American Cigar Co., had begun his career as a buyer and, with an initial capital of $500, had built up a successful trade. W. R. Harris, another vice president of the American Tobacco Co., and later Chairman of the Board of the British-American, was a Welshman, taken from the auditing department of the Pullman Palace Car Co. to become auditor of the Duke corporation. The Dulas, originally from Lenoir, N. C., were experts in plug manufacture and had come to him through the Drummond Tobacco Co. D. C. Patterson, now president of the Imperial Tobacco Co. of Canada, had been Mr. Duke's chief bookkeeper and aide when he was establishing his New York factory.

Rufus L. Patterson, president of the American Machine and Foundry Co., had worked with Kerr, inventor of the first bag-making machine, and had himself invented various devices for packing and labeling tobacco. W. W. Fuller, chief counsel, had been attorney for W. Duke, Sons & Co. and their local adviser, as had his brother, Frank L. Fuller. Junius Parker, associate counsel, was also a North Carolina lawyer, who after many years in the legal department of the American Tobacco Co., became Chairman of the Board. Charles A. Penn, vice president of the American, was from Reidsville, N. C., coming of a family long identified with the tobacco business. W. W. Flowers, vice

JAMES B. DUKE

president of Liggett and Myers, entered the Duke factory soon after his graduation from Trinity College. Clinton W. Toms, recently made president of that company, first attracted attention as superintendent of schools in Durham, and was later manager of the local plant. George G. Allen, a native of Warrenton, N. C., who began as a bookkeeper and accountant in the New York office, is now American head of the British-American Tobacco Co. and president of the Duke Endowment. These are only a few examples of the hundreds of men who rose to places of importance.

"Give the other fellow a chance," was one of Mr. Duke's cardinal principles. Constantly telling his chiefs to "build up understudies," to one department head he said, "If in five years you haven't half a dozen men under you who are better than you are, you have fallen down on your job." Then, after a pause, he added: "Because, by the time you have half a dozen men who are better than you are, you will be five times as good as you are now." He had no patience with those in responsible positions who strove to keep others down. "A man in developing others is developing himself," was his view. "It is a small man who is afraid to lose his job to somebody else." Thus the entire organization was kept alive and growing, never permitted to stagnate.

"When there's anything big to be done, get the right man for the job, and leave it to him—hold him responsible," was his policy—and they seldom failed to measure up to their responsibilities.

Having no use for loafers, either in or out of his employ—and this applied to all the Sons of Idleness, from the do-nothing rich to the ragged tramp, sponging on thrifty housewives—Mr. Duke remarked: "If a

MEN AND THEIR JOBS

man who is physically able won't work, he should be made to work. The lazy loafers should be sent to jail."

"Sizing up" men was as natural to him as breathing, not only in selecting some one for an important task, but in hiring hands for factories, machinists, superintendents, salesmen. He made a study of men. Even closest associates were not free from his kindly but searching scrutiny. More severe regarding himself than with any employee, this characteristic cropped out at the most unexpected moments.

Living most of his life as a bachelor, with scant thought of providing for a family, his approaching marriage necessitated a rearrangement of his personal affairs, and the drawing of a new will. The task was entrusted to his chief counsel and they spent days together at the Duke farm in New Jersey, considering the matter. In such concerns he insisted on the utmost particularity. After stating, in general, to whom and how he wished his property left, he studied each paragraph, inquiring just what effect it would have.

One Sunday afternoon, after a drive through the estate, as they were dozing away in the big cushioned chairs Mr. Duke roused suddenly and said:

"Fuller, what kind of a man are you, anyhow?"

Coming to himself with a start, the lawyer, surprised, said: "I don't know just what you mean, Mr. Duke."

"What kind of a man do you think you are? I'd like to know what you think of yourself."

This was no idle query. Mr. Duke was in deadly earnest. "I don't want you to demean yourself," he explained, "or praise yourself too highly; but just to tell me what you think."

Not an easy task—for a man to paint his own por-

JAMES B. DUKE

trait and unburden his thoughts regarding his own personality. But the attorney did it, carefully, thoughtfully, conscientiously.

Then Mr. Duke said, "Now I'll tell you what kind of a man I think I am." Setting forth clearly, one after the other, his characteristics, the various phases of his personality, he pointed out what he considered his good and bad points, faults and virtues.

There was no false modesty about it, no attempt to gloss over faults or weaknesses. It was simply a case of personal appraisement—of a man standing off, looking at his personality in a clear, cold light, sitting in judgment upon himself.

Mr. Fuller recalls, even now, the impression it made upon him, as the most singular and illuminating instance of self-analysis in his experience.

In 1889, when the American Tobacco Company was in process of formation, though the articles of agreement, charter and other documents had been drafted by eminent New York attorneys, Duke sent copies to the firm's lawyers in North Carolina, to learn if they could pick any flaws in them. Mr. Fuller, who was local counsel for W. Duke, Sons & Co., did find a provision that appeared more than doubtful; which, he believed, would tie the manufacturer up in a way which might embarrass and hamper him.

The New York legal lights who had drawn the documents scouted the idea that there was anything wrong with them. Mr. Seward, the leading counsel, and his firm were regarded as authorities on corporations. Mr. Markowitz, his partner, had, in fact, written what was then the standard if not the only comprehensive book on corporation law as applied to such combinations.

But Duke was not satisfied. Sending for Fuller, he told him to state his objections to the attorneys.

MEN AND THEIR JOBS

Seward, the son of William H. Seward, Secretary of State under President Lincoln, was president of the Union Club, and took Fuller there to discuss the matter. Courtesy itself to his guest, Mr. Seward explained the points involved, but loftily waved aside his legal objections. Unconvinced, the Carolinian was at the same time unwilling for the agreement, involving millions, to be upset on his lone advice.

Finally the point was submitted to Mr. Beaman, law partner of Senator William M. Evarts and Joseph H. Choate, afterwards Ambassador to England, who gave his opinion that the Durham attorney was right. Though the other manufacturers insisted on including the provision, and for a time this threatened to upset the entire combination, Duke had his way, the agreement was modified, and he admitted, in after years, that the young attorney's advice had "saved him a lot of trouble."

Deciding, some years later, that he would like to have the North Carolinian as his legal adviser, Mr. Duke, sending for him, set forth the large amount of work and responsibility involved, and then said:

"Do you think you are a big enough man for this job? Do you think you can swing it?

"Consider well before you decide," he said in friendly caution. "You have to go up against the biggest men in your profession here. You'll be pitted at times against the biggest lawyers in New York and this country. I can't keep anybody in that place if he doesn't make good. You have a good practice, are doing well where you are. If you fail here and have to go back, it will hurt you. Now, don't answer hastily. Think the matter over, and if you think you are big enough to handle it, I'll take the risk and give you the job."

JAMES B. DUKE

Taking the responsibility, Mr. Fuller accepted the position of chief counsel of the company, moved to New York, and for many years was Duke's adviser and aid.

One of the first things Mr. Duke asked on his arrival was: "Do you know how to spend money?" An unexpected question. Never having much money to spend, the lawyer replied that he had devoted more thought to saving than spending.

"Well, you have to spend money to make it," Mr. Duke explained. "You can't ever get anywhere by merely saving it. That's all right in small things, but you can't do anything on a big scale that way. You have to spend a lot of money here to do anything worth while, and the first thing to learn is how to spend it."

Convinced that spending millions in advertising, introducing goods and making them popular with consumers was one of the chief elements of success; that buying established brands, acquiring companies, improving plants and processes, building up trade in new regions was all money well spent, no one was more insistent on keeping down manufacturing expenses to a minimum. Spending a million dollars in advertising a brand, or ten millions in acquiring factories, he would figure down to a fraction of a cent the cost of producing a pack of cigarettes or a two-ounce tin of smoking tobacco. And this fraction might, and sometimes did, cover all the advertising costs, and make the difference between a handsome profit and a loss.

Another thing he insisted upon was at all times knowing, not guessing, the exact status of every branch of his business. He had installed, due to Mr. Harris, the most accurate and detailed system of accounting. Many manufacturers knew only at the end of the year exactly what were their gains or losses. The Duke concerns received daily reports on "Sales by Brands by Towns," and could tell at any moment the sales in every city and section, which brands were in the ascendancy and which were declining.

Buying out a Western factory making popular products, the former owner was left in charge but the American accounting system was installed. In thirty days this disclosed that the manager's pet brand was losing money while others he thought less of were making good profits. Refusing to believe it, he continued spending money lavishly on his favorite. After three months, finally convinced by the figures, he turned his energies to the profitable goods.

Accounting and reports were in such detail that each brand showed cost per unit, running into five decimal points, of every item entering into its manufacture—tobacco, wrapping of package, casing or sweetening material, shipping cases, down to the straps and nails. Labor in cutting tobacco, operating machines, putting goods in cases and handling them after they were packed was recorded, carried out to the last decimal, even if it was .00035 per thousand. Costs of any given article in the various factories were carefully compared, and manufacture eventually assigned to the plant where the article could be most economically produced and handled.

Mass production, volume, giving the largest possible values for the money, were his hobbies. Forcing through any project decided upon, imposing his views upon the largest financiers as readily as on his own employees, he would, in considering business matters, listen to any one who had a useful suggestion, even his office boy. Questioning the chef on his private car, talking to his chauffeur as well as his banker, he would get opinions from every angle.

JAMES B. DUKE

But he "thought things out" for himself. Decision usually came in the privacy of his home, often late at night after he had retired or in the morning before arising. "I can think better in bed," he remarked, regarding this habit of his. Enthusiastic over projects that aroused his interest, he was careful not to permit enthusiasm to run away with his judgment.

Quick to act in emergencies, shooting out orders like bullets from a gun, telling what to do and expecting it to be done immediately, he was never a quibbler or trimmer, but struck straight from the shoulder. Scorning pretense, he held that a busy man "had no time to put on frills."

"Mr. Duke was the fairest man I've ever known," Mr. Allen says, "as fair to the man who was absent as to the one who was present. He hated injustice. But if any one tried to take advantage of him, he never got a second chance. It was the rarest thing for him to speak ill, even of his worst enemy. The strongest expression I ever heard him use was to refer to some one who had tricked him or abused his confidence as a 'dinged yellow dog.'

"He had the greatest power of concentration—bringing out all the essentials of a subject—of any man I have ever known. That was what enabled him to dispose of important matters promptly and effectively.

"One method he had of 'educating' employees was to ask them questions about the business. If they didn't know, he would ask again. Those who hadn't taken the trouble to inform themselves were marked men.

"In discussions he would often take the opposite side, to see what argument the other man would bring out. Open to conviction, he was quick to reverse himself when he found he was wrong, saying, 'Well, I think you are right about it; we will do it that way.'

MEN AND THEIR JOBS

"Ambition, willingness to learn, attracted his attention, and he was especially interested in boys who, like himself, had come from the country. 'The best men come from the back-woods churches,' he remarked. 'The country boy can come to town and soon learn all the town boy knows, but the town boy can never get all that the country boy has had.'"

CHAPTER THIRTEEN

Harnessing Rivers to Serve Southern Industries

Down in the Carolinas, mainly along one river, the Catawba, is a development second in importance only to Muscle Shoals. Far up in Canada, on the Saguenay, engineers and workmen are developing a power that will rival Niagara, bringing into existence the largest enterprise in the Province of Quebec. Both are due to Mr. Duke, who, after making his fortune in tobacco, poured millions into water-power.

With numerous hydro-electric and six steam-electric plants, the Southern system has a generating capacity of 900,000 horsepower and distributes annually over one-and-a-half billion kilowatt hours of electricity through 3,500 miles of transmission lines. More than three hundred cotton mills, approximating 6,000,000 spindles, are driven by this power—over one-half of all the spindles in the Carolinas, more than a third of the total in the South, one-sixth of all the spindles in America. Electricity for other industries, for lighting and domestic uses, is supplied to eighty cities and towns, illuminating streets, driving trolley cars and interurban trains, serving a large population.

Built up in twenty years, most of it in the last decade, so far as financial backing and provision for construction were concerned this was a one-man proposition.

Carolinians never tire of relating how this series of enterprises grew out of a sore foot, a doctor's talk and the dream of a young engineer. Perhaps too much has been attributed to the combination of circumstances, but that was the way it began.

His foot paining him so he could scarcely walk, Duke sent for his physician. Erysipelas developed, not a violent case but severe enough to confine him to his

SOUTHERN WATER-POWERS

home. As he sat there, day after day, the bandaged foot propped up on a pillow, the doctor was almost his sole companion. Unused to illness, impatient at being kept from his office, something was needed to engage his active mind.

Having invested in a power plant in South Carolina, near his former home, Dr. W. Gill Wylie, his physician, spoke of the possibilities along the Catawba. By high-tension wires electricity could be transmitted long distances, distributed over a wide area. The young engineer in charge of construction, W. S. Lee, seemed to know his business and saw opportunities for a number of developments.

One plant in which Duke had invested some years previous had proved a failure, too small to bother with. But a chain of them, pouring out a steady stream of power, was something worth considering. Oceans of water were going to waste while Carolina mills bought coal from other States to stoke their boilers. Here was "white coal" in abundance, enough to run them all.

Hydro-electric generation on a large scale was a fascinating idea. Eager to know more about it, he asked who could tell him. "Lee," said the doctor. Send for Lee, then; let him bring his plans and discuss the project.

Summoned at once, the young engineer arrived promptly, in response to the doctor's telegram. Expecting little from a single interview, he welcomed the opportunity. Capital was the one thing needed, and here was the man who could furnish it, if he "took the notion."

"The first time I ever saw Mr. Duke was at his home in New York," Mr. Lee tells me. "I went there with Dr. Wylie, and we talked for a couple of hours. As I came in, Mr. Duke said: 'Doctor, is this that fel-

JAMES B. DUKE

low Lee who you say can do so much in power?' Knowing he would wish a diagram of what was proposed, I had made the preliminary plans. Examining them carefully, asking many questions, he inquired what it would cost. I told him about $8,000,000. I thought that was about the biggest amount I had ever heard of, but it seemed to attract him."

The Great Falls property in which he had invested eight or ten years previous had been almost abandoned. But a small plant was operated on the Raritan River to light his New Jersey farm, and he and Dr. Wylie began talking about that and how he enjoyed working with it.

Water power for service in industrial areas, the discussion soon revealed, was what interested him. Electric transmission at high voltage being in its infancy, financiers had been reluctant to invest the large sums involved. But Duke, alive to anything which promised encouragement to industries in the Piedmont, was willing to take the risk, if practical plans could be devised.

The initial scheme was to link up the Great Falls of the Catawba and the Mountain Island plants. Lee had made a map showing the transmission lines tying these stations together, giving continuity of service. Mr. Duke, he discovered, had been thinking along that line before. This was an opportune time to bring the matter to his attention.

Putting the engineer through quite a category of questions, he asked about the distances between plants, the practicability of connecting the work; the towns in that region, and the possibilities of industrial development.

Branching out as far as eighteen miles from the Catawba plant near Rock Hill, the company whose

GREAT FALLS AND FISHING CREEK STATIONS, SOUTH CAROLINA

THE MOUNTAIN ISLAND POWER PLANT, NEAR CHARLOTTE

SOUTHERN WATER-POWERS

project Lee was engineering was then building into Charlotte. There was another site down the river—now known as the Wateree, near Camden—which could be taken into the system. South Carolina capitalists had had Lee investigate this station, but seemed unable to produce the funds required. The property had been optioned and could be bought for about $100,000.

Turning to Dr. Wylie, Mr. Duke said: "Doctor, if you will give Lee $50,000, I'll give him $50,000, and we'll send him down and buy that property."

Coming to New York, delighted at the opportunity of presenting his plans, hardly hoping to accomplish more than the promise that they would be given consideration, Lee departed with two checks for $50,000 each—$100,000—and an order to buy the Wateree site and begin work.

Lee was only 32 years old. Mr. Duke had never seen him before that day. But, giving the young engineer his full backing, he left to his judgment how the project was to be developed. The property bought, additional funds were furnished from time to time as required, and the Wateree station, thirty miles from Columbia, was constructed.

That interview, which marked Mr. Duke's entrance into the field of water-power, occurred in the late autumn of 1904. Surveys were begun on a broad scale, other properties acquired, and a few months later, in June, 1905, the Southern Power Company was organized.

Plunging into water-power development heart and soul, Mr. Duke was studying every phase of it. All the major plans were discussed with him, and at times he would insist on going into the utmost possibilities of whatever matter was under consideration. Dams, which they were striving to make better and stronger

JAMES B. DUKE

than was customary, excited his especial interest. Studying the entire subject at his direction, the engineers made a comprehensive report on the evolution of dams —the earliest and how they had been built, all the later types devised, down to the most recent designs which experience and scientific knowledge had proved successful.

Considering various methods that might be used, Mr. Duke often suggested things that had been tried out, some of them long ago. Not in any sense a trained engineer, his mind would follow automatically a discussion of engineering problems. When he said emphatically, "that can't be done," his engineers would usually find it was impracticable.

"I know that in many cases he never had studied or heard of the things brought up," said Mr. Lee; "I could tell that from his manner of approach. But readily grasping the idea, his mind passed on to the next step."

Disliking "conferences" and talk that "didn't get anywhere," Duke would say impatiently, "Cut out the town meetings," when there seemed to be too much talk and not enough action. Many important instructions were given verbally. Deciding matters almost immediately, when the facts were before him, he would direct the man in charge to "Do it, and do it quick."

Plants that cost millions were authorized without the scratch of a pen. If the plans were satisfactory he would say, "All right, go ahead." His "O.K." was all the authority needed. It was as good as a check for the funds required.

"I do not recall that there were ever any formal or written instructions given me during my many years of association with Mr. Duke," Mr. Lee remarked. "It was his policy to designate one man to begin and

SOUTHERN WATER-POWERS

complete a thing rather than start a debating society or hold a town meeting over it.

"He had a wonderful power of making decisions. Sometimes these seemed to be almost off-hand, with hardly any consideration. But they were as accurate as they were swift. Generally he had gone into the matter thoroughly, had the points fixed in his mind and was sure of his ground. He merely thought faster, more accurately, and grasped the points of a situation more quickly than most men. And, once he had decided, he acted promptly." "Action was his middle name," as another friend expressed it.

A sharp questioner, probing direct for the essentials of a subject, Mr. Duke was never a ready talker. While discussing business matters he had a habit, as he sat at desk or table, of tearing paper into little pieces. This, somehow, seemed to help the process of thought with him. Sometimes the floor was littered with the bits of paper. But when, arising, the litter was brushed aside, he was ready for action.

"If you were to ask me," said Mr. Lee, "what built the Southern Power system, I would say: First, Mr. Duke's careful analysis in detail of any matter brought before him; second, his quick and positive decision; third, his intuitive knowledge and habit of studying the various phases of anything in which he was interested."

Use of electricity for power purposes was then in its early stages, transmission over any considerable distance being largely experimental. There was no assurance that, if the power were developed on a huge scale, users could be found for it, or that this power could be successfully transmitted over a sufficiently large territory to assure an ample market.

But having broad visions of what could be done in the South, Duke was convinced that the extensive tex-

JAMES B. DUKE

tile development in the Fall River section of Massachusetts could be and would be duplicated in the Carolinas, if low-priced power was available. And he proceeded to provide it.

The Southern Power Company, when organized in 1905, absorbed the Catawba Power Company with its 10,000-horsepower plant at Indian Head Shoals. Construction of a large hydro-electric plant at Great Falls, S. C., was begun immediately, and before that was finished work was under way on a plant of similar capacity at Rocky Creek. The former was put into commission in April, 1907, the latter in 1901. Next was the plant at Ninety-Nine Islands, on the Broad River, completed in May, 1910; followed by Lookout Shoals in North Carolina, Fishing Creek in South Carolina, completed in 1915 and 1916, and the Bridgewater development in North Carolina, finished in 1919, the Wateree plant near Camden, S. C., also going into operation that year. Then came two more large plants, the Dearborn, Great Falls, S. C., and the Mountain Island plant, twelve miles south of Charlotte, put in commission in 1923.

A 45,000-horsepower station was completed at Rhodhiss early in 1925, as was the new Catawba plant with a capacity of 80,000 horsepower. Meanwhile construction was begun on another hydro-electric of 60,000 horsepower at Rocky Creek and also upon an additional steam-electric plant at Salisbury, designed for a generating capacity of 100,000 horsepower.

Industries were few and scattered when these developments were begun, the importance and value of electric power were not fully appreciated, and for a long while there was a surplus of power. During recent years the requirements have exceeded the available

SOUTHERN WATER-POWERS

supply and new plants have had to be erected continually to meet the demand.

From one small power-house developing less than 10,000 horsepower, and forty miles of transmission lines, the Southern Power system has grown until to-day its plants generate 900,000 horsepower, and its transmission system embraces 3,500 miles of lines. At the beginning serving only thirteen cotton mills with fewer than 150,000 spindles, to-day this power drives more than three hundred cotton mills and numerous other factories.

Interested in cotton as well as tobacco manufacture the Dukes owned several large mills and invested in others, Benjamin N., as well as Brodie Duke, being particularly interested in this field. In addition to his power and other enterprises, "J. B." built the most important interurban electric railway in the Carolinas, the Piedmont and Northern, running from Charlotte to Greenville, S. C., his companies also operating street railways in a number of towns.

Electric service available at low cost for manufacturing establishments, stores and homes has wrought a revolution in that territory. Wherever the high-tension lines have gone factories have arisen, villages expanded into towns and towns into cities, bringing prosperity and the creation of new pay-rolls, giving work and wages to thousands. Farmers have profited through the wider markets for foodstuffs and other agricultural products, and the entire region has shared in the benefits.

The pioneer in hydro-electric development on a large scale in that region, the Southern Power Company supplies several times as much current to industries as all other public utilities combined. Its annual output of electricity is equivalent to the energy produced from

JAMES B. DUKE

more than two million tons of coal. Cotton manufacturers figure that the use of electric power instead of burning coal in their individual plants means a saving of more than $5,000,000 a year. Money invested in boilers and engines is "dead" capital, in so far as production is concerned, while the factory using electric power puts practically its entire capital into productive equipment, the expense of motors and accessories being but a fraction of the cost of a steam plant.

Everything considered, not less than $9 and probably $10, authorities estimate, is added to the general wealth by every dollar invested in water-power. Industries new or enlarged account for most of this, but there is also an immense incidental investment, in housing, stores and other features of an industrial community. Thus the advantages brought through Mr. Duke's electric enterprises have aggregated perhaps ten times the amount of capital put into them—and he invested many millions.

In Mr. Duke's boyhood North Carolina was one of the poorest parts of the country. Property had been destroyed, wealth swept away by war. Reconstruction was almost as destructive.

Not succeeding in enlisting Northern capital or obtaining outside aid, the "Tar Heels" began developing their own resources. Small tobacco factories and cotton mills were established with the few dollars that could be scraped together, profits were reinvested in the plants, and additional capital was mainly from local savings. So the people of the State, on the whole, own its industries. Growing into important establishments, some of these factories, like the Duke and Bull Durham plants, the R. J. Reynolds Company at Winston, the Cannon mills, near Concord, became the largest of their kind.

NINETY-NINE ISLANDS STATION, ON BROAD RIVER

RHODHISS POWER STATION AND COTTON MILLS

SOUTHERN WATER-POWERS

Leading the South in industries, both in value of product and numbers employed, the capital invested in North Carolina now totals close to a billion dollars, as is shown by this official report:

	Number	Capital Invested	Value of Product
Cotton mills	386	$168,292,000	$252,078,000
Cordage mills	5	1,035,000	1,728,000
Silk mills	2	3,000,000	2,350,000
Woolen mills	5	1,890,000	3,723,000
Knitting mills	131	33,994,000	29,058,702
Furniture factories	117	15,000,000	50,000,000
Tobacco factories	17	50,198,170	251,555,000
Tire and rubber manufacturers	3	1,600,000	3,500,000
Miscellaneous manufacturers			357,918,298
Total			$951,911,000

Producing one-fourth of the tobacco manufactured in the United States, its tobacco manufacturers pay to the Federal Government annually some $118,000,000 or more in internal revenue taxes, New York, next in rank, paying less than half that sum.

Excelled in cotton manufacture only by Massachusetts, North Carolina has a larger number of cotton mills than that stronghold of the textile industry. Cotton manufactures have increased ten-fold in value, reaching more than $250,000,000 annually; the number of employees has increased 123 per cent, and the capital employed 712 per cent. Here are the largest hosiery and towel mills, the largest denim and damask factories in America.

Furniture making is another thriving industry, High Point being the center of furniture manufacture in the South as Grand Rapids is in the North.

Agriculture has kept pace with manufacturing. Farm values more than doubled in the decade covered by the

JAMES B. DUKE

last Federal census, increasing from $537,716,210 to more than $1,250,000,000, and the State has advanced in twenty years from twenty-fourth to fourth place in value of crops.

Making a compilation of comparative increase of wealth in twenty-three States, the U. S. Department of Commerce discovered that North Carolina showed the largest proportionate advance, 175.7 per cent. In road improvement, schools and colleges the "Tar Heels" have set the pace for their neighbors. Smooth, well-graded highways stretch from the mountains to the sea. More than a hundred million dollars have been expended in roads, and a system constructed that compares well with any in existence.

Once near the bottom of the list, having a higher percentage of illiteracy than any State save one, North Carolina now stands ninth in the Union in school attendance, and first among the Southern States. Inaugurated some thirty years ago, the educational revival has resulted in establishing a model school system, with over 800,000 pupils enrolled. Building for years "a school-house a day," there are now nearly seven hundred high schools, in addition to the thousands of common schools.

This has been accomplished, in the main, by Carolinians themselves, by men "born and raised" there. Almost the entire population being of native stock, principally descendants of English and Scotch-Irish settlers, here is the smallest proportion of foreigners in any part of the United States, the population of 2,559,123 including, according to the last census, only 7,272 foreign born, three-tenths of one per cent.

Immigration has fertilized the majority of our commonwealths, but this one's growth has been due almost entirely to natural increase, its birth rate being greater

SOUTHERN WATER-POWERS

than that shown by any other State from which the Census Bureau collects data, 30.2 per 1,000 population.

What has been responsible for this notable improvement in what was long regarded as a backward State? Many things have contributed to it. Progressive leaders in town and country, in business establishments, schools, colleges and the professions have done their part. Pulpit and press preached the gospel of good roads, better schools and larger industries. Factories, stores and farms, with their wages, yields and profits, provided the means. Industrial and educational development moved hand in hand.

The tobacco and cotton industries have been perhaps the most important factors, and their growth has been immensely stimulated by the supply of electricity. "Cheap power, ample resources and an abundance of enterprise and muscular energy are the facts that are rejuvenating the South, bringing it back to the place of dominance which it once occupied," said the American Exchange-Pacific Bank, in summing up a recent survey. And that has been especially the case in this part of the South.

Electricity of more than a million horse-power is now generated and distributed by hydro-electric plants in the Carolinas, equaling the combined power of this character generated for commercial and community use in the other Southeastern States. Ninety per cent of the cotton mills and tobacco factories, fifty per cent of the furniture factories and knitting mills are electrically driven.

Due to many different elements, no single factor has contributed more to the growth of the Carolinas than these water-power developments and resulting enterprises.

Large as were Mr. Duke's material contributions, his

JAMES B. DUKE

real passion, Governor Angus W. McLean of North Carolina declared, was "based on spiritual values, as expressed in manhood and womanhood." Bringing back his riches to his mother State, he "laid them in her lap that they should be used to bless and benefit her children and children's children in seeking the enduring things of life."

"The material benefits of Mr. Duke's generosity are already apparent," the Governor pointed out, "but no one can visualize the benefits which he has bestowed on future generations any more than one can see in the tiny acorn the spreading oak, except through the eyes of faith and anticipation. The division of his munificent bequests—part for hospital work, the relief of suffering, and part for education, the growth of the soul, shows most eloquently what interests lay nearest his heart in the last years of his life. For the next hundred years—even longer—there will not be a citizen of the State, young or old, who will not feel the benign influence of his contribution to the great work of making North Carolina a better State in which to live."

CHAPTER FOURTEEN
Taming the Waters of the Saguenay

IN the swift fall of the Saguenay, as it flows from Lake St. John, in Upper Quebec, Mr. Duke found the means of generating an almost unlimited supply of electricity. There in the Canadian wilds, a hundred miles north of the City of Quebec, is proceeding steadily, step by step, one of the most extensive power developments on the continent.

The largest single installation ever undertaken is that at Isle Maligne, which will produce 540,000 horsepower. The ten units at Chute à Caron, when the dam and power house there are completed, will generate 800,000 horsepower. At that point is being established the largest of aluminum plants. The Premier of Quebec announced, in June, 1925, four months before Mr. Duke died, that the plans provided for the greatest industrial establishment ever projected in the Province, calling for the expenditure of $75,000,000 to $100,000,000 in development and construction.

Some 8,000 workmen will be employed, when the aluminum plant is in full operation. To house them and their families a model town is being laid out, providing for hundreds of cottages, schools, churches, stores and all the modern conveniences. With other enterprises which the power plants will attract, Canadians are predicting that in a few years there will grow up a city of 35,000 to 40,000 population in what not long ago was a wilderness.

For generations men had looked upon these rapids, recognizing their boundless potentialities, but realizing also the almost insuperable difficulties to be overcome before this tremendous force could be utilized. Engineers did not, of course, take any stock in the local tradition, handed down from the time of the early explorers, that the "dark, mysterious river," as the Indians called it, could never be brought under human control. From an engineering standpoint, with the advance of hydro-electric science, this was regarded as feasible. A huge project, requiring not only immense capital but the "nerve" to put through an untried enterprise and the business ability to make the investment yield returns, no man or corporation had been found to attempt the venture until Mr. Duke entered upon the undertaking, with all the energy and resources at his command.

Organizing the Quebec Development Co., he began acquiring properties in 1913, but owing to conditions, the active work of construction did not begin until after the war. The physical task, impounding the waters of a vast lake, changing channels, constructing dams, erecting power-houses, building railroads and bridges, planting a city in the wilderness, was difficult enough. But a more puzzling problem to financiers was how the power could be utilized profitably.

"I am not worried about disposing of the power," Mr. Duke said. "It is only a question of patience and a little time."

Confident that cheap electric energy, wherever developed, would attract users, he did not wait for customers but went after them, investigating what industries were the largest users of electric power, which were best suited to conditions there. If they could not be attracted, he would establish similar ones of his own.

Joining forces with Sir William Price, of Montreal, and associates, he organized the Duke-Price Power Company, and entered upon the development at Isle Maligne. Price Brothers and Co. already had a paper

ISLE MALIGNE, THE 540,000-HORSEPOWER STATION ON THE SAGUENAY

mill at Kenogami, near by, and he contracted with them for a considerable amount of power. Acquiring from the Price Brothers Company the site at Chute à Caron, farther down the river, he formed an alliance with the Aluminum Company of America, the largest single users of hydro-electric power, resulting in construction of the big aluminum plant. When he became a director of the Aluminum Company, in which Mr. Andrew Mellon and his brother are largely interested, the Secretary of the Treasury was quoted as saying that he considered Mr. Duke's judgment, experience and vision as worth more to them than the property they had acquired. Arthur V. Davis, the president, and other officials of the Aluminum Company became prominent factors in this Canadian enterprise.

How Mr. Duke happened to invest huge sums in Canada is worth relating. For, in a way, it did simply "happen." Canada was not his destination. He was headed for the Pacific Coast when a friend induced him to go to Quebec and take a look at the Saguenay. The tickets for Seattle were canceled. Quebec acquired its greatest asset, and Seattle will never know what it missed.

In connection with water-power Mr. Duke had been greatly interested in the electro-chemical industry, especially the fixation of nitrogen and manufacture of fertilizers. On various trips to Europe he had secured certain rights and processes for the fixation of nitrogen from the air. Dr. Eyde, of Norway, originator of the Birkland-Eyde process, a leading authority on the subject, visited America in 1912, and Mr. Duke, W. S. Lee, of the Southern Power Company, and others had several conferences with him.

Mr. Duke finally decided to make a trip out to the West Coast, to inspect water powers with a view to

JAMES B. DUKE

finding some which could be economically developed for the manufacture of nitrogenous compounds. Leaving New York in September, 1912, the party of six or eight proceeded to Canada, visiting Massena Springs, looking over the Lachine Falls and the St. Lawrence River, and going to Ottawa.

There they were met by Thomas L. Wilson, widely known as "Carbide" Wilson, because of his enthusiasm over power development for electro-chemical use. In fact, he had a small plant in Canada used as a laboratory, and had done some work on the Saguenay and Shipshaw rivers, near Chicoutimi. He and his associates were insistent that Mr. Duke and his party change their itinerary, and make a trip to that region.

So the party concluded to go to Chicoutimi, and from there visited and inspected the falls and rapids of the Saguenay, seven to ten miles up the river. With a drainage area of 30,000 square miles, the normal flow of this mighty stream is equivalent to flood conditions on the Carolina rivers, rushing down the rapids at the rate of 35,000 cubic feet per second. Here was all the power a man could ask.

"We went in a duck boat up to the end of tidewater, landed and then walked up trails on the banks of the river for possibly two miles," Mr. Lee relates. "This large river breaks through regular gorges at that point and was a very impressive scene. As we passed these various falls and walked around among the bushes, Mr. Duke stopped and said: 'Lee, I'm going to buy this.' He had been there less than thirty minutes, and that was his first sight of the place. But his mind was made up. He decided to go into it there and then."

This particular fall forms a part of the rapids of the Saguenay, extending from Chicoutimi to Lake St.

John, a distance of about thirty-seven miles, in which the river drops 318 feet. The lower part was owned by Mr. Wilson and his associates, and was acquired by Mr. Duke from them. The remaining portion of the falls, extending from Chute à Caron, was bought from J. B. Haggin and others associated with him. Mr. Haggin at that time was 96 years of age and his son 76. Mr. Duke referred to his son as "the boy."

Nearly two years were consumed in acquiring these properties. After that three or four years were spent in buying the various farms and power rights, changing roads, building bridges and moving churches, for a large area had to be cleared. More than two thousand farms were purchased, in whole or in part, to complete the necessary water and flowage rights of the Saguenay project. These were in a French-speaking region and belonged to the "habitants." Dealing with these French-Canadians, getting them to sell the farms and houses which their people had occupied for generations, was no easy matter.

In the meantime surveys were made and plans perfected for development of the entire falls on the most efficient and comprehensive basis. In addition to securing water rights from the Wilson, Haggin and Price interests, the purchase of land and sweeping changes in the community necessitated securing from the Provincial Government the right to impound Lake St. John, above the river. This northern lake covers an area of nearly four hundred square miles and is twenty-five to thirty miles across at certain points.

The Saguenay, which is a tributary of the St. Lawrence, flows out of the lake by two channels, known as the Grand and the Little Discharge. Nine miles below these channels unite and thirteen miles further downstream reach tidewater.

JAMES B. DUKE

Complete utilization of the river, which has a fall of more than 300 feet from the lake to tidewater, requires two developments in order to use all the fall economically. One of these is located at Isle Maligne, seven miles from Chicoutimi, and the other at Chute à Caron, twenty miles further down the stream.

Isle Maligne, the last of the numerous islands in the Grand Discharge, is a mile and a quarter long. This divides the stream bed into two rocky gorges through which the water rushes with tremendous force, and here it was decided to locate the power house.

Unusual problems were to be solved. In winter the ice is two to three feet thick on the lake, and the Little Discharge is practically dry. Some means had to be devised to draw water into the turbines directly from the lake's natural storage. The arrangement finally adopted draws the water from an average of twenty feet below the lake's surface, insuring an uninterrupted flow.

The power house was located at the downstream end of the island, and the right channel closed at its upstream end by a spillway. Other spillways were provided, and an earth dam erected in a ravine on Alma Island, between the two channels, so as to extend the lake to the intake of the power house. More than half a million cubic yards of masonry were used in construction.

Isle Maligne was inaccessible, so far as freight transportation was concerned. Hebertville, the nearest station on the Canadian National Railway, was fourteen miles away. There was a road running from St. Joseph d'Alma, the nearest settlement, but the grades were steep, a covered bridge was the only crossing over the Grand Discharge, and the highway was impracticable for heavy traffic.

TAMING THE SAGUENAY.

A railroad had to be provided before work on the power station could be started. Construction of a line eleven miles in length from Isle Maligne to Hebertville was begun. Camps were set up, scores of houses erected for the workmen, and hundreds were employed in grading, laying cross-ties and rails, and building the three steel bridges. Heavy winters had to be faced, not a few handicaps overcome, but the railway was built in record time. Authority to begin construction on the general project was given in December, 1922. The railroad was completed to the terminal, at the Grand Discharge, by the middle of the following August. Three months later the cantilever bridge across the river was completed and trains were running into Isle Maligne.

This was but one part of a work that employed thousands of men and involved some of the most extensive construction of the kind ever undertaken. Controlling the river is the key to the entire project. Spring floods if not held back, would come pouring down, sweeping away everything in their path. A year's construction work might be wiped out in a day. By impounding Lake St. John and damming the stream at Isle Maligne, the entire flow is controlled and could be practically stopped for a few days while foundations were being laid or some big piece of construction put into place.

At Chute à Caron the fall is nearly twice as great as at Isle Maligne, with almost double the power, but the upper works had to be virtually completed before construction could be begun on the lower development. The larger work, which will require, it is estimated, some four years for completion, is now under way. In this the aluminum interests are the leading factors.

A new corporation, the Alcoa Power Company Limited, has been organized by the Aluminum Company of Canada, the Canadian subsidiary of the American corporation, for the undertaking. Below the power site at Chute à Caron is coming into existence the new city of Arvida, named for Arthur V. Davis, president of the Aluminum Company, which will house the staff, the army of workmen who will be employed and their families. Town planning experts and landscape architects have laid out the area on the most advanced lines with provision for thousands of residences, business houses, schools, a cathedral, hospitals, and even a country club and golf course.

This model city is being built, section by section, as the growth of population requires, and the population will increase as the aluminum factory expands. The initial unit of the plant is already in operation, a hundred thousand horsepower being transmitted from Isle Maligne. Other units will be completed as the demand grows. The turbines on the Saguenay will furnish all the power required for the aluminum factory, as well as for other industries that may be established. In addition, when the Chute à Caron plant is completed, there will probably be a considerable surplus of power available for transmission to Quebec and other parts of the province, though in time the industries attracted to this region may eventually require all the 1,300,000 to 1,400,000 horsepower.

Various factors have entered into this great development, but it was made possible, initiated and carried forward by Mr. Duke, and stands as a monument to his courage, vision and energy. This extensive engineering enterprise, one of the largest of the kind on record, has been carried out by the men he selected, W. S. Lee, who from the beginning was his chief engineer in his Southern power developments, and F. H.

45,000-HORSEPOWER HYDRO-TURBINE, ISLE MALIGNE, CANADA

TAMING THE SAGUENAY

Cothran, who has been in charge of the Canadian construction; by the Mellons, Mr. Davis, and the Aluminum interests he enlisted. Mr. Cothran, with Mr. Lee as consulting engineer, has directed the building of the dams, power-houses, railways and bridges. So the untamable Saguenay has been harnessed, and a new industrial empire added to Canada.

Remarking upon the magnitude of the Saguenay River project and the financial resources required to swing such a proposition, the New York *Herald*, in a striking editorial, said:

"The vast North American waterpowers that are spilled unused into the lakes, bays and seas are an economic waste that can be expressed only in hundreds of millions of dollars a year lost to man. This natural and inexhaustible power of the streams and rivers can save the coal supplies and roads that are now in darkness, and add to the wealth of the nation and the world in an unceasing volume. Public sentiment and business vision have come to a realization of the possibilities of this problem only recently, so that the work of water power development is merely at its beginning.

"All over the country and Canada, wherever the genius and daring of men like Mr. Duke can turn wasted water into heat, light and power that can be applied to productive industry and to improved living conditions, there are perpetual benefits to be conferred on nations and people. Coal burns away and the earth becomes empty of it. As the forests make room for agriculture to provide food for increasing populations the timber supply is diminished. But the springs and brooks that provide the power of the great waterfalls go on forever."

CHAPTER FIFTEEN

Creating a Wonderland—Homes in City and Country

Loving green fields, streams, flowers, fountains, horses and cattle, never enjoying life in the city as much as in the country, Mr. Duke in his homes and farm gratified his taste for beauty in nature and art.

For five years after coming to New York in the early eighties he had lived in hall bed-rooms, eaten in restaurants and hardly considered his personal comfort. Not until the close of 1889, when the cigarette manufacturers had been brought together and his trade firmly established, did he really give any attention to personal enjoyment.

Fond of horses, he first bought a team—two spanking fine roadsters and a brougham. To drive them Alex Herndon, a tall, yellow negro, was taken from the shipping room and installed on the box. Mr. Duke cared nothing for display, in the office or on the road. But Alex had no such modest ideas. He was no mere driver, but a "coachman," and had to be appareled as became his rank. Wearing a coachman's hat, with a cockade on the side, and a moonstone pin the size of a small toadstool in his scarf, "Big Alex" was a conspicuous figure around the streets. "I believe I spend more time keeping up with Alex," Mr. Duke said, "than he does in driving the team."

Desiring a home of his own, something he had not yet possessed, he bought, in July, 1893, the John Veghte place, a farm of 327 acres in New Jersey, near Somerville. He devoted his attention to farming and dairying, and at one time owned a herd of 250 registered Guernseys. Interested in fine horses, in a few years stables and a half-mile trotting course were con-

CREATING A WONDERLAND

structed on the estate, as well as a model dairy, stocked with the best breeds of cattle for butter and cream.

Adding to his holdings from time to time, Mr. Duke finally owned twenty-two hundred acres, and made this the "show place" of New Jersey, one of the finest estates in America. Few areas were less adapted to artistic conversion. The land was flat and uninteresting, the soil poor, composed principally of shale and clay. But the difficulties seemed only to add to his zest in the transformation.

"Duke Farms" was his pride, developing it his favorite diversion. The property was transformed into a veritable fairyland. Landscape gardeners, architects, horticulturists, sculptors, workers in stone and stained glass were brought from Europe. Armies of workmen were employed. For years the place was a litter of steam shovels, donkey engines, pumping stations, workhouses and bagged nursery plants.

Hills were piled up, valleys and forests created, and a chain of lakes excavated covering seventy-five acres. Transplanting hundreds of trees, placing miles of shrubbery was as much in the day's work as grading and surfacing the winding roads which threaded the estate. Native trees were planted by hundreds and for quite a period 100,000 trees and plants were imported annually from abroad.

Water was one of Mr. Duke's passions. He never tired of watching its flow or seeing crystal columns and misty spray thrown high into the air. Streams were turned into new channels, flowing through grassy banks, lined with shrubs and flowers. Attractive stone bridges were built, spanning river and brooks with graceful arches.

Fountains were placed on every hand, thirty-five or more of them, rivaling in beauty if not in numbers

JAMES B. DUKE

those of Fontainebleau and Versailles. One was an exact copy of the fountain in the Place de la Concorde, in Paris. Water to supply lakes and fountains was drawn from the Raritan River, filtered, pumped into a large reservoir, and after being distributed to the lakes was returned, by an ingenious system, to the power plant.

Flowers delighted him and there were acres of them at Duke Farms—elaborate formal gardens, reminiscent of Italy; masses of the old-fashioned blossoms he had been fond of since childhood. His greenhouses not only supplied his estate and town-house with flowers and plants, but the gardeners raised, under glass, oranges and melons which were served, fresh from trees and vines, at his table. Rare plants, as well as the more familiar species, interested Mr. Duke, who took a particular pride in his orchids, buying and growing unusual specimens and new varieties. His orchids and roses were features of numerous exhibitions and won prizes time and again at the national flower shows.

Sculpture attracted him, and statuary was placed at various points around the grounds. Studying effects, sites and vistas, he spent hours in deciding where these should be placed. In marble and bronze, most of them were by foreign artists, some productions of unusual merit.

An ardent admirer of McKinley, Mr. Duke ordered a large statue of the martyred President made in Italy. In bronze, three times life-size, this was cast in Florence, brought to America and set up on the estate. Thousands of dollars were spent and the location changed time and again before Mr. Duke found a site that suited him, with a fitting approach.

Millions were lavished on construction. The residence, originally the Veghte home, was enlarged to a

A GLIMPSE OF "DUKE FARMS," THE WONDERLAND CREATED IN NEW JERSEY

CREATING A WONDERLAND

pretentious structure of some fifty rooms, with a palm room and three conservatories. Later a new mansion was erected, one of the largest and most elaborate dwellings in that section.

Ranges of greenhouses were constructed, covered with 110,000 square feet of glass. In them was an almost endless variety of rare plants. One house was filled with orange trees. Plants and flowers were produced in abundance, and considerable space devoted also to fruits, peaches, nectarines, grapes and melons.

When the major work was completed and the farm had been converted into a rarely beautiful park, the estate was thrown open to the public. Mr. Duke wished every one who passed that way to enjoy it. But, as is often the case, the privilege was abused. Residents of the neighborhood were considerate, but visitors pouring in from other points trampled lawns, picked rare flowers and broke down shrubbery. Finally in August, 1915, an automobile party from Pennsylvania invaded the estate, picnicked on the lawn in front, trampled flower beds and left the place littered with bottles, boxes and newspapers. That was more than the owner could tolerate. While a large part of the estate was left open to visitors, their privileges were restricted.

Much as this transformation of a Jersey farm into a wonderland of forest, streams and fountains delighted Mr. Duke, he was more interested in creation than in possession. "It was always the unfinished part that held his interest," a friend remarked. "He took more pleasure in painting the picture than he did in its beauty when finished."

"I wonder how many trees and shrubs you have planted and transplanted," Mr. Allen remarked one day, as they were discussing Duke Farms.

JAMES B. DUKE

"More than two millions," was the quick answer.

"Do you really know how many?"

"Yes, I have a complete record in my office."

He knew the number and the exact cost of every item.

Generous to employees, he would not tolerate any delay or interference with his plans. Faithful workmen who wished to work must be protected at any cost. Only one strike occurred in the years of construction in the estate, and he ended that immediately. In September, 1907, the tobacco magnate "made a record as a strike-breaker," as Somerville dispatches to the New York newspapers stated, by landing seventeen union hod-carriers in the county jail, breaking the back of what was intended to be an extensive strike before it was an hour old.

Mr. Duke and his bride had just returned from an automobile tour through the Eastern States. A large addition was being built to the residence, and wishing it finished as soon as possible, the owner was personally superintending the construction. To hurry the work along, the contractors imported additional bricklayers. But they failed to get enough hod-carriers to serve them, and Italian day laborers were employed. The union hod-carriers, also Italians, went on strike and gathered around, threatening to attack the non-unionists and stop the whole force.

Mr. Duke, incensed, got into action at once. Laying down the law to the strikers, he telephoned for the police and almost before they knew what was taking place the trouble-makers were rounded up, placed in the "Black Marias" and were on their way to prison. That was the last strike he was ever troubled with.

Hospitable enough, he resented unfairness even in

CREATING A WONDERLAND

his charities. Planning a Sunday school picnic, a neighboring minister asked if the affair could be held in the park. Certainly, Mr. Duke said, and if they would make it a union picnic, for the children of all the neighboring churches, he would gladly pay all the expenses, for stands, band music and refreshments. When the bills were brought in, the charge for tables and seats seemed exorbitant. The lumber was still on the ground, and Mr. Duke had his carpenter measure it. Charged for considerably more than had been delivered, he discovered that the lumber had not been bought, but was to be returned, and the money used for church purposes.

With scarcely a thought, Duke would have given ten times as much to the church. But he refused to be "done out" of any amount, however small. "The parson took back his memorandum for 'correction'" a friend who was at the Somerville farm related, "and at the same time received a hair-raising lecture on the evils of cheating the poor children of a whole community out of money given for their pleasure, to pay the debts of grown-ups, even though it was for a church."

Remaining a bachelor until he was forty-eight, Mr. Duke in 1904 was married to Mrs. Lillian N. McCready, who had been the wife of William D. McCready, a New York broker. A year later, naming as co-respondent one of her former suitors, he was granted a divorce by the courts of New Jersey. Though he was the innocent party and under no further obligations, Mr. Duke provided liberally for her support. Never seeing her again, to the end of his life this unhappy incident was to him a closed book.

On July 23, 1907, he married Mrs. Nanaline Lee

JAMES B. DUKE

Holt Inman, widow of Walter Inman, of Atlanta, Ga., and in this union found his greatest happiness. Five years later a daughter was born to them.

Upon his wife and only child, Doris, who was born November 22, 1912, Mr. Duke lavished his affections. It was for them that he built one of the finest residences in New York. The white marble palace which stands on Fifth Avenue at Seventy-eighth Street, overlooking Central Park, was constructed and equipped with all that architectural genius and decorative art could afford.

The furniture, largely of Louis XV and Louis XVI design, included examples of the best periods of France. In the main hall hung notable works of famous British painters, Gainsborough's "Lord Gwydyr," Hopner's "Mrs. Deninson" and Raeburn's "English Gentleman in Red Coat." An Ispahan palace rug covered the floor, the sofa was of Beauvais tapestry and near by stood two statues by Couston, his "Girl Playing the Flute" and "La Musique."

Hopner's "Lady Charles Fitzroy" and Freeman's "Prince Hoare," paintings of rare merit, adorned the walls of the drawing room, which was furnished in the style of Louis XVI, and contained rare Japanese vases and an attractive terra cotta figure, Clodion's "Little Girl with Tambourine."

In the dining room were Regence tapestries, a Bavonnières tapestry screen, and Chinese temple jars of the Yung Chang period. A large Gobelin, "Le Memorable Judgment de Sancho," hung in the second floor hall, which also contained a notable painting, the "Marchioness of Wellesley with Her Sons."

These were by no means all the art treasures Mr. Duke owned. Valuable Gothic panels and tapestries of the sixteenth century and the French renaissance, works

"ROUGH POINT," THE SEASIDE ESTATE AT NEWPORT

THE FIFTH AVENUE MANSION, OVERLOOKING CENTRAL PARK

CREATING A WONDERLAND

of Flemish and French artists, "Betrothal Scenes," "Musical Festivities," "The Hunt" and others were among his treasures.

"Rough Point," the Dukes' summer home at Newport, is one of the most attractive estates in that resort of wealth and fashion. Spending the summer in Newport for several seasons, leasing one or another well known mansion, in 1922 they bought this residence from the Princess Anastasia of Greece.

Built by Frederick W. Vanderbilt in 1886, "Rough Point" was occupied by his family for a number of years, the dwelling enlarged and the grounds beautified. In 1906 the property was sold to Mr. and Mrs. William B. Leeds, who were there only one summer. After Mr. Leeds' death the mansion was owned by his widow, who spent most of her time abroad, in Paris and Athens, eventually marrying the brother of the King of Greece, and becoming the Princess Anastasia. Although she did not reside in Newport for years before the house was sold, the place was kept in fine condition, and remained, as it is now, one of the most notable places on Bellevue Avenue.

After becoming chairman of the British-American Tobacco Company in 1912, Mr. Duke spent much of his time in London, but had no permanent residence there. At the beginning of 1914, not many months before the World War began, he leased Crewe House, on Curzon Street, Mayfair, his arrangement with Lord Crewe being for a lease of six months, with the option of purchase. But soon after England declared war, he gave up his London residence, returned to America, and remained in this country.

"Crewe House," one of the few detached residences in Mayfair, has a large and attractive garden, containing thirty apartments. When the building was reno-

JAMES B. DUKE

vated after a fire in 1911, a new dining room and a picture gallery were built at the back of the house. The structure ranks with the most imposing and elaborate mansions in that favored quarter.

But one of Mr. Duke's greatest enjoyments was in a more modest establishment than this. His business centering in New York and London, immersed in affairs he had resided away from his native State for thirty years. But "the tar was still on his heels," as they say in North Carolina. He had always cherished the idea of some day going "back home." As he began developing Southern water power on a large scale, the idea grew upon him. His power and other interests centering not in Durham, the home of his youth, but in Charlotte, he erected in Myers Park, Charlotte's residential suburb, a handsome home-like structure, "Lynnewood," where he found the companionship of neighbors and friends and the Southern atmosphere he missed in the larger cities.

The nearest stream of any size, the Catawba River, being twelve miles away, pipes were laid, pumping apparatus installed, and a lofty fountain constructed. Standing on his lawn, throwing into the air a column of water eighty feet high, this was the most conspicuous and attractive feature of the landscape. Driving for miles around to gaze at it, people told each other how many thousands of gallons it spouted, marveling at the way in which money was literally "poured out" to secure this effect. It did cost a pretty penny, but Mr. Duke regarded it as a good investment for him, an entrancing sight, delighting his eyes and soul.

CHAPTER SIXTEEN
The Man as Others Saw Him

WHAT manner of man was this Southern farmer's son who had become one of the masters of industry and finance?

"In form and feature Mr. Duke looks a well-bred Scot, robust, standing erect six feet two inches in height. The large head, covered with red hair, has a broad brow, straight nose, firm, good-tempered, kindly mouth, clear eyes, which look at you reposefully without criticizing you. A fresh, healthy coloring sets off the strong face and shows his British ancestry," Mr. Fuller, his associate and counselor, wrote of him, when he was in the midst of large affairs.

"His dress is simple and expresses no vanity. In manner he is positive, never petulant, but always reasonable; taciturn, but ready and eager to state his reasons for any opinion or judgment. He does this with a power spontaneously springing from the merits of his position, and is prepared to argue with logical cogency when necessary; willing to yield if shown to be in error, without a trace of obstinacy or pride of opinion seeking the truth regardless of its source. So just a man, he does not flinch from acknowledging as his own errors and unsuccessful expedients or enterprise first suggested by himself, and is careful to credit successful suggestions to those who made them. Possessed of a memory remarkable for its tenacity and accuracy, he is able to summon instantly to his aid all that he ever knew or saw or did or heard bearing on the subject under consideration.

"Self-reliant, quick, cautious from prudence, not timidity; he is cool and courageous in action, and magnanimous in victory. Wise, he discerns a flatterer from

JAMES B. DUKE

afar, but values praise from sincere admirers. Although much sought after by other successful men for association in great enterprises, he is entirely free from vanity or self-conceit. Modest and retiring in his manners, in social life his speech is without cant or hypocrisy. Intolerant of deception or any form of lying or dishonesty, the frankest, most candid of men, he never takes refuge in a falsehood. If unable or unwilling to disclose to a questioner facts which he prefers to hold in reserve, he never hesitates, but politely declines to speak on the subject at all.

"A most thorough man, in intimate touch with every branch and all departments of the great business he manages, so competent and versatile that among the officers and departmental heads of his enterprises it is frequently remarked, and never disbelieved, that he could take the position of any man in the organization and do his work better than the incumbent. . . .

"In political association Mr. Duke is a Republican, because he believes that the economic policy of that party is the accepted sentiment of the country and assures more happiness to more people. While his sympathies naturally rise and fall with those of the people among whom he was born and where he passed his young manhood, his judgment guides his action. A patriotic American, he loves his whole country and follows with alacrity his duty in helping to make it first in every heart.

"The legend tells that a great king of old had a messenger at his elbow when he prepared a feast to whisper to him that he was only mortal. In prosperity it is a hard lesson to repeat. The chief office of the American Tobacco Company is furnished in elegant massiveness, but opposite the large chair set for the president there hangs, in singular contrast, on the walls,

AS OTHERS SAW HIM

the picture of the first log-house factory of the Dukes' and standing beside it the venerable founder of the business. The president had it placed there to remind him of the struggles of his youth, and to give him patience with the humbler things that come before him. He did not choose to forget, and wanted to remain humble as well as to achieve great things.

"Mr. Duke has given freely to the benefactions cherished by his father, but his governing idea in giving is to give work. He delights in undertakings that will give work to those who want to help themselves, and believes its divine radiance is felt in widening waves of influence, and that every worker won is a missionary to the idle.

"If there is any chord that rings highest in his thoughts it is this eagerness to give those who would have it work. Work for its own ennobling and saving sake, work for the unselfish care of others. He has proven that he could be a great minister of finance, but he has scant patience with the school of finance that makes money breed money by artificial methods. He likes the bustle of the market place. The developed mold of his mind requires huge metal. Whether this consists of big business abroad or terracing the meads and meadows of broad acres into smooth lawns and setting plantations and making parks with vistas of classic statues for his own home, the effective way of helping some one to help himself is the plot of his work. Like the motion of the sea, it never tires, but inspires.

"When he believes he is right, and when he has asked his ever-recurring question, why? and is satisfied with his answer, the criticisms of those who do not comprehend his actions, or, comprehending, choose to distort them, neither disconcert nor divert him. He un-

JAMES B. DUKE

derstands that the man who reforms business as well as politics pays the penalty. He is not bookish, has few theories or fancies. His study is men and their deeds.

"His judgment of men seems intuitive and unerring. From the highest executive officer to the head of the humblest department, he knows that the men to whom he gives his unstinted confidence will repay it with a single devotion. He returns this devotion with boyish sincerity.

"The hundreds of young men sent out by him to home and foreign markets bring back with pride what they are sent to get, and his kindly praise is valued by them above their earnings. He is proud of and rejoices in the fact that there is no royal road to promotion in his service, but that merit clears the way for any possessor.

"Nothing gives him greater gratification than to see the men employed in the company becoming his partners by investing their savings in its securities—in which they know there is no 'water' (to use the slang of the Exchanges) save the sweat from the faces of the men whose brains made them worth their claims in gold. They are another name for the magnificent physical properties that ornament the great countries of the world and the intelligent toil which has made their products a necessity wherever luxury gives innocent enjoyment.

"In creating a monumental, permanent capital, and in directing this aggregate to generating returns, Mr. Duke has become possessed of a princely fortune, and lives in manly opulence. He allows no parasites or prodigals, who calmly take for granted their superiority, to grow rich by his favor or fatten at his expense. The idle rich do not interest him, but the man with a

AS OTHERS SAW HIM

single talent, well employed, commands his attention and admiration."

High praise, you may say, high praise indeed; yet no more than Mr. Duke's associates thought he deserved.

If any consider this too eulogistic, the tribute of friendship, inspired by admiration and intimate association, let us look upon another picture, presented not by one of his associates, but by a journalist who had never seen him before, Ben Dixon McNeill, and published in a newspaper which fought the trust consistently and had never been sparing in its criticism, the Raleigh *News and Observer*.

It is a picture of Mr. Duke among the "home folks" down in North Carolina in the latter years of his life, when he was constructing power plants, encouraging cotton mills and building up the Southern Power Company. He was under attack at the time, for his power system had been assailed as his tobacco companies were, and he had gone into the courts to defend the right to charge rates that would be profitable and pay dividends on his investments. Opponents were charging that he was trying to "grab up all the water powers" and create another monopoly. Many of the "down homers" were not friendly then. He was being "roasted" by opposition newspapers. But he went his way steadily, paying no attention to the attacks, confident that some day they would understand what he was trying to do—devote all this to the service of his people.

"Buck Duke is approachable," McNeill wrote. "Anybody who has the temerity can go up to him wherever he is and introduce himself. He is not surrounded by any company of guards and flunkies like others of the small company of America's half-dozen richest men. A dozen people interrupted him in a day's time in Shelby last Wednesday. Among them were newspaper men gathered there in their annual convention.

"John D. Rockefeller, whom he admires profoundly as the great American of all time, is as well known in Ocracoke as he is in Wall Street, Charles M. Schwab a little less well known, and Henry Ford, another man greatly admired by Mr. Duke, is a sort of a household standby in millions of homes. But this Tar Heel, who ranks about third among them in the measure of his wealth, nobody knows.

"And yet any one of them is harder to get at than Duke. None of them ever goes into a little courthouse and sits down among the folks and looks on while a case is being heard. None of them ever slips out into the grand jury room to smoke. None of them is ever seen walking about the streets of a small town with none to shield him from the public. Buck Duke is his own shield.

"People who are used to being interviewed have a lot of set phrases that they hand out from time to time. Most of their ideas are so well known that nobody has to go to see them to interview them. But Buck Duke, once he gets started, rambles along, talking about anything that pops into his head, saying what he thinks about it. Sensation lurks in his words. One minute he is like to be commending a farmer for keeping his weeds down, and the next he is saying something that would stand financiers on their heads.

"After all, it is rather fortunate for him that he doesn't give interviews. He is too straightforward when he talks."

In a whole day there were three things that he confessed a pride in, McNeill recalled, a joy that had the

AS OTHERS SAW HIM

ring of spontaneity in it—his limousine that had served him eleven years, his fountain at Charlotte, and his daughter. "Now and again his conversation drifted back to his little girl. In his heart there is no dollar mark on her."

"I paid $11,000 for this car and I have driven it 100,000 miles," Mr. Duke remarked. "A while back I bought another car, an American car that cost me $4,900. I drove it 30,000 miles and threw it away. It cost too much—fifteen cents a mile to ride in it, and this one has cost me only seven and a half cents. Buy good automobiles and good men, buy good anything. They pay profits."

"Kaleidoscopes have gone out of fashion, but talking with James Buchanan Duke is like looking through one of these archaic contrivances for eight hours," said his interviewer. "He is not a conversationalist. His mind works constantly like a great dynamo in one of his power plants. For a mile he may ride and say not a word, and then a spark will come up from him, unrelated to anything that he has said before.

"It may be to remark that Henry Ford is one of the greatest merchants in the world or that somebody had better watch the Chinese or that Theodore Roosevelt was a dinged fool or that Frank Page ought to build his roads an inch thicker or that a man goes fishing only because he thinks he will get something for nothing, or that there ought to be a tax of twenty-five cents the gallon on gasoline to make people quit riding so much.

"Or perhaps that he has a profound contempt for politicians or that John D. Rockefeller is the greatest American, or that some day, and because of his own foresight, a town will reach from Gastonia to Charlotte or that he would like to see coöperative marketing win out in tobacco so they will not plant more than the

JAMES B. DUKE

world can smoke up, or that he can't see why the newspapers keep after him.

"About the height of misapplied energy is trying to direct, or divert, the Duke mind when it is functioning. No use whatsoever to dry to draw him out on something. He will answer in a flash if the question goes home, but often as not it will pass beyond him. His mind moves with terrific velocity and just crumples up anything that gets in its way. And then there are surprising interludes of recollection from his boyhood, of times when he pulverized leaf tobacco with a stick, 'flailed it out,' as he expressed it, and then with his father, peddled it out over the country. He came to Raleigh, he went to Fayetteville, and to all the towns about in this section, and as he rode behind the slow-moving team, he dreamed dreams.

"'I always knew that I was going to be rich. As early as I can remember, that idea has been in my mind,' he shot out. 'I saw Elwood Cox not long ago, and he was reminding me of how I used to say that I was going to be rich when I was at that Quaker School.'

"But why be rich? Why have hundreds of millions of dollars? Somewhere inside him, flashing up sometimes dimly, there is the notion in Buck Duke that his wealth came to him by divine right. Possession vested in his hands means prosperity for hundreds and thousands of people. In the vast reaches of those mill villages, that are crowded into the forty miles between Shelby and Charlotte, his own genius has made work possible for thousands.

"'Americans don't work enough. They are too careless. They can't make this car. No man ought to be allowed to live if he will not work. No matter if he has millions or if he has nothing.' He called off num-

AS OTHERS SAW HIM

bers of idling millionaires, devastating them with a gesture. Work. That is the passion of Duke's life.

"'If you like the thing you are doing, it is enough. You will succeed at it, and you don't need to do anything else.' Fish? Well, maybe for some who have not learned to work. These mill people here can swim and frolic in Mountain Island lake when it is done.

"Millions have come to him because he worked for them, and because he had the judgment to buy the right sort of men to work for him. He believes that very firmly. 'Cheap men don't pay. Build up your organization with costly men. Let them make profits. Give them part of yours and you will get it back.' Time and time over he reiterated that philosophy of business. 'They pay me good profits,' he would say of some of his best men.

"Why should these people, these mill operatives, these mill owners even, hound him about his water power? Had not these streams tumbled down out of these mountains for centuries and none noticed them? Had he not invested his money in them when men called him foolish? They were here hundreds of years before he bought them. Even now there are other streams. He has not bought them all. If they are not satisfied with him, he will cancel any man's contract. He actually made that proposal during the week.

"'I have never made a cent out of it, and I never expect to make a penny out of it.'

"Duke waved his hand in the direction of a great hydro plant. That statement has often been made in the last year. 'If it was just power I want to develop and sell, I have got a site in Canada that would develop two million horse power, and I could sell every bit of it on the ground.'"

JAMES B. DUKE

"Wedded as you are to dividends, what does it mean that you have sunk eighty million dollars in something here that will never yield you a penny?" the newspaper man asked.

"I was born in North Carolina and I am sixty-six years old," Mr. Duke said. "It is time I was beginning to think about a monument. I want to leave something in the State that five hundred years from now people can look upon and say that Duke did that. Every man owes something to the State he was born in, and this is what I want to leave North Carolina.

"Twenty-five years from now,"—he continued. Then he painted, with surprising vividness for a man to whom books are for lawyers and preachers, a picture of what Piedmont Carolina will look like. It was a great vision—a country, a whole State, that will no longer pay tribute to coal barons, a country where agriculture and industry go hand in hand, driven alike by the mystery that Ben Franklin pulled down out of the clouds.

"I am going to leave it—" But at the end of the sentence he put in again, how he would denounce the writer if it were printed. "Men's wills are not printed before their leave-taking, anyhow," the newspaper man wrote. "North Carolina can wait for the reading of the will of Buck Duke."

"That fountain yonder is mine." He pointed across the gentle hills of Myers Park to where a column of water shot fifty feet above the tops of the trees. The sun caught it and flung back a rainbow. Presently the Rolls-Royce swung into the driveway before his mansion and the fountain came into full view. The stranger could feel Duke's eyes upon him, watching for some sign of approval.

AS OTHERS SAW HIM

"It was a surpassingly wonderful sight," McNeill said. "Duke had planned it all himself. Somewhere down in him there must be something more than dollar marks. There is something human and warm in a man that could lay out those grounds and set that house among them. He wandered off down the terrace to look at it. It was water in motion, and after all it may have been symbolism. Maybe it reminded him of water gushing through mighty generators out on the Catawba River."

"Do you think I am a dangerous man to have loose in the State?" Buck Duke asked it quietly, almost wistfully, one might have thought. "There was nothing of the driving, ruthless, powerful, pitiless master of one of the world's greatest industries, nothing of the man who could make his world tremble," the journalist wrote. "There was conviction in his voice, he who had—by his own words—brought agriculture out of its bondage, and who, back again in the State where he had begun his career, salvaged its waste rivers and made them available for millions."

Strangers might have considered him rather cold and reserved, but his intimates knew Mr. Duke as a warmhearted, loyal friend, considerate as he was able, constantly looking out for their interests. Probably no man of his time wrote so few personal letters, which gives to this, written to Mr. B. N. Duke, who was seriously ill at St. Petersburg, Florida, in February, 1919, an added significance:

"My Dear Brother:

"I have received your two letters and was very glad to hear from you and to know that you continue to improve. You must not get impatient. It has taken you a long time to get into this condition and will require time to get cured. . . .

JAMES B. DUKE

"At any time I can serve you don't fail to call upon me. I have your interest at heart and it has always been a pleasure to help you in any way I can. You are the dearest brother in the world, and my heart goes out to you in your many afflictions. I know that you have always been ready to serve my every interest and desire and I cannot write or even tell you of my love and deep appreciation of what you have been to me since we were little boys together.

"We are having plenty of water and the power company is doing well. The construction work is moving a little better. The country, yes the whole world is in a very chaotic condition and I think it will be a long time before normal times will return.

"Please excuse all mistakes in this letter as it is the first I have attempted in ten years.

"With a heart full of love and affection, I beg to remain,
"Your devoted brother,
"J. B. DUKE."

Employees and business associates were devoted to him. Mr. Allen, who was closely associated with Mr. Duke and succeeded him as chairman of the Duke Endowment, said of him:

"One of his traits of character which I always admired intensely was the way he overlooked the numerous adverse criticisms by those who misunderstood him, many of them from sources within his native State, and went on preparing for and carrying out the great plans which he had in mind. Despite such evidences of lack of appreciation, he realized that he was doing the right thing and determined that nothing should cause him to swerve from the course he had mapped out. At times, when his attention would be called to some of these things, instead of showing resentment, as most men would have done, he would smile and say: 'Pay no attention to them.' This characteristic, to my mind, was one of the surest possible evidences of his greatness."

Broad in his beliefs, seeing the good in all denominations, he held firmly to the faith of his fathers, saying he considered the Methodists "more broadminded than others." But when Mr. Allen advocated bringing the different denominations together in a harmonious whole, Mr. Duke opposed the idea.

"No," he said; "that would be the biggest kind of mistake. Competition in religion keeps up the interest."

One night, not many months before his death, he heard a sermon over the radio that impressed him by its logic and eloquence. The possibilities of broadcasting such a discourse excited his imagination. Next morning he expressed his ideas to his associates at his office. That was to build a great church, a cathedral for all the people, with the best organ and choir that could be procured. He would invite the ablest ministers from this and other countries, regardless of denomination, to preach there. With a powerful radio station, he would broadcast the services so that millions could listen in and any one in the land could enjoy the loftiest sermons and most inspiring music. That was one of his ideas he did not live to carry out as he had planned, but which may be translated into reality where the cathedral-like chapel and School of Religion form the very center of the numerous structures of Duke University.

"He was a man with a big, warm, melting heart," Mr. Allen says. "He indulged in few amusements, but was fond of good motion pictures and had each of his homes equipped with machines so that he could enjoy selections of his own choosing with his family and friends in the privacy of home. I recall, after enjoying with him and others in his home in Charlotte

JAMES B. DUKE

a picture through which ran a touch of pathos, that when the lights came on, there were tears in his eyes, and his first remark was:

"'I liked that picture because it made me feel like crying, and I am not ashamed to cry.'

"Whenever subjects arose which he believed had a bearing on the national welfare, on which he had decided views, he would often say:

"'I wish I had a talent for public speaking so that I might go out and present this subject to the people in the light in which I see it.'"

Detesting publicity, he never made a public speech in his life, but friends considered him, in business councils and private conversation, one of the most effective speakers they ever heard.

"It so happened that I was with him in England in 1914, when the great war was declared," Mr. Allen recalls. "The very next day I heard him counseling his British friends to plow up their parks and sow wheat. He foresaw the war might be long. He knew England was largely dependent upon imported foodstuffs and he foresaw the possible difficulties of shipping, to say nothing of what was likely to be the mounting cost of all necessities of life.

"So strong were his convictions that immediately upon returning home he had hundreds of acres of his own land in New Jersey plowed and sowed to wheat. But it was a couple of years afterward before Europe awoke to the realities of the situation and commenced to make strenuous efforts at home. That was only one instance of his farsightedness and the practical interest he took in public affairs."

Mr. Duke's personal characteristics which vividly impressed those in daily contact with him have been strikingly set forth by Clinton W. Toms, president of

AS OTHERS SAW HIM

the Liggett and Myers Company. In thinking of him there comes to mind, Mr. Toms says:

"His power of concentration—his ability to put into any one task his whole power and then to turn around and do the same thing with another entirely different problem.

"His enthusiasm—not the hurrah kind, but the intelligent, forceful expression of a great personality.

"His faculty of putting emphasis where it belonged, readily discerning between the essential and the non-essential.

"His power to inspire men to be something and to do something, creating within them a real ambition to succeed. Often by praise and then again by fair and just criticism, even though at times it might be severe, he enabled men to overcome a weakness—and they were grateful to him.

"His consideration for men—those who worked under him were always given more than due credit—and his desire that those who tried to do their part should be liberally rewarded.

"His big-heartedness—a kind and sympathetic nature.

"His love and admiration for his father and his brother.

"His great faith—a genuine faith—a firm belief in the Eternal; a strong confidence in the Church and the Christian religion."

CHAPTER SEVENTEEN

A Business Man's View of War Problems

AT the very beginning of the World War, in 1914, Mr. Duke was convinced that the United States would inevitably be drawn into the conflict, and that the change in financial conditions would make New York the banking center of the world, and on his return to America he urged upon his banking friends the importance of preparing to finance foreign operations on a large scale.

"Send to London for the best experts we can get in international banking and foreign exchange," he advised. "We are novices in this, while they are the ablest and most experienced on earth. You know hardly anything about foreign banking and financing. They know everything about it. Let them show us how to do it."

The titanic struggle being primarily a contest not of armies but nations, the effective use of economic as well as military resources would count mightily in the final decision. Food was the vital factor in England, as any one, in his opinion, should realize, and he was amazed when the British authorities delayed taking strenuous measures to increase food production.

"Starve England!" was the German cry, the submarines centered their attacks on vessels carrying supplies and munitions, and the plan came perilously near succeeding. British admiralty officials admitted, early in 1917, that there was scarcely more than a few weeks' surplus food supply in England and, unless the submarine campaign was checked, Great Britain might be compelled to admit defeat. Fortunately the U-boats were curbed, shipping was increased by rapid building, making up for losses in sinkings, and the flow of food

WAR PROBLEMS

was uninterrupted. But at times it was seriously endangered.

When the United States entered the war, Mr. Duke hoped that this country might avoid the mistakes made by the Allies, and not "muddle through." As the struggle continued, and our officials met with the same trying experiences in supplying armies, training troops and providing transports that other nations had gone through, he was deeply stirred.

Waste, running into billions, would entail heavy financial burdens, to be borne by the people for years to come. But more serious was the possibility that our resources would be so taxed that America's forces might not be brought to bear in time to be decisive.

Congestion in transportation, the taking over of the railways by the Government; failure of the fuel supply, delaying shipping and imposing upon the civilian population "heatless Mondays" and other hardships—all these, he felt, could have been avoided.

He could not understand why a nation which did not hesitate to draft its youth by millions into armies, calling on them to risk their lives in its service, should not dare to draft men for necessary labor in connection with the war. In common with many other Americans, he considered it a supreme injustice for the government to favor civilians who remained safely at home, working for high wages, exempt from the draft, while at the same time millions of ardent young patriots were drafted to be transported across the seas, exposed to the hardships of the trenches, with no compensation except their beggarly thirty dollars a month.

War profiteering of both capital and labor seemed to him so unpatriotic and needless that he thought people should be aroused to the importance of checking this wild waste.

JAMES B. DUKE

Never pushing himself forward in public affairs, he was moved in this emergency to prepare the only article he ever designed for publication, making practical suggestions which he believed would save the nation billions of dollars and put the entire war service on a more efficient basis.

"In the last analysis," he wrote, "this war is a contest of material resources, and great as those of our country are they may prove inadequate unless properly conserved, fostered and utilized. I was in England when the war started and I advocated then that every park throughout the British Isles should be cultivated so as thereby to supply more home-grown food, lessen the outflow of gold and relieve the burden on shipping. How much better it would have been if such action had not been postponed until forced by dire necessity! From that day to this I have given constant and most anxious consideration to the war and its varied problems, because I realized that the Allies were fighting our battles and that in all likelihood sooner or later we would be fighting Germany either with the Allies or alone.

"While the government has done many things which I commend, notably in the Draft Law and the Federal Reserve System, I am convinced that in the conduct of the war it is pursuing some policies which are fundamentally wrong. Their harmful tendencies must now be apparent to all, and so far they are but an earnest of the calamitous consequences that may ensue unless other methods are adopted—for as yet we are but upon the threshold of our war activities.

"I say this in no spirit of antagonism whatsoever, for I believe our public officials are earnestly endeavoring to administer our affairs to the very best of their ability. These things, however, seem so plain and certain to me that I am constrained to give expression to my views in the hope that so doing may prove a constructive criticism from which some benefit may flow.

"Running the railroads I regard as a more difficult job than that of running the United States Government. It is gigantic from every viewpoint, whether of number of men employed, varying conditions encountered, quantity of tonnage moved, amount of capital invested, extent of trackage, equipment and terminal facilities, or annual receipts and expenditures. Hardly less can be said of carriage by sea. Their complexities and exactions beggar description. From time to time have arisen those who advocated Government Ownership, but the magnitude of such an undertaking, even in normal times, has appalled the stoutest hearts, not to mention the well grounded fear that, despite all efforts to the contrary, political influence would, sooner or later, seep into, cripple and mar. No one body of men, however brilliant, can get the best results.

"Why, then, when by official admission the Government is being simply overwhelmed in the performance (with its own share of delays, troubles and failures) of those functions which under our system are its peculiar province and rest within its expert knowledge, should it additionally encumber itself with the administration of affairs in this great new and untried field for which it has neither time, faculty nor experience? When I consider the vital character of transportation it seems to me almost a crime even to think of interference on the part of untrained hands. This is no time for experiments. It is a time when, of all others, the Government should follow the safe and certain course, which in this case means the giving of the freest hand and greatest scope to our practical railroad men, for who but they are adequate? If we have to train our

JAMES B. DUKE

boys in order that they may fight efficiently at the front, does it not go without saying that the Government cannot do this job half as well as those geniuses who have spent their lives in this service?

"The deplorable railroad situation of to-day is not due to inefficient management. The marvel is that they have endured so much and so long. Instances of inefficiency are the exception, not the rule. It is due to the harassing State and Federal restrictions which for many years have bound them hand and foot. Our railroad men have been the peers of any. America has led the world in railroading. It is a tribute to their prowess that England, Russia and other countries have turned to America for assistance in their hour of railroad need.

"Is it not patent to all that the sensible thing to do is to strike off these shackles, turn back the railroads, restore them to their rightful position and give our railroad men an opportunity to truly and greatly serve their country?

"For a number of years we have tried price regulation with respect to our railroads. Our laws did not stop, as they should have, at forbidding rebates and other forms of discrimination, but went further and declared that their commodity, transportation, could be sold only at the price allowed by the Inter-state Commerce Commission. Now, despite the rise in the cost of labor and of all supplies and raw materials, the railroads have knocked in vain at the door of the Interstate Commerce Commission for such increases in rates as would take care of this increased cost of doing business and yield a return on their capital comparable with the return upon the capital of other enterprises. Of course, railroad securities ceased to be an attractive investment, rendering it impossible to procure the additional funds necessary to meet the requirements of even

WAR PROBLEMS

normal times. Is it any wonder, then, that they were not equipped to measure up to the war emergencies?

"Failing to profit by the experience of the railroads, the government last year fixed the price of coal. The consequences are now, unhappily, being too well realized by everybody. Instead of thereby enabling requirements of coal to be obtained at what the government considered a proper price, we have seen our ships waiting in harbors when shipping was the greatest need of the hour, our factories shut down when they should have been most productive, our schools and churches closed, and even our families shivering in their homes, because coal could not be had at any price.

"Now the Government is restricting the price of food products and I see no reason for expecting any greater measure of success in this field.

"These problems are being tackled from the wrong end. Had the railroads been allowed to properly increase their rates they would have had no difficulty about their financing, and I feel sure they would have proven themselves ready and able to handle our transportation in all respects adequately and well. If the law of supply and demand had been allowed to work its natural course with respect to coal, new mines would have been opened, old mines worked to their utmost capacity, and I am confident our supply of coal for every purpose would have been abundant. The same thing is equally true of our food products.

"No better results will be gained with respect to our food products by the effort of the Government to curtail consumption. In this respect it has followed the course of England, France and Germany; but the conditions are not at all similar. In the countries mentioned there are no vast areas of idle land such as we have in the United States, so their only alternative was to restrict consumption. In this country adequate food

JAMES B. DUKE

supplies for ourselves and our allies can be secured much more certainly, much more easily and far more satisfactorily to all by concentrating our whole efforts and necessary funds on increased production, rather than by resorting to the meager and doubtful expedient of curtailing consumption.

"It is true that this course would likely for a while, at first, result in high prices, but with regulations preventing artificial shortages, nature's law of supply and demand would inevitably restore prices to their proper level. And any large profits temporarily made would be a comparatively small price to pay for insuring ample supplies, and would be cheerfully borne by our people, who are now fretting under the critical conditions brought about by these restrictive measures.

"Though the money cost of the war is already colossal, it is only a small part of what the sum total will likely be. Yet even now all government bonds issued for this purpose are selling below par, the market value of our securities has dwindled from a fourth to a half without regard to their earnings and this shrinkage in values is being extended to real estate through the calling of loans by savings banks and insurance and trust companies, who now find better returns for their money in other directions.

"I cannot view these things without great alarm, because it means that our financial structure is being disrupted and, if continued, our money resources may prove inadequate to our needs. Our estimated wealth of some $250,000,000,000 when we entered the conflict, is fast shrinking to half that amount, so that if the war should eventually cost us some $50,000,000,-000, as it very likely may, that would be 40 per cent of our probable wealth at that time—a tremendous burden upon the country, especially when we consider the already heavy amount of public bonds afloat.

WAR PROBLEMS

"The enormous and unparalleled inheritance taxes and surtaxes is one of the foremost causes of this condition of affairs. They should no longer be called taxes, for they have been carried to a point where they are, in effect, mere penalties visited upon the successful business men of this country.

"But far above and beyond this consideration, they do great affirmative harm to all the people, whereas they raise, comparatively, only small revenue and under a proper system of financing would be unnecessary. You cannot thus cripple men whose activities or investments produce large incomes without at the same time, and to an even greater extent, hurting all of our enterprises and the individuals who are engaged in and dependent upon them. You are pulling down the pillars of our business temples.

"Reservoirs of wealth in the hands of individuals are just as necessary as in the hands of banks and insurance and trust companies, because individuals can take risks and undertake enterprises which such institutions cannot. Instead of the government making possible, as at this time it should, the fullest coöperation of all such men, it is carrying such class legislation into the very terms of the latest Liberty Loan Bonds, seemingly utterly oblivious of the certain and disastrous consequences to society at large.

"This is a great, elemental truth, often overlooked and disregarded, but which should be pondered well and fully realized by the masses of our people. It is the secure foundation upon which rests alike their welfare and their happiness. If nobody had accumulated wealth we could not have had our extensive railroad systems whose mileage exceeds the combined total of the other countries of the world, our great business enterprises with their big factories and trained organizations carrying our products to all parts of the earth, our thriving cities, our great universities, our well equipped hospitals, all of which owe their existence to individual success.

"Take even the bread that you eat. Few carry a week's supply in the home. The farmers produce it and many months elapse before it is consumed. During this period it has to be financed through the hands of the miller, the wholesaler and the retailer until it reaches the consumer. This is possible only through reservoirs of wealth; and the same thing is true of cotton, corn, steel, coal, tobacco, copper and other products.

"Contrast America and Russia. American growth and development have been at once the wonder and admiration of the world, and it is because America has been the land of opportunity, giving the very largest scope and incentive to individual initiative and endeavor. Her men of affairs to-day were the poor boys of yesterday and the poor boys of to-day will be the captains of industry to-morrow. Russia, on the other hand, has stifled opportunity through the heavy hand of government regulation reaching out into all walks of life. There was no incentive to individual endeavor and no mighty works have been done there. Stagnation has been her portion and ignorance and poverty the heritage of the masses of her people. And this is but an illustration. History is replete with just such instances, if we will only read its pages and learn.

"The following tabulation will make even clearer just what I mean:

Net value of estate subject to estate tax	Net income on 5% basis subject to taxation	Amount of income tax to be paid	Balance of income after payment of income tax	Amount of estate tax to be paid	Approx. no. yrs. required for balance of net income to aggregate amt. of estate tax
$ 5,000,000	$ 250,000	$ 69,680	$180,320	$ 680,000	3¼ yrs.
10,000,000	500,000	192,680	307,320	1,720,000	5½ "
15,000,000	750,000	327,680	422,320	2,970,000	7 "
20,000,000	1,000,000	475,180	524,820	4,220,000	8 "
40,000,000	2,000,000	1,130,180	869,829	9,220,000	10½ "

WAR PROBLEMS

"Observe, first, that it will take the entire net income of such estates from three to ten years respectively to pay the income tax and accumulate a sufficient fund to meet the estate tax, leaving no income whatever for any other purpose, not even for outstanding business obligations, to say nothing of personal expenses. Owners of such estates are thus completely bereft of power to be of the material aid which they might otherwise render. Worse, this is bringing premature divisions of estates, thereby taking out of the hands of the builders and locking up in the hands of fiduciaries fortunes which otherwise might be utilized in initiating and expanding business enterprises. Thus, these tax laws are in a measure defeating their own object and should be abolished. If additional reason be necessary it is found in the enforced liquidation of estates in the short period allowed to raise the cash necessary to pay these exorbitant inheritance taxes, which is not only ruinous to the estates themselves, but so demoralizes prices as to be most hurtful to others as well.

"Observe, second, that large estates which have enjoyed an average income of say five per cent after paying such excessive surtaxes have left only from 2 to 3¾ per cent for their net annual return. This has induced large sales of all classes of property, resulting in gradual but tremendous declines in values, because the people who are not so treated by our tax laws cannot absorb the offerings and carry the financial load entailed. With the gravest anxiety I contemplate the consequences to the United States of a continuance of such unwise policies. Witness already the difficulty the industries of the country are having in procuring necessary capital to meet increased cost of doing business.

"Observe, also, that the 4 per cent Liberty Loan

bonds, as a net result, yield such persons only a return varying approximately from 1¾ to 3 per cent. In brief, it places the government in the anomalous position of seeking to borrow money for its war purposes from its citizens at grossly discriminative rates of interest. It was said this was done to keep the rich from putting their fortunes in tax exempt securities. But how small, comparatively, such a saving would be. And it may result in such an increased rate of interest upon war bonds as that the excessive interest charges will overbalance any such saving. Remembering the combined total of state and municipal securities which Congress cannot tax and the 3½ per cent Liberty Loan bonds which Congress did not tax, will there be any saving whatever? Was there not already a plenty and to spare of tax exempt securities, if people were of a mind so to utilize them? And yet for such a consideration the government has handicapped its raising of funds by subjecting the bond issues to such forms of taxation.

"It is absolutely necessary that the war be financed almost exclusively through bond issues and that there should be raised by taxation only sufficient money to pay the interest on these bonds and establish a liberal sinking fund for their final redemption, in addition to the revenues necessary to meet the normal expenses of the government. The government, no more than an individual, can 'eat its cake and have it too.' It cannot continue to sell bonds to those whose incomes are too largely taken by taxation.

"This taxation, as regards manufacturing and producers, should be in reality a tax on the excess of war over pre-war profits—not one merely so in name, as at present; and it should be classified with respect to the various lines of endeavor, such as steel, transportation,

WAR PROBLEMS

coal, textiles, explosives, chemicals, tobacco and other products. My reason for this classification is that there are some businesses which show excess profits that are not due to the war and they should not be taxed to the same extent as are those whose tremendous excess profits are due directly to the war. This method has always appealed to me as being the fair and equitable means of raising the major portion of the necessary additional taxation, because it places the burden on those who are reaping the benefits. Here England has set us a conspicuous example to follow, and has found the revenues from such sources and 25 per cent income tax ample, as we will here if we allow business to proceed along normal lines. The measure of the tax upon such excess should be only our absolute requirements—80 per cent, as in England, if this be necessary, but leaving as a reward to incite individual endeavor all that existing conditions will allow. If this form of taxation and a reasonable income tax and surtax (say 25 per cent maximum) do not suffice, it should be supplemented by a tax upon the distributors (not producers) of commodities by way of a percentage upon their turnover, and not by way of a direct consumption tax.

"While we are forcing men to fight, we are leaving them to work when and where they please. This is not only utterly inconsistent and grossly inefficient; it is rank disloyalty to our soldiers. For no one will deny that it is futile to send troops to France unless they are properly equipped and maintained there. It is idle to say that the labor problem will solve itself. No one can read our papers, study our conditions, see the idlers and loafers on our streets and hear the cry for labor that comes from all industries without being convinced that all is not well in this particular.

JAMES B. DUKE

"Our Draft Law did not go far enough. It should also have included, for purposes of labor, every man, woman and child over 16 years of age and mentally and physically fit. I saw in the New York *Times* an interview with Senator France of Maryland descriptive of a Bill he had introduced in Congress to remedy this situation. What he said has my heartiest approval. He is proceeding along the right line. We are serving just as truly, as honorably and as patriotically in tilling the soil or working the mine, or running the train, or wherever our lot may be cast, as in 'going over the top' on a shell-scarred field in France. What is toil in field or factory to risk of life in battle? No good American should object to any measure which will insure the essentials of victory, and none other has a right to be heard."

CHAPTER EIGHTEEN

Trinity—New Life in an Old College

How the Dukes began their benefactions to education is an interesting story. Founded half a century before, the Methodists had decided that their college, Trinity, had struggled long enough in the woods of Randolph County, and must be moved to a more central location. Bids were invited and Raleigh made the largest offer, twelve acres of land and $20,500. But the site was limited, the amount pledged not sufficient to erect a single building. Gen. Julian S. Carr, president of the "Bull Durham" company and a trustee of Trinity, strongly favored its location in Durham.

Benjamin N. Duke, who was one of the trustees of the Masonic Orphanage at Oxford, had been considering buying Blackwell Park and building there an orphan asylum. Rev. R. F. Bumpass, his pastor, suggested that a greater service would be to acquire the park as a site for Trinity College.

Meanwhile another factor had entered into the situation. The Baptists having decided to establish a female university, various towns were competing for the institution. Durham had offered a site and $50,000. Raleigh pledged half that amount. The commission decided, however, that the "tobacco town," with its numerous factories, was no proper place for a girls' school. Raleigh's bid was accepted and the Baptist Female University located there. Durham's pride was hurt, the whole town was indignant, and at a mass-meeting held in Trinity Church citizens freely expressed their feelings.

Washington Duke was present, and though not given to the heated language used by some of the speakers,

JAMES B. DUKE

felt deeply this slight to his town. Turning to Mr. Albright, the postmaster, a leading Baptist, who sat beside him, Mr. Duke remarked that if his own church, the Methodists, would bring their college to Durham, he would give $50,000 more than Raleigh offered.

Rev. Dr. E. A. Yates, pastor of Trinity Church, overheard the conversation and next day called upon the manufacturer, asking if he really meant what he said. This was quick action, picking up a casual remark and turning it into thousands of dollars. But Mr. Duke was as good as his word.

Turning to his son, Benjamin, Mr. Duke asked his opinion.

"Go ahead, father," was the reply; "it is a good cause."

Visiting Trinity at the previous commencement, Mr. Duke had been impressed by the college and its young president, Dr. John F. Crowell, and remarked to a friend, "Crowell is all wool and a yard wide." He confirmed his offer. Dr. Crowell was notified, and hastened to Durham.

"Yes," Mr. Duke told him, "I'll give that myself, if you will bring the college here. Try it out."

The amount required for initial buildings was set forth, and the manufacturer promised to stand by them to the extent of $85,000.

Securing a site was the next problem. The old fair grounds and race track, sixty acres, at the edge of the town, owned or held under mortgage by Carr, appeared to be the best property available. "Let's go to General Carr and see if he will give us the race track," was the next move. Enthusiastic over Mr. Duke's offer, he said: "Yes, I will—gladly," when asked to donate the fair-grounds.

They had an ample site, and a promise of $85,000

TRINITY COLLEGE LIBRARY

"EAST DUKE" BUILDING

for construction. But some of the trustees and leading Methodists doubted whether that would justify the change.

Dr. Crowell had builders go to Randolph and make an appraisal of the existing Trinity property. There was really but one large college building, a three-story brick structure, containing offices, recitation rooms, dormitories and an auditorium. "We can duplicate that building, of practically the same material, for $14,000," the contractors reported. So even the doubters were convinced that Trinity could not lose, so far as property values were concerned.

Raleigh withdrew from the race. Durham was decided upon. But there was "one more river to cross." Not a few ministers and laymen were firmly opposed to removal. "Old Trinity" was dear to them, many of them had been educated there, and they questioned the wisdom of changing its character or location.

Dr. Crowell had drawings prepared, showing his conception of a college such as could be created on the new site—departments of Religion, Science, Law, provision for the various classifications of learning—a vision of a great institution.

The final contest was waged at the Methodist Annual Conference. Centering their fire upon the young president, who had recently come to the South from Yale, opponents openly resented the youthful professor's "coming down here from the North and telling us what to do." "You are only showing us pictures," one speaker scornfully remarked: "things that can't be done, and we never will be able to do."

Crowell stuck to his guns. These were not merely pictures, he pointed out; they were the expression of an ideal, something not possible at the time, but that might be done in the distant future. But they could

JAMES B. DUKE

make a beginning toward it; could establish a larger college in a favorable situation, that would grow with the years. Pleading that they "deliver Trinity from the bondage of its birthplace, afford it a wider field, bring it out into a broader world," his speech won the day. The conference voted, by a large majority, to accept Durham's offer and establish Trinity there.

Work was begun at once. The fair-grounds were cleared, contracts let, and laborers set about transforming the race-track into a campus. The funds offered were barely enough to erect and equip the initial buildings, but the college authorities set bravely ahead.

The nation was in the grip of a financial panic. Money was more than "tight," it was almost impossible to obtain in substantial amounts. "Those were the hardest times I ever saw," Dr. Crowell said. Banks tied up deposits. "We'll give you $10 a day and no more," was told depositors. But the Dukes and Carr stood by Crowell, furnishing the means to pay for materials and meet the weekly pay-rolls. Bank balances were drawn upon almost to the breaking point, yet when cash for other things was almost unobtainable they always managed to provide enough to keep the college forces moving.

As construction went forward, day by day, there were difficulties enough and one serious mishap. As the main building, named in honor of Mr. Duke, was nearing completion, the tower collapsed, taking down with it brick, stone and mortar. But the structure was quickly rebuilt, the buildings at length completed, and in the autumn of 1892 Trinity opened its doors for students on the new site.

From that day to this Trinity's progress has been steady and continuous. Now the college founded in the woods of Randolph, taking the name of its benefactors, is blossoming forth into a university.

TRINITY COLLEGE

Born in a log-cabin, nurtured by forward-looking men, Trinity was imbued from its inception with the pioneer spirit that does not hesitate to venture into wider fields. Founded by Quakers and Methodists, who combined to establish a school, in 1838, with Brantley York as teacher, the college has a tradition of liberalism, tolerance and breadth of thought that has been maintained through all the years.

Forceful as he was cultured, Dr. York believed in the saving grace of education as well as religion, and inspired pupils and parents with his own zeal.

"Union Institute," as the school was originally called, acquired more than a neighborhood reputation. The diminutive building was outgrown. The entire community "turning to," a larger house, twenty by forty feet, was erected on a lot of its own, a mile southwest of the old site. This, too, was built of logs, but solidly constructed, and a proud day was that when the boys and girls, headed by Dr. York with English Blair as "captain," lined up and marched in double file from the old to the new school-house.

A year or two later, in 1841, a two-room frame building was erected, with a hall between, and an assistant employed—Braxton Craven, a young man of promise and talents, then not more than nineteen or twenty years old. Laboring together in close fellowship, they built up a school of real merit and value.

When Dr. York, his sight impaired, departed for other fields, later founding York Collegiate Institute, the reins fell into the hands of his associate. A man of broad vision, Craven had ambitious plans. Well-equipped teachers were sadly needed, North Carolina had no college devoted to their training. Here was an opportunity to render a wider service.

In 1851 Union Institute was granted a new charter and incorporated as "Normal College," which was further amended the following year, making the Governor chairman and other officials members of the Board of Trustees. Affiliated with the State, this was perhaps the first institution especially for the training of teachers established in the South. Ahead of its time, however, adequate support was lacking and in a few years the experiment failed.

But Craven could not permit the enterprise for which he and Dr. York had labored through years of struggle to die. Enlisting the support of his church, he turned the institution over to the North Carolina Conference, in 1856. Coming under direct patronage of the Methodists, it was chartered in 1859 as Trinity College, with Craven as president.

For a quarter of a century Trinity was conducted under his guidance, he serving as president continuously except for the last two years of the war when his place was taken by Prof. Wm. T. Gannaway. Not a few Southern colleges were swept away by the Civil War and reconstruction, but Trinity survived, due to the unfailing devotion and energy of one man—Braxton Craven. He kept it alive, and through all the years never lost his faith in the institution.

With insufficient income, scanty support from any source, the little college had a hard struggle. Its crude buildings and small faculty offered few attractions. But the instructors were earnest, consecrated men who inspired students with their own sense of responsibility and duty, and the product was a high type of useful manhood.

Though wealthy families were inclined to send their sons to the State University at Chapel Hill, to Randolph-Macon or the University of Virginia, Trinity's graduates included some of the "best blood" in the State. A few of those who entered, like Walter Hines

TRINITY COLLEGE

Page, could not abide the rather primitive conditions. The future Ambassador to England, who went there in 1871 from Bingham School, wrote letter after letter to his mother, criticizing the college, his instructors and fellow students, and begging that he be allowed to leave. Departing in the middle of his term, in December, 1872, he went to Virginia, entering Randolph-Macon. But such cases were rare.

The buildings were old and barn-like, the faculty inadequate; but Trinity was doing a work of genuine value to Church and State, supplying able ministers, teachers, lawyers, training men who became leaders in business and the professions.

The seeds of greater things were in the college, which grew steadily, if slowly, in patronage and usefulness. Hundreds of men who became prominent and influential looked back with pleasure and gratitude to the days they spent at "Old Trinity," and sat at the feet of its Gamaliel. Both of the present United States Senators from North Carolina, F. M. Simmons and Lee S. Overman, were educated there, and the roll of its alumni in the seventies and eighties includes many men of prominence in civic and religious life.

With the death of Dr. Craven, in 1882, came a crisis in the life of the college. Prof. William H. Pegram was made chairman of the faculty, serving until June, 1883, when Dr. M. L. Wood was elected president. But Dr. Wood, after a year, resigned. For three years the chairman of the faculty, Prof. John F. Heitman, was the chief administrative officer. A few men of means had become interested in the institution, however, and in December, 1884, three of the trustees, Gen. Carr, Col. J. W. Alspaugh and James A. Gray, of Winston, assumed the financial management, contributing $5,000 annually for maintenance.

JAMES B. DUKE

Three years later Dr. Crowell, a brilliant young graduate of Yale, was elected president—probably the first Northern man chosen, after the Civil War, to head a distinctively Southern college. Bringing to the institution rare energy and breadth of view, his election was an evidence of the broader spirit that prevailed.

Removal to Durham marked the beginning of a new era for Trinity. When Dr. Crowell, after years of progressive administration, resigned in 1894, there came to the presidency one of the most ardent spirits and eloquent preachers the South has known, Rev. Dr. John C. Kilgo. Under his administration Trinity rapidly expanded. Devoted to him and the institution, the Dukes gave liberally to the college, erecting additional buildings, beautifying the grounds, and providing considerable endowment.

Not only in material and educational ways did Trinity expand. Breadth of view, freedom of thought and opinion were held as basic principles by faculty and students. They were not maintained without more than one long and bitter struggle. There were stormy periods when the very existence of the college was threatened.

Perhaps the severest test came in 1903 when Dr. John Spencer Bassett, the Professor of History, in an article in the *South Atlantic Quarterly* on "Stirring Up Race Antipathy," himself stirred up a veritable hornet's nest by this remark concerning Booker T. Washington:

"Now Washington is a great and good man, a Christian statesman, and, take him all in all, the greatest man, save General Lee, born in the South in a hundred years; but he is not a typical negro."

Dr. Bassett was not, primarily, eulogizing the colored educator, but pointing out that he was a marked

TRINITY COLLEGE

exception, one among millions, having in mind the Tuskegee educator's service to his fellow freedmen, his rise from slavery to the leadership of his race. But the comparison with General Lee, the placing of a negro, no matter from what point of view, above the famous white men of his time, was heatedly resented. The historian was violently attacked by newspapers and many individuals, who demanded that he resign or be expelled. Parents were urged not to send their sons to Trinity so long as the instructor remained. A boycott was threatened.

No one, perhaps, was more surprised at this outburst than Dr. Bassett himself. He had not intended any disparagement of the leaders of his own people. But refusing to be intimidated, he would neither recant nor resign. Opposing any invasion of academic freedom, his confreres stood by him to a man.

In a strong address to the Board of Trustees, President Kilgo declared that "coercion of opinion in all times has been a miserable failure"; that "tolerance is the foundation virtue upon which American civilization has been built and developed," and said:

"Bury liberty here, and with it the college is buried. It were better that Trinity College should work with ten students than that it should repudiate and violate every principle of the Christian religion, the high virtues of the commonwealth, and the foundation spirit of this nation.

"Personally, I should prefer to see a hurricane sweep from the face of the earth every brick and piece of timber here than to see the college committed to policies of the Inquisition."

The faculty, in a notable address, set forth their views, concluding:

"This college has now the opportunity to show that its campus is undeniably one spot on Southern soil where men's

JAMES B. DUKE

minds are free, and to maintain that the social order of the South need not be shielded from criticism, because it has no reason to fear it, because it is not too weak to bear it. Money, students, friends are not for one moment to be weighed in the balance with tolerance, with fairness, and with freedom."

After a session lasting until three o'clock in the morning, the Board of Trustees voted, eighteen to seven, not to accept Dr. Bassett's resignation, and adopted resolutions stating that—

"The search for truth should be unhampered and in an atmosphere that is free. Liberty may sometimes lead to folly; yet it is better that some should be tolerated than that all should think and speak under the deadening influence of repression. A reasonable freedom of opinion is to a college the very breath of life; and any official throttling of the private judgment of its teachers would destroy their influence, and place upon the college an enduring stigma."

Unknown to the Board, the resignations of every member of the faculty had been placed in the hands of the President, to be presented in case of adverse decision against their colleague. Dr. Edwin Mims, now of Vanderbilt University, long a member of Trinity's faculty, recalls this as one of the most courageous instances of collegiate action on record in the New South.

President Roosevelt, in an address at Trinity the following year, declared:

"I know of no other college which has so nobly set forth, as the object of its being, the principles to which every college should be devoted, in whatever portion of this Union it may be placed. You stand for all these things for which the scholar must stand if he is to render real and lasting service to the State. You stand for academic freedom, for the right of private judgment, for the duty more incumbent upon the scholar than upon any other man, to tell the truth as he sees it, to claim for himself and to give to others the largest liberty in seeking after truth."

This declaration of collegiate independence, which met with the warm approval of the Dukes and other staunch friends of the college, blazed the way along which Trinity has progressed for nearly a quarter of a century and expressed the ideals of the larger career which is just beginning.

Washington Duke, to the end of his days, was Trinity's loyal supporter, contributing large sums to the institution. Giving $180,000 for buildings when the college was established on its new site, in 1896 he presented $100,000 as a permanent endowment fund, adding a like amount in 1898, and another $100,000 in 1900, besides other substantial contributions. His gifts were continuous and his interest in the college unfailing.

At his death on May 8, 1905, Dr. Kilgo said of him: "He earnestly desired to do something to push back the shadow of ignorance from the minds of men, to send forth a clearer and a fuller light of knowledge, and to do this he endowed Trinity College."

On the campus at Trinity stands a statue of him, dedicated with this tribute:

WASHINGTON DUKE

1820-1905

Animated by lofty principles he ever cherished the welfare of his country with the ardor of a true patriot; diligent in business he acquired riches, but in the enjoyment of them did not forget to share with the less fortunate; a patron of learning he fostered an institution which placed within reach of aspiring youth the immortal gift of knowledge; and when the activities of his early life and the sterner struggles of his

JAMES B. DUKE

maturer years had passed, he entered upon a serene old age, cheered by a lowly piety and sustained by an unfailing trust in God, who in all the vicissitudes of life had kept him single in his aims, sincere in his friendships and true to himself.

> "Friend of Truth, of soul sincere,
> In action faithful, and in honor clear."

In 1910, when President Kilgo, elevated to the highest honor of his denomination, resigned to become a Bishop of the Methodist Episcopal Church, South, he was succeeded by William P. Few, who had been a member of the faculty for fourteen years and dean for eight years. Continuing also from the preceding administration were Robert L. Flowers, now secretary and treasurer of Duke University; William H. Wannamaker, dean first of Trinity, then of the University; William H. Glasson, now dean of the Graduate School of Arts and Sciences; William I. Cranford, for seven years dean of the college, with others of a small but able faculty, including that honored veteran of "Old Trinity," William H. Pegram.

Under the guidance of President Few and these associates, and others who joined the staff in the intervening years, Trinity's patronage was so largely increased, its program of construction and instruction so widely extended, that the transition from college to university was more the entering upon a broader phase than the creation of a new institution.

After Washington Duke's death, his sons increased their contributions, which had been more than liberal. Replacing the main building, burned in 1911, they added twenty-seven acres to the college property, providing for beautification of the campus, new buildings and various other improvements. Two years later they jointly contributed $800,000 to endowment.

THE CO-ORDINATE COLLEGE FOR WOMEN, DUKE UNIVERSITY, WHICH WILL INCLUDE TRINITY BUILDINGS

TRINITY COLLEGE

Their individual gifts were even larger. Beginning in 1898, B. N. Duke gave hundreds of thousands for new buildings, dormitories, gymnasiums, athletic grounds, lectureships, current expenses and endowment. Alspaugh, Bivins, Lanier and Branson Halls, the Asbury and other structures are due to him, and he also gave $100,000 to the Southgate Memorial and considerable sums to other buildings. The library, erected in 1902, and Jarvis Hall, built in 1912, were erected by James B. Duke, who gave generously to college purposes and in 1922 contributed $1,000,000 more for endowment.

Angier B. Duke, son of Benjamin, and his sister, Mary Lillian, now Mrs. Anthony J. Drexel Biddle, Jr., of New York, both graduates of Trinity, gave $25,000 to Alumni Memorial Gymnasium. Angier, who was president of the college Alumni Association and had previously donated $30,000, at his death in 1923 bequeathed $250,000 to the endowment fund. Mrs. James Edward Stagg, granddaughter of Washington Duke, erected the stone pavilion and Miss Anne Roney, another relative, provided the fountain and surrounding garden which adorn the campus.

The benefactions of the family reached their climax in 1924 when James B. Duke in creating his Endowment gave $6,000,000 for land and buildings and practically one-third of the Endowment's net income, bringing the total of the Duke benefactions given within the lifetime of the donors to approximately $20,000,000. At his death, less than a year later, he bequeathed directly $17,000,000 more to Duke University, the successor of Trinity, and ten per cent of his residuary estate, making this one of the most richly-provided-for institutions in America.

CHAPTER NINETEEN
True Friends of the Colored Race

IN Durham stands a hospital, attractive, excellently arranged, well conducted, with an equipment many larger institutions might envy. Conducted by negro physicians with negro nurses and internes, it is devoted to the care of colored patients.

Named in honor of Abraham Lincoln, this hospital was erected through the liberality of Southern white men. Founded twenty-five years ago, at the entrance of the first building, which the present structure replaced, was a marble tablet, inscribed:

MEMORIAM
LINCOLN 1901 HOSPITAL

With grateful appreciation and loving remembrance of the fidelity and faithfulness of the Negro slaves to the Mothers and Daughters of the Confederacy, during the Civil War, this institution was founded by one of the Fathers and Sons

B. N. DUKE   W. DUKE
J. B. DUKE

Not one act of disloyalty was recorded against them.

JOHN MERRICK, President
A. M. MOORE, Founder and Supt.

Behind this is a story that has an interest of its own. Strongly opposed to slavery, Washington Duke himself owned one slave. When "Ben" and "Buck" and Mary were small and Brodie just growing up to working age, some one was needed to assist in caring for the children and to "help around the house." White servants were almost unknown then in the South, "free negroes" were few, and Mr. Duke bought a colored girl, Caroline.

Devoted to the family as only the old-time servants

AID TO COLORED RACE

of her race can be to their "white folks," Caroline, as has been recorded, went with the younger Dukes to their Grandfather Roney's place, when their father and elder brother entered the Confederate army, and remained with them during the war. When slavery was ended, Caroline had no idea of leaving the "chillun." Freedom meant nothing to her without them. Going back to the farm, she remained with the Dukes and served in their household until the children were grown, until "Miss Mary" was married, "Marse Ben" an important manufacturer with a handsome home of his own, and "Marse Buck" a "big business man, way up yonder in New York."

Mr. Duke never forgot Caroline's faithfulness. Having given her two small houses, one to live in and the other to rent, he bequeathed in his will money and stock sufficient to maintain her in comfort all her days.

Remembering Caroline and thousands like her, negro men and women as loyal in slavery as they were in freedom, and for whom their "white folks" cherished an enduring affection, the Dukes were sincere friends of the colored people and never lost an opportunity to help them.

Washington Duke had in mind the erection of a monument on the grounds of Trinity College, to the memory of the slaves and their devotion to the Southern people during the war. A modern hospital for the white population had been erected and presented to Durham by his partner, George W. Watts. The negroes had no hospital. Their leading physician, Dr. Aaron Moore, was striving to establish such an institution, but the negroes, poor as they were, could not, with all the pennies they put aside, accumulate enough to make a real beginning toward it. Dr. Albert G. Carr, the Dukes' family physician, contended that

JAMES B. DUKE

Durham should have a hospital for colored as well as white citizens. Mr. Duke's barber, John Merrick; his butler, W. H. Armstrong, and his cook, Addie Evans, all talked with him about what their people were trying to do.

The negroes needed a hospital, Mr. Duke concluded, more than they did a monument. That would be a memorial of practical use to them. Coming to the rescue, he and his sons made up the amount required, $13,000; a building was erected and the hospital opened in 1901. Later the Dukes gave $20,000 additional.

When, in 1921, a larger building was required, James B. and Benjamin N. Duke gave $75,000 of the $150,000 raised for the purpose, the colored people contributing $25,000, white residents a similar amount, and the city and county governments appropriating $12,500 each. The Dukes, Mr. Watts and his son-in-law, John Sprunt Hill, donated a site of four acres, the old Stokes home, in the suburbs, and the negroes were given a hospital which is their refuge and pride.

That is only one of many instances of the Dukes' helpfulness. They were liberal contributors to colored charities, schools and every movement for the welfare of the race.

In creating his Endowment, James Duke did not forget them. Funds were provided for black as well as white orphans, colored institutions will share in the funds for hospitals, and a share of the Endowment's income, he specified, should go to the college for colored students at Charlotte.

Booker T. Washington wrote that the negro residents of Durham seemed to be more prosperous, and he found fewer signs of poverty among them, than almost anywhere else in the South. "Of all the

AID TO COLORED RACE

Southern cities I have visited," he said, "I found here the sanest attitude of the white people toward the black. I never saw in a city of this size so many prosperous carpenters, brickmasons, blacksmiths, wheelwrights, cotton mill operatives, and tobacco factory workers among the negroes."

Even W. E. B. Dubois, violently denouncing Southerners in general for their treatment of his race, found no cause for complaint here. "There is in this small city," he wrote, "a group of five thousand or more colored people whose social and economic development is perhaps more striking than that of any similar group in the nation."

If any one doubts whether the two races can dwell, side by side, in harmony; if any one contends that the negro "has no chance" in the South, let him go to Durham. There the negroes have not only excellent churches and schools, prosperous stores, barber shops, carpenter shops and small businesses; they own and run banks, building and loan associations and various other enterprises.

They have a life insurance company with assets of nearly $2,000,000, policy reserves of over $1,800,000, and insurance in force of more than $41,000,000. Chartered in 1898, this has been in successful operation for nearly thirty years. In 1890 they organized a fire insurance company, with $200,000 capital and a larger surplus, which does business in five States, carrying risks amounting to $7,000,000. Some record for a people who only a generation ago emerged from slavery!

In many of these enterprises John Merrick, the local barber, was the moving spirit, and it was largely through James Duke that he made his start.

Going into Merrick's shop for a shave, Mr. Duke,

impressed with the prosperous appearance of the place, remarked:

"John, you have too much sense to be a mere barber. Why don't you make money among your own people?"

"But how, Mr. Duke?"

"Well, for instance, why not establish an insurance company?"

That seemed a practical idea. The negroes were strong for insurance. Hardly one of them, man or woman, but belonged to some "lodge" or fraternal order which promised death or sick benefits. But these were far from justifying their high-sounding names. The most that the majority accomplished was to insure an imposing funeral with long lines of mourners, affording the numerous "brothers" and "sisters" the opportunity of marching in full regalia.

Merrick himself was a high officer and owned an interest in one of these societies—the "Royal Knights of King David," which had lodges and members in seven States.

But the "King David" order, with its knights and royalty, was not substantial enough for John. He desired a real insurance company, and in 1898, with half a dozen others, organized the North Carolina Mutual and Provident Association, each paying in $50, giving a cash capital of $350. But plain insurance, with no lodges or parades, did not seem to appeal to colored patrons. The other "investors" thought the scheme would never succeed. So Merrick and Dr. Moore bought out the other partners, reorganized the company, and placed it on a solid basis.

Beginning with small industrial insurance, they were soon writing straight life and endowment policies, and in five years the annual income increased from $900 to $70,912. By 1911 the company owned its own

AID TO COLORED RACE

home, a six-story building, had hundreds of agencies and was doing business in ten States. Not a bad showing for a company born of a chance remark in a barber shop.

In the meantime, a bank had been established, with Merrick as vice president; and a fire insurance company organized. To aid in financing negro enterprises, in 1921 the Durham Commercial and Security Company was organized. When, in 1924, leading colored men of various States organized the National Negro Finance Corporation, with Robert R. Moton, who succeeded Booker Washington at Tuskegee, as its president, Durham was selected as its center.

The rise of the colored citizens of this Southern city to affluence and leadership, recounted in detail by Dr. Boyd, of Duke University, in his "Story of Durham," in an inspiring record, significant not only to the South but to the nation.

What made this possible? Enterprise, of course, no little genuine ability; but quite as much the spirit of tolerance that has prevailed; the disposition of residents and leading business men to aid their colored fellow citizens in every worthy undertaking.

Long ago, in 1890, Washington Duke expressed this in a message he sent, in place of a speech he had been invited to deliver, to a negro educational convention:

"Five years more and I shall have lived three quarters of a century. Not long before I was born, Napoleon thundered at Waterloo, as the Old Guard melted itself before the hollow squares of the English army and England's Iron Duke conquered the world's most magnetic leader. Since then the destiny of nations has been changed. I have seen countries of Europe racked by terrible wars and here in our land I have witnessed the greatest revolution of them all—the emancipation of your race. I have always had a friendly feeling to-

JAMES B. DUKE

ward you, and now address you in the spirit of a friend, wishing if I can to help you overcome the hard conditions of your lot.

"I have no doubt that each of you would like to be a successful man. It is right that you should feel so, for a proper ambition is God's call to a higher life, but how shall that success be gained? Be industrious, do not always be looking for an easy, soft place. I have made more furrows in God's earth than any man of forty years of age in North Carolina. And when you have made yourself industrious, you must be frugal. Establish it as a rule always to spend less than you make. I never closed a year's work in my life without being happy in the knowledge that I was better off than I was when it began. Be sure to put away every week part of your earnings in a savings bank. And when people begin to find out that you are industrious and reliable they will offer you positions of profit. Do honest work for your honest dollar, put it in your pocket, and at night when you lie down with it under your pillow the eagle on its face will sing you to sleep, because it knows you have earned it and can spend it properly.

"Be men of honest, upright lives; support your churches and your schools; regard your minister as your best friend and your school teacher as your next; work honestly for your money and give some of it to help support these institutions, cease to rely upon outside help, for you must work out your own salvation. Ever since I was twelve years old I have been trying to make the world better by having lived in it. Let this be the rule of your lives. I have never failed to give freely to the support of the gospel; I have regarded it as a part of my life. If I am anything, if my life has been successful, if from small beginnings I have brought myself to a successful point in life, then I say to you that it was by following these rules that I have gained it."

Mr. Duke's sons had the same ideals, giving expression to them in contributions to hospitals, orphan asylums, colleges and schools. The negro race has had no better or more sincere friends.

CHAPTER TWENTY

Millions for Education, Hospitals, Churches and Orphans

FORTY millions to education, charity and the relief of human suffering—a perpetual endowment that, increasing annually, will eventually reach eighty millions—was the princely gift which James Duke made to his native State and section. Large as the amount, the money was not a true measure of his munificence, for in creating this trust he gave himself, his organizing genius, the experience of a lifetime in affairs.

"What will Mr. Duke do with his fortune?" was a question that had been discussed for twenty years. Here was the answer.

The secret had been so well kept that the news of the largest benefaction the South has known came as almost a complete surprise. The announcement was made at his home in Charlotte, N. C., on December 8, 1924.

The millions set aside were devoted to purposes which were near his heart. Dreaming for years of creating in the South a university comparable with the leading institutions of the East and North, one that eventually might rank with Yale and Harvard, in carrying out this project he inevitably turned to Trinity College, with which his family had been closely identified for a quarter of a century.

Colleges of other denominations, as well as the Methodists', were provided for—Davidson, the Presbyterian college near Charlotte, which Woodrow Wilson once attended; Furman University, the Baptist institution at Greenville, S. C., and Johnson C. Smith University, the negro institution at Charlotte.

Relief of sickness and suffering, bringing about improved health conditions and better means for the treatment of disease, appealed strongly to Mr. Duke. Knowing the scarcity of hospitals in that section, the handicaps under which they were laboring, he provided for them liberally, allotting nearly one-third of the Endowment's net income for this purpose.

Ten per cent of the income was to be expended for the benefit of orphans, white and colored, in North and South Carolina. Knowing of the trials of aged ministers as, worn out in service, they faced hardships in their declining years, and the struggles of the farmers to maintain proper houses of worship, he provided for all these—for building churches in sparsely settled rural districts, for pensioning superannuated preachers and aiding their widows and orphans.

Devoted to various purposes, mainly in the region served by his power companies, his beneficences were so distributed that thousands would share in their benefits.

In pursuance of a plan long contemplated, the initial announcement stated, he had determined to create and establish a trust for certain charitable purposes embracing property having a value of at least $40,000,000, and which would include, among other securities, approximately three-fourths of his holdings in the Southern Power System, the income from which during the course of the next few years would aggregate approximately $2,000,000 per annum and thereafter considerably more, increasing with the growth of the country and of the power systems.

The trust was to be administered by fifteen trustees, constituting a self-perpetuating body, the first including Mrs. Nanaline H. Duke, his wife; George G. Allen, of Hartsdale, N. Y.; William R. Perkins, of Montclair, N. J.; William B. Bell and Anthony J.

CHAPEL CAMPUS—CENTRAL BUILDINGS PLANNED FOR DUKE UNIVERSITY

MILLIONS FOR EDUCATION

Drexel Biddle, Jr., of New York; Walter C. Parker, of New Rochelle, N. Y.; Alex. H. Sands, Jr., of Montclair, N. J.; William S. Lee, Charles I. Burkholder, Norman A. Cocke and Edward C. Marshall, of Charlotte, N. C., and Bennette E. Geer, of Greenville, S. C.

Directed to expend $6,000,000 in acquiring land and erecting and equipping buildings for the establishment of an institution of learning in North Carolina to be known as Duke University, the trustees were empowered, if Trinity College saw fit to adopt that name, to spend that sum in expanding and extending Trinity.

To increase the trust estate, twenty per cent of the income was to be withheld and added to the principal until such additions aggregate $40,000,000, the remainder of the income to be expended and distributed as follows:

Thirty-two per cent to Duke University; thirty-two per cent for maintaining and securing hospitals, primarily in North and South Carolina, on the plan of paying to the hospitals a sum not exceeding $1 per free bed per day occupied free, and in addition building and equipping hospitals; ten per cent for the benefit of white and colored orphans in the two States; six per cent for assisting and building Methodist Episcopal churches in rural districts of North Carolina; four per cent for the same purpose in South Carolina.

Two per cent was allotted for pensioning superannuated Methodist preachers and the widows and orphans of deceased ministers in North Carolina; five per cent to Davidson College, five per cent to Furman University, four per cent to Johnson C. Smith University.

On his return to Somerville, N. J., in formally turning over the endowment fund to the trustees, Mr. Duke, in probably the longest personal statement he

JAMES B. DUKE

ever made, set forth his ideals and purposes in making this endowment, which are given in full in the Trust Indenture published as an appendix to this book.

In the development of water power in the Carolinas, he had observed, he said, how utilization of such a natural resource which otherwise would run to waste both gives impetus to industrial life and provides a safe and enduring investment for capital, and his ambition was that the revenues of such developments shall administer to the social welfare as their operation administers to the economic welfare of the communities they serve. With these views in mind, he recommended the securities of the Southern Power System as the prime investment for the funds of the Endowment, not to be changed except in response to the most urgent and extraordinary necessities, and requested the trustees to see to it that at all times these companies be managed and operated by the men best qualified for such a service.

Duke University had been selected as one of the principal objects of this trust because he recognized that "education, when conducted along sane and practical lines as opposed to dogmatic and theoretical lines, is, next to religion, the greatest stabilizing influence." Requesting that this institution secure for its officers, trustees and faculty men of such outstanding character, ability and vision as will insure it a place of real leadership in the educational world, he advised that great care and discrimination be exercised in admitting as students only those whose previous records show character, determination and application evincing whole and real ambition for life.

Advising that the University courses be arranged first with special reference to the training of preachers, teachers, lawyers and physicians, "because these are most in the public eye and by precept and example can do most to uplift mankind," he stressed as next in importance instruction in chemistry, economics and history, "especially the lives of the great of earth, because I believe that such subjects will most help to develop our resources, increase our wisdom and promote human happiness."

Hospitals had been chosen as another of the principal objects of his benefaction because he recognized that they have become indispensable institutions, not only in ministering to the comforts of the sick, but in increasing the efficiency of mankind and prolonging human life. "So worthy do I deem the cause and so great do I deem the need," he said, "that I very much hope that the people will see to it that adequate and convenient hospitals are assured in their respective communities, with especial reference to the poor who are unable to defray such expenses of their own."

Orphans were included in an effort to help those who are most unable to help themselves, a cause in which he felt all good citizens should have an abiding interest. "While, in my opinion," he commented, "nothing can take the place of the home and its influence, every effort should be made to safeguard and develop these wards of society."

Lastly, he made provision for what he considered "a very fertile and much neglected field for useful help in religious life"—assisting aged ministers and the widows and children of clergymen, and aiding in the building and maintenance of churches in rural districts. "Indeed, my observation of the broad expanse of our territory makes me believe," he said, "it is to the rural districts that we are to look in large measure for the bone and sinew of our country."

Urging the trustees to administer well, within the limits set, the trust committed to them, he concluded:

"From the foregoing, it will be seen that I have en-

JAMES B. DUKE

deavored to make provision in some measure for the needs of mankind along physical, mental and spiritual lines, largely confining the benefactions to those sections served by this water-power development. I might have extended this aid to other charitable objects and to other sections, but my opinion is that so doing would probably be productive of less good by reason of attempting too much."

Since early manhood Mr. Duke had had in mind the devotion of his fortune to the benefit of others, and in later years it was his chief concern. The power systems he had created provided the machinery for a constant flow of dividends. What were the best purposes to which it could be devoted? What did the Carolinas need most?

Having very clear ideas as to what should be done, he wished to know precisely what conditions were and how they could be remedied, how his funds could be expended so every dollar would count.

How many orphans are there, and how can they best be cared for? What is needed in hospitals? How can we help build churches in country neighborhoods? How many aged ministers are there who need aid? What will be required to build and maintain the kind of university we desire?

Surveys were made, statistics compiled, the field gone over thoroughly. Experts were consulted, and he and his personal staff studied for months the questions involved. The entire plans were put on a business basis, figured out to the last decimal. He would not be content until he felt sure they would work out in practice and function efficiently regardless of the lapse of time or changing conditions. No easy task for all concerned.

"This is a harder job than I thought it would be," he

MILLIONS FOR EDUCATION

remarked. "I'm beginning to think it is almost as difficult for a man to give away his money rightly as it is to make it."

At last, satisfied with the plans, one part of his ambition was realized—to do something great for humanity and his own people while he was yet alive. The Indenture creating this trust is in itself a notable document, evidencing the care with which he provided for every detail. The original endowment was but the beginning. Mr. Duke was continually thinking of other things that might be done. His plans were continually expanding.

Physicians being needed as urgently as preachers and lawyers, and North Carolina having no medical college of the first rank, Mr. Duke determined to establish one. At his home in Charlotte, his associates were working with him on the methods of carrying into effect the provisions of the Endowment. Sending for Dr. Few, president of Trinity, he asked question after question as to the establishment of a medical school and hospital, cost of buildings, operating expenses, and what such an institution could accomplish. Bequeathing in his will $10,000,000—$4,000,000 for buildings, $6,000,000 for endowment—to create at Duke University the largest medical school south of Baltimore, later a codicil was added, leaving $7,000,000 additional to the university for other purposes.

By these and other donations and bequests the amount originally given in the Endowment was greatly increased. Through the cumulative provisions of the trust, the original fund will, in time, be doubled, and the total of Mr. Duke's benefactions will eventually be considerably more than $100,000,000. Only two men in our history—John D. Rockefeller and Andrew Carnegie—have given more.

CHAPTER TWENTY-ONE

As He Came to the End of His Days

STRICKEN with severe illness in the summer of 1925, Mr. Duke suffered an almost complete physical breakdown. Unable at first to discover the cause, physicians finally diagnosed it as pernicious anemia, a wasting disease for which medical science has, as yet, found no cure.

His strength gradually failing, in July he was compelled to take to his bed, and ill and suffering, for months was confined to his room, under the constant care of doctors and nurses. But they could not keep his mind from personal and business affairs.

At "Rough Point," his Newport estate, when his illness became serious, he remained there for several weeks, being brought later to his New York residence, No. 1 East Seventy-eighth Street.

In the South the severest drought on record prevailed. Shortage of water in the Catawba and other rivers curtailed the service of the power plants. Factories were shutting down or running on reduced time, throwing workmen out of employment, and seriously affecting towns and industries.

The streams which drove his turbines had for generations furnished an abundant supply of water. Years might elapse before their flow would fail again, but he was determined to provide against that contingency. Large steam plants must be built, to supplement those already erected, and supply ample electricity whenever the water powers failed.

Sites were selected, engineers rushed the making of surveys and drawings, millions of additional capital were provided, and preparations made for construction on an extensive scale.

THE END OF HIS DAYS

On his last visit to Charlotte, early in July, Mr. Duke remarked that the drought seemed providential, coming as it did when he was yet alive, and could devise means of meeting such emergencies in the future.

As he lay ill his mind constantly turned to the water-power situation, and the steps that were being taken to meet it. The doctors had told him he must not be disturbed by any thought of business, but this was too important. Noticing one night that he was wide awake hours after he should have been asleep, his attendant asked what was the trouble.

"Please don't disturb me," he said; "I'm building a steam plant down South."

Unable to rest until assured that this undertaking was being carried out to his satisfaction, engineers and officials were summoned. Gathering them around his bedside, he inspected the blue-prints, checked up the estimates, went into all the details of construction. Satisfied with the plans, he urged them to press the work to completion.

He was even more interested in the progress of Duke University, and every move in connection with it had to be reported to him. Now and then, thinking of some new feature that could be introduced, some improvement that might be made, he would immediately give orders that it be done.

Restless at a late hour, he seemed impatient at the efforts of his attendant to make him more comfortable. Rising in bed, and motioning her away, he said: "Nurse, don't disturb me now; I am laying out the University grounds."

Eleven days before his death, he sent for Mr. Allen. He seemed to be perturbed, laboring under some compelling emotion.

"Allen," he explained, "I have not provided suffi-

JAMES B. DUKE

cient funds for carrying out the complete plans I have in mind for the University. I want to arrange to give an additional $7,000,000 to complete the building program."

His legal adviser was called in, and a codicil was added to his will, providing for this additional bequest.

Very weak at the time, following an attack of pneumonia, he seemed to be improving until suddenly a relapse occurred. Two days before his death he sank into a coma from which he never revived, passing away at six o'clock on Saturday evening, October 10, 1925.

The simple funeral service held at his New York residence the following Monday, conducted by Rev. Dr. Raymond L. Forman, pastor of St. Paul's Methodist Church, was attended only by members of the family and intimate friends. Following the solemn ritual of the Methodist Church, the minister read John G. Whittier's poem, "Eternal Goodness," whose concluding verses voice humanity's hope and trust:

> "I know not what the future hath
>   Of marvel or surprise,
> Assured alone that life and death
>   His mercy underlies.
> And so beside the silent sea
>   I wait the muffled oar;
> No harm from Him can come to me
>   On ocean or on shore.
>
> "I know not where His islands lift
>   Their fronded palms in air;
> I only know I cannot drift
>   Beyond his love and care.
> And thou, O Lord, by whom are seen
>   Thy creatures as they be,
> Forgive me if too close I lean
>   My human heart on thee."

DUKE UNIVERSITY STUDENTS—THE GUARD OF HONOR AT ITS FOUNDER'S FUNERAL

THE END OF HIS DAYS

There was no sermon or eulogy, but in his fervent prayer Dr. Forman gave thanks for the life of this good man who, piling up his material mountain, had climbed up to its summit and there, viewing life as a seer, in a prophetic vision had seen the future need, and "out of a wise mind and compassionate heart invested his goods to serve the generations yet to come, in Christ's name." Wherefore "a countless host of friends in the North and all the Southland mourned the loss of a great benefactor."

Reading the twenty-third Psalm and the fourteenth chapter of St. John, the minister concluded with Elberton's hymn:

> "Now the laborer's task is o'er,
> Now the battle day is past,
> Now upon the farther shore,
> Lands the voyager at last.
> Father, in Thy gracious keeping
> Leave we now Thy servant sleeping."

Taken to North Carolina for interment, his body lay in state at Duke University, students, members of the faculty, friends and employees filing reverently by the bronze casket.

The funeral, held on the morning of October 13th, was the largest Durham had ever known. Thousands lined the streets and gathered around Duke Memorial Methodist Church, which the brothers had erected, and where the services were held. A blanket of golden roses, ferns and orchids covered the casket. The chimes in the tower rang solemnly. Mr. Duke's favorite hymns were sung, "How Firm a Foundation," "Abide With Me" and "Nearer, My God, To Thee." Rev. Dr. Edmund D. Soper, dean of the School of Religion, read the service and offered a brief prayer. The honorary pall-bearers were the trustees of the

JAMES B. DUKE

Duke Endowment, the men he had selected to carry on the work planned for the future.

Fourteen hundred students of Duke University formed a guard of honor from church to cemetery, bearing wreaths of flowers which they banked around the tomb—an impressive scene. With the simple, solemn words of the burial service the body was placed in the Duke mausoleum. James B. Duke was at rest beside his father.

Tributes to his memory came from many States and countries. Premier Taschereau, of Quebec, declared that Mr. Duke's death was "an irreparable loss" to the Canadian province. Colonel John H. Price, associated with him in his Northern power developments, spoke of the great things he had done for Canada. All parts of the Carolinas joined in honoring his memory.

Mr. Duke's career, the New York *Herald Tribune* stated, "had all those characteristics which in the public mind are now associated with captains of industry. The wealth he piled up he looked upon as a means of public service, as the American fortune builder nearly always does. To his native state he has been a benefactor in a double sense in that after contributing largely to its growth and prosperity as a manufacturer he has turned back so large a share of his wealth to give it the trained leaders in the learned professions of whom it stands in need. Mr. Duke was a thorough-going American—a constructive factor in business and a broadminded citizen who had won both local and national respect."

Terming him "America's Tobacco King," the New York *World* said:

"The late James B. Duke's fortune was built by business enterprise upon a scale unique in the South. The family of which he was the ablest member began establishing the Pied-

THE END OF HIS DAYS

mont tobacco industry in the same post-war years in which young Carnegie in Pittsburgh was revolutionizing the steel business; in which Rockefeller in Cleveland was organizing the Standard Oil; in which Frick was making Connellsville the nation's coke center, in which Agassiz and Higginson were building the Michigan copper industry. Duke consciously took Rockefeller for his model. He saw no reason why the tobacco business could not be organized with the same boldness as the oil business.

"The qualities of shrewdness and energy that stamped these Northern men marked Duke as well. He was quick to seize opportunity in such shapes as the pasteboard cigarette box and the cigarette-rolling machine; he saw the value of nation-wide advertising; and he pushed his consolidation schemes until the Government had to break up the trust he headed. More than any other man he made America a nation that smokes cigarettes by the hundred million. Having given the South a tobacco industry it had never dreamed of, he turned to other fields of Southern development.

"Indeed, Duke will be longest remembered as one of the builders of the New South and especially of the New North Carolina. It would be hard to name a rich American who has done so much to re-create his native State. He gave $40,000,000 to a university which he hoped would yet rival Harvard and Yale. He led in the development of its water-power and helped make it second only to Massachusetts in the number of its cotton spindles. North Carolina, recently one of the poorest and most backward of States, is now one of the busiest and most progressive. Duke may yet stand as the first representative figure in a great new Southern industrial era."

These were examples of hundreds of editorial comments, in every part of the country.

Filed soon after his death, his will revealed the careful, thorough way in which he had planned the devisal of his estate. Liberal provision had been made for his wife and daughter, as well as other relatives.

JAMES B. DUKE

One unusual feature was the creation of "The Doris Duke Trust," to which was assigned more than 125,000 shares of the Duke Power Company, valued at many millions, and certain other securities. Two-thirds of the income is to be paid to his daughter and only child, Doris, and one-third to his nieces and nephews and their descendants, the trust to continue until twenty-one years after the death of the last beneficiary now living, the principal then to be distributed. In case neither these nor their lineal descendants are surviving at that time, the funds and properties are to go to the Duke Endowment.

Another trust was created, with the same trustees and practically the same powers, setting aside one-third of the residuary estate, the income to go to his daughter, one-third of the principal to be paid to her when she is twenty-one years of age, the second third when she has attained twenty-five, and the remainder when she is thirty years old. Two million dollars was left to his cousins and other kin, so that even his most distant relatives would be included. In addition, associates, his office staff, servants, those who worked with and for Mr. Duke, were left various sums, none being forgotten.

The original will, executed at Somerville, N. J., on December 11, 1924, made a specific bequest of $10,000,000 to the medical school and hospital at Duke University, and provided that the residue of the residuary estate go to the Duke Endowment on the same terms as the original trust. But the codicil, executed on October 1, 1925, provided that $7,000,000 of this be used "in building and equipping Duke University and acquiring and improving property necessary for the same." Ninety per cent of the income, revenues and profits accruing from the remainder were to be de-

THE END OF HIS DAYS

voted, it was specified, to maintaining and securing hospitals, and ten per cent to the University.

His last will and testament was as characteristic of Mr. Duke as any act of his life. Both in his Endowment and bequests Mr. Duke sought to provide for activities which were not being and probably would not be adequately supported by others. One imperative need was for better medical service, especially in rural regions, which he sought to supply in two ways: First, by establishing a medical school of high grade for training physicians and nurses; second, by aiding existing hospitals and encouraging the building of new ones.

Cities in the South, as in other parts of the country, possess excellent hospitals and a plenitude of physicians. But many counties have no hospital facilities whatever, and the passing of the country doctor has deprived sparsely settled sections even of the services they previously enjoyed.

Dr. W. S. Rankin, director of the Hospital and Orphan Section of the Endowment and who was previously secretary of the North Carolina State Board of Health, has gone through that entire region, preaching the gospel of hospitalization and better medical service.

Too many physicians in urban centers, Dr. Rankin points out, tends to discourage professional understanding, sympathetic purposes and coöperative enterprises, and encourages high charges, split fees, over-specialization and excessive references from one specialist to another. Too few physicians in rural areas means inadequate medical care, unrelieved suffering, untimely death.

A county with a hospital and twelve doctors, it is contended, can enjoy far better medical service than one with twenty doctors and no hospital, and the poten-

JAMES B. DUKE

tial saving of $40,000 a year which would be paid the eight additional physicians would enable that county to build and maintain a hospital.

The Duke Endowment cannot assist individual patients or physicians. Nor can it relieve a town or community of obligation to care for its sick and suffering; but it can assist materially communities which assume their share of the responsibility. First, the Endowment pays hospitals one dollar a day for each charity patient treated free of cost in a free bed, the allotments applying in proportion to the need. Second, the surplus, after such charity payments, may be used to aid in building and equipping hospitals.

Ordinarily the trustees, it is estimated, will have available $700,000 or more annually, $400,000 for maintenance in assisting charity cases, and $300,000 for construction and equipment. With the cumulative growth of the fund's capital the amount will continually increase.

Observing the interest already aroused, health authorities are convinced that through the Duke Endowment there will, in time, be wrought a decided improvement in medical service throughout a wide region.

No less potent is its influence in the upbuilding of country churches. The Rural Church Section, under the direction of Rev. J. M. Ormond with headquarters at Duke University, has a building as well as a maintenance fund. Stimulating congregations to do things for themselves, intelligent direction and inspiration are accomplishing more than mere monetary assistance ever could, and this policy seems likely to bring about a transformation in the churches themselves as well as in the buildings that house them.

Empowered to contribute as much as fifty per cent of the cost of an improvement, the trustees find that

THE END OF HIS DAYS

the average required has been but a fraction of that proportion. In fact some of the smallest contributions have yielded large results.

Standard types of churches have been designed, a model one providing for four rooms—one for worship, the main auditorium, and three for Sunday School departments. Regarding the Sunday School as the keynote of church effectiveness, these schools are systematized in three types—"A," graded in seven departments from beginners to adults; "B," having five departments; and "C," with three departments. Assisting forty-four churches which were below the minimum to reach the "C" type requirement was accomplished by the Duke fund in 1926 at a cost of only $40,000.

Encouraging consolidation of churches is another important activity. In one section there were four Methodist churches within a radius of three miles, all on a good road. Bringing them together replaced three weak, struggling units with one strong congregation and a creditable structure. Similar instances have occurred time and again.

Churches isolated by changes in roads and communities are being rebuilt in more convenient locations. Attractive brick and stone structures are replacing weatherboard houses. The old "plank" churches, like the log cabins they succeeded, are giving way to modern structures. Excellent schools, good roads, scientific farming have wrought revolutionary changes in rural life, and the church must keep pace with them.

"I see no reason why, within fifteen years, we should not reconstruct the churches in rural North Carolina," a leader in this movement remarked.

Giving for a decade or more before his death $25,000 annually to Carolina country churches, Mr. Duke also for many years contributed, through Dr.

JAMES B. DUKE

Few, president of Trinity, thousands of dollars to aid superannuated clergymen and the widows and orphans of ministers. Now this fund is enlarged and at Christmastide there goes out to each of these beneficiaries a welcome check, accompanied by a sympathetic letter, bringing joy to the homes of these veteran itinerants.

Last, but not least, the orphanages, children's aid societies and organizations which care for the fatherless all share in the benefits of the Endowment. Convinced that this was one field in which others could be depended upon to do their full share, Mr. Duke's earnest hope was that not one of these little ones should suffer for lack of sustenance and care.

CHAPTER TWENTY-TWO
Bringing into Being a Great University

ON a broad plateau in the rolling, wooded lands west of Durham, not far from the campus where Trinity College has stood for thirty-five years, will soon be rising more than a half-mile of imposing buildings—administrative structures, study and lecture halls, dormitories, chapel, library, auditorium, hospital—all that is required for the instruction, accommodation and recreation of students.

In what was almost an untouched forest, architects, landscape gardeners, engineers, stone-masons, bricklayers—an army of workmen—will be engaged for years in preparing the grounds and carrying out this extensive project. For a university, perhaps the largest ever created at any one time, is coming into being.

Over four thousand acres are included in the site, and the buildings of a dozen colleges could be placed in this vast campus. Diversified grounds, studded with trees, afford distinctive sites and attractive settings. There is room and to spare for athletic fields, golf links, baseball diamonds, football ovals, tennis courts, running tracks, without disturbing the park-like character of the tract, which stretches for miles through the suburbs.

Eleven buildings of Georgian type, red-brick trimmed with marble, are under construction on the former Trinity campus, grouped around a quadrangle. But these compose only one unit, a fraction of the institution—that for the Co-ordinate College for Women, to which will be devoted also the present Trinity College buildings.

The University proper, of which Trinity is the

undergraduate college for men, will be located more than a mile away, linked with the women's college by a winding boulevard. Here will stand the schools of science, law, chemistry and physics, medicine and theology, the dormitories and numerous buildings required to house hundreds of students and provide for the faculty and various departments.

Seeking the most fitting type of architecture, Horace Trumbauer, the Philadelphia architect selected by Mr. Duke to design these structures, made extensive studies of the best examples of collegiate architecture both in this country and abroad. As a result the Gothic of English colleges was adopted for the principal group, not only by reason of its appropriateness for a university but as best suited to the rugged landscape. In this Mr. Duke was entirely in accord. Work was begun on the preliminary plans, and at last, after many months of preparation, the final studies have been completed, ready to be embodied in physical form.

A Gothic chapel whose tower, inspired by that of Canterbury Cathedral, rising to a height of 240 feet, will be the most prominent figure of the landscape, will be the central feature. To the right and left, on a three-quarter-mile eminence, the other structures will be placed. A deep ravine, now covered with sedgebrush and scrub-pine, extending along the entire front of the plateau, forms a natural basin for a lake. With fountains and cascades on either slope, encircled by a parkway lined with flowers, shrubs and trees, this can be transformed into a scene of rare beauty.

Along the lines that radiate from the center, on what architects term the subordinate axes, will stand the principal structures, in related groups, placed in appropriate settings. All of the same general type of architecture, constructed in one continuous operation,

CHAPEL, TOWER AND ADMINISTRATION BUILDING

INTERIOR OF CHAPEL, DUKE UNIVERSITY

CREATING A UNIVERSITY

this must result in a harmony that could hardly be attained under other conditions.

Viewed from the front, to the left of the Chapel will stand the Auditorium and class-room structures, the Union Building and dormitories; on the right the Religious Education Building, Library, Law, Chemistry, Botany and Zoölogy, and Physics buildings and the Medical School and Hospital.

Many details are yet to be determined; plans may be changed to meet conditions, necessarily modified here and there to suit requirements, but these have advanced so far that an approximate picture can be given of the construction proposed.

A strikingly beautiful interior is planned for the Chapel, the nave, 80 feet high and 35 feet wide, extending 132 feet from the entrance to the chancel arch, and the total length, including the chancel, being 174 feet. Aisles will extend on either side of the nave, and large clerestory windows light the chancel. With vaulted ceiling, the interior will be of cut stone, illuminated by stained-glass windows made in the natique manner.

The Auditorium, in a building of its own near the Chapel, is designed to seat fifteen hundred, with a stage equipped for drama or other entertainments.

The Union, the center of social life, will comprise a student lounge, dining rooms for students and faculty as well as visitors, and meeting-rooms for University organizations. A large room for receptions and other social functions will occupy a considerable part of the second floor; and the post office, college store, barber shop, bowling alleys, kitchen and service rooms will be located in the basement. Divided into houses for one hundred students each, with commons room and a suite for a matron or professor in each, accommodations for twelve hundred are provided in the dormitories now to be erected.

The School of Religion, at the right of the Chapel, which with the Class-Room Building on the opposite side, will form a fore-court of which the memorial tower will be the central feature, will contain a chapel of its own, thirty by sixty feet, seating two hundred.

Adjoining and communicating with this will be the Library, its entrance through a tower at the intersection of the two main quadrangles. With one room of exceptional length, 32 by 117 feet, on the first floor, the library will contain periodical and map rooms and numerous studies. The main reading room, 32 by 105 feet and 45 feet high, on the second floor, will communicate with the stack-room, which, extending through all floors, is designed for a capacity of 800,000 volumes. Catalogue and delivery rooms, as well as administrative offices, are conveniently located. Graduate reading and seminar rooms will occupy most of the third floor, with numerous cubicles for special study.

One feature of the Law Building, adjoining, will be a library of 200,000 volumes capacity. A museum and lecture hall are included in the designs for the Chemistry Building, which will be mainly occupied by laboratories for chemical research. Facing this will stand the Botany and Zoölogy structure, and near by the Physics Building, each of these including a library of its own as well as class, study and lecture rooms and instructors' offices.

The Medical School and Hospital, terminating the east end of the campus and designed as a single group, have been planned on the most advanced lines, including a hospital of three-hundred-bed capacity, with every facility for the care of patients and the training of nurses as well as medical students.

CREATING A UNIVERSITY

Of stone construction, the roofs of slate, the buildings will be fireproof throughout, heated by steam from a central plant. To the southwest will be located the gymnasium, football field and stadium. The serpentine boulevard, a mile and a half in length, will afford a convenient connection with the Trinity campus.

Five years or more will be required, experts estimate, to construct and equip these buildings, ten years to convert the tract into the ideal landscape designed and complete all the construction work that is contemplated. Not a brief period, but only a day in the life of an institution like this.

Acres of foundations are to be dug; millions of brick baked and laid; endless stretches of timber sawed and planed for floors and ceilings, miles of walls plastered and decorated, rooms built by hundreds. Roads are to be graded and surfaced, wide stretches of lawns and hillsides sodded, forests of trees, myriads of shrubs and flowers planted. A mammoth undertaking, this creation of a university "to order."

No business enterprise ever more thoroughly engaged Mr. Duke's genius and energy than this child of his dreams. Seeking an adequate site, he first planned to extend the Trinity campus, buying sufficient land adjacent for the larger institution. But a high price was demanded, far more, in his opinion, than the land was worth. He refused to pay it. Duke, the owners thought, "had to have this tract," was rich enough to pay any amount, and eventually would be compelled to accept their terms.

While the eyes of the town were on this property, his advisers were seeking another site. There was plenty of undeveloped land near the edge of the city. The largest tract, untenanted, most of it never cultivated, belonged to a man who, as long as he lived, refused to sell a single acre. After his death, the heirs not being able to agree, the courts ordered the property sold. Prof. Robert L. Flowers, vice president and treasurer of the University, who was acting for Mr. Duke in the negotiations, was convinced that this tract and the other acreage desired could be acquired without paying an excessive price. Mr. Duke was rather dubious about this, remarking that, once the owners learned any particular area was being considered, the prices would go sky-high; but he finally told Prof. Flowers to "go ahead and see what you can do."

Acting through local real estate dealers, pledged not to disclose an inkling of the transactions, one piece of property after another was bought, and the entire community was surprised when announcement was made that all the land needed for the university, thousands of acres, had been acquired.

Mr. Duke was delighted. A site far more extensive and better adapted to the purpose than that first contemplated had been obtained, and at a fraction of what the owners demanded for the other property. Meanwhile, impatient to "get started," he was formulating plans for buildings, developing grounds, clearing the way for construction. Particularly interested in landscaping, regarding Frederick Law Olmsted as the country's leading landscape architect, he entrusted that part of the undertaking to the Olmsteds, making numerous suggestions which they were quick to adopt.

Tramping over the property, penetrating into every nook and corner of it, he consulted with architects, builders, landscape experts, learning their ideas and giving them his own, visualizing not only the conception as a whole, but the most technical details.

The buildings must not only be well designed and solidly constructed, but the most attractive that could

MEDICAL SCHOOL AND HOSPITAL, ONE OF THE MAJOR GROUPS OF UNIVERSITY BUILDINGS

CREATING A UNIVERSITY

be produced. "I am looking to the future," he said, "how they will stand and appear a hundred years from now." Considering what was the best stone to use, the comparative merits of the leading varieties were tested, from New England granite to Georgia marble—appearance, durability, tensile strength, cost of material, quarrying and transportation. Not satisfied with these technical comparisons, he insisted on viewing each variety in finished form, to "see how it would look."

Carloads of various specimens were bought, transported to Durham, and walls of the most promising materials erected on the college grounds. The most attractive proved to be from New England, costly, the long haul entailing heavy expense for transportation. Mr. Duke believed that stone quite as good could be found nearer than this, and had Professor F. C. Brown and others investigate the neighboring deposits. Professor Brown discovered in Orange County, only a few miles away, a stone that in strength and coloring, as well as other qualities, seemed to compare well with any that had been considered. Options on the quarries were secured, and several carloads taken to the college and erected beside the other test walls.

To the surprise of architects and builders, the local stone proved superior to that from distant regions. Attractive in appearance, with soft touches of color that relieved the sameness of gray granite, it proved precisely what was sought. Highly pleased, Mr. Duke bought the entire deposit and surrounding property, presenting the university with a quarry of its own. With an almost inexhaustible supply of stone within easy reach there will be an immense saving in freights as well as in the cost of the thousands of tons required.

Creating a real university, however, means more than material construction, as some educators were ready enough to exclaim and editors not slow to point out when the Duke Endowment was announced. One writer in *The Nation*, reciting that Oxford, Cambridge, Bologna, Salamanca and Paris began far less grandly, went so far as to say:

"Mr. Duke in his naïve way believed that he could build a great university as he could build a factory—by going out and buying the brick and stone, the machinery and tools, and the workmen to operate them. He forgot that he was dealing in the most elusive commodity in the world. He could no more create ideas in this wholesale fashion than he could later create a market for them: Thus he started to build his university at the wrong end. He was distressed because North Carolina had no great school; he did not stop to discover the reason for this lack. He assumed that it was want of money—and of money he knew he had plenty. But a careful examination of the ideas which have come out of North Carolina in the last two hundred years might have told him more. If North Carolina had no great university, it might have been that she had no desire for one. Now that one has been wished on her, it remains to be seen what she will do with it."

These captious critics might have saved their breath and ink. No one realized more keenly than did Mr. Duke himself that, without high ideals, competent instructors and a broad, progressive policy, his effort and expenditure would be in vain. Costly buildings and extensive grounds were only the setting, large endowment the means for the institution he planned. Far more important was the human product.

"Get the ablest men, no matter where they come from, for the heads of the different departments," his trustees were instructed. Urging them to pay more attention to the faculty than to buildings or any other material thing, he said: "Get the best executives and educators, no matter what they cost. I want Duke to

TYPICAL DORMITORY GROUP—ARCHITECT'S DESIGN

THE UNION CLOISTERS—DUKE UNIVERSITY

CREATING A UNIVERSITY

be a great national institution, ranking with Harvard, Yale or any other university in the country."

Quality, not quantity, was his ideal—not mere numbers, but an earnest student body, developed by thorough training. Having no sympathy for the thousands who go to college to "have a good time," devote their time to sports and social affairs and "edge through" with no more study than is required to attain degrees, he frankly told his advisers that he did not wish Duke University cluttered up with such idlers.

"Unless a boy has ambition and a determination to be something in life, he will never amount to anything, no matter what is done for him," Mr. Duke remarked. His purpose, he emphasized, was to afford opportunity for the worthy and ambitious, those who "want to make something of themselves."

Striving to make provision, as he set forth, for mental and spiritual as well as physical needs, to create an educational institution of the highest rank, his plans were as broad as the realm of human knowledge, his sympathies as wide as humanity itself.

In the locality where he was born and reared, in the wide region whose industries he developed, there are springing up new hospitals and churches, colleges are expanding, orphan asylums opening wide their doors. Aged ministers worn out in devoted service, widows and orphans, unfortunate victims of injury and illness bless their benefactor.

Almost within sight of the marble tomb where he sleeps beside his father will stand the institution that bears his name. Those entrusted with administration of the endowment he created, the expenditure of the funds he provided, are earnestly endeavoring to carry forward his plans in the spirit in which they were conceived, laying the foundations broad and deep. With

JAMES B. DUKE

splendid buildings, richly endowed, having all knowledge for its field, Duke University will have every opportunity to translate into reality the dreams of its founder.

What the future holds the wisest cannot tell. But, established with all that generosity could provide or forethought ensure, the Duke Endowment gives promise of enduring for ages, pouring out its largesse continually, extending its benefits to generations yet unborn.

INDENTURE AND DEED OF TRUST ESTABLISHING THE DUKE ENDOWMENT

INDENTURE AND DEED OF TRUST ESTABLISHING THE DUKE ENDOWMENT

(With Additions Thereto by the Will of James B. Duke, Probated October 23, 1925.)

THIS INDENTURE made in quadruplicate this 11th day of December, 1924, by and between JAMES B. DUKE, residing at Duke Farms, near Somerville, in the County of Somerset, and State of New Jersey, United States of America, party of the first part, and NANALINE H. DUKE, of Somerville, N. J., GEORGE G. ALLEN, of Hartsdale, N. Y., WILLIAM R. PERKINS, of Montclair, N. J., WILLIAM B. BELL, of New York City, N. Y., ANTHONY J. DREXEL BIDDLE, JR., of New York City, N. Y., WALTER C. PARKER, of New Rochelle, N. Y., ALEX. H. SANDS, JR., of Montclair, N. J., WILLIAM S. LEE, of Charlotte, N. C., CHARLES I. BURKHOLDER, of Charlotte, N. C., NORMAN A. COCKE, of Charlotte, N. C., EDWARD C. MARSHALL, of Charlotte, N. C. and BENNETTE E. GEER, of Greenville, S. C., as trustees and their successors as trustees under and in accordance with the terms of this Indenture, to be known as the Board of Trustees of this Endowment, parties of the second part,

WITNESSETH:

That in order to effectuate the trusts hereby created, the first party has given, assigned, transferred and delivered, and by these presents does give, assign, transfer and deliver, the following property, to wit:

122,647 Shares of Stock of Duke Power Company, a corporation organized and existing under the laws of the State of New Jersey.

100,000 Ordinary Shares of the Stock of British-American Tobacco Company, Limited, a corporation organized and existing under the laws of Great Britain.

JAMES B. DUKE

75,000 Shares of the Common "B" Stock of R. J. Reynolds Tobacco Company, a corporation organized and existing under the laws of said State of New Jersey.

5,000 Shares of the Common Stock of George W. Helme Company, a corporation organized and existing under the laws of said State of New Jersey.

12,325 Shares of the Stock of Republic Cotton Mills, a corporation organized and existing under the laws of the State of South Carolina.

7,935-3/10 Shares of the Common Stock of Judson Mills, a corporation organized and existing under the laws of said State of South Carolina.

unto said trustees and their successors as trustees hereunder, in trust, to be held, used, managed, administered and disposed of, as well as all additions and accretions thereto and all incomes, revenues and profits thereof and therefrom, forever for the charitable purposes, in the manner and upon the terms herein expressly provided, and not otherwise, namely:

FIRST

The trust established by this Indenture is hereby denominated The Duke Endowment, and shall have perpetual existence.

SECOND

Each trustee herein named, as well as each trustee selected hereunder, shall be and remain a trustee so long as such trustee shall live and continue mentally and physically capable of performing the duties of a trustee hereunder, subject to resignation and to removal as hereinafter stated. The number of trustees within two years from the date of this Indenture shall be increased to, and thereafter remain at, fifteen, such increase being made by vote of the trustees at any meeting. He suggests, but does not require, that, so far as practicable, no one may be selected trustee if thereby at such time a majority of the trustees be not natives and/or residents of the States of North Carolina and/or South Carolina. It is the wish of the party of the first part, and he so directs, that his daughter, Doris Duke, upon attaining the age of twenty-one years, shall be made a trustee hereunder, for that purpose being elected to fill any vacancy then existing, or, if there be no such vacancy, added to the trustees thereby making the number of trustees sixteen until the next occurring of a vacancy, whereupon the number of trustees shall again become and remain fifteen.

Subject to the terms of this Indenture, the trustees may adopt and change at any time rules and regulations which shall govern in the management and administration of the trust and trust property.

Meetings of the trustees shall be held at least ten times in each calendar year at such time and place and upon such notice as the rules and regulations may provide. Other meetings of the trustees may be held upon the call in writing of the chairman or a vice-chairman or any three trustees given in accordance with the rules and regulations, at such place and time and for such purpose as may be specified in the call. A majority of the then trustees shall constitute a quorum at any such meeting, but less than a majority may adjourn any such meeting from time to time and from place to place until a quorum shall be present. The affirmative vote of the majority of a quorum shall be necessary and sufficient at any such meeting to authorize or ratify any action by the trustees hereunder, except as herein otherwise expressly provided. Written records, setting forth all action taken at said meetings and the voting thereon, shall be kept in a permanent minute book of the trustees, and shall be signed by each trustee present at the meeting.

The trustees shall select annually from their number a chairman and two vice-chairmen, and a secretary and a treasurer, who need not be trustees. Such officers shall hold office for one year and thereafter until their respective successors shall be selected. The compensation of the secretary and treasurer shall be that fixed by the trustees.

The trustees shall establish an office, which may be changed from time to time, which shall be known as the principal office of this trust, and at it shall be kept the books and papers other than securities relating to this trust.

By the affirmative vote of a majority of the then trustees any officer, and by the affirmative vote of three-fourths of the

JAMES B. DUKE

then trustees any trustee, may be removed for any cause whatever at any meeting of the trustees called for the purpose in accordance with the rules and regulations.

Vacancies occurring among the trustees from any cause whatever (for which purpose an increase in the number of trustees shall be deemed to cause vacancies to the extent of such increase in number of trustees) may be filled by the remaining trustees at any meeting of the trustees, and must be so filled within six months after the vacancy occurs; provided that no person (except said Doris Duke) shall remain or become a trustee hereunder who shall not be or at once become a trustee under the trust this day being created by the party of the first part by Indenture which will bear even date herewith for his said daughter and his kin and their descendants, so long as said latter trust shall be in existence.

Each trustee shall be paid at the end of each calendar year one equal fifteenth part of three per cent of the incomes, revenues and profits received by the trustees upon the trust properties and estate during such year, provided that if any trustee by reason of death, resignation, or any other cause, shall have served during only a part of such year, there shall be paid to such trustee, if alive, or if such trustee be dead then to the personal representatives of such trustee, such a part of said one-fifteenth as the time during which said trustee served during such year shall bear to the whole of such year, such payment to be in full for all services as trustee hereunder and for all expenses of the trustees. In the event that any trustee shall serve in any additional capacity (other than as chairman or vice-chairman) the trustees may add to the foregoing compensation such additional compensation as the trustees may think such trustee should receive by reason of serving in such additional capacity.

No act done by any one or more of the trustees shall be valid or binding unless it shall have been authorized or until it shall be ratified as required by this Indenture.

The trustees are urged to make a special effort to secure persons of character and ability, not only as trustees, but as officials and employees.

THE DUKE ENDOWMENT

THIRD

For the purpose of managing and administering the trust, and the properties and funds in the trust, hereby created, said trustees shall have and may exercise the following powers, namely:

To manage and administer in all respects the trust hereby created and the properties and funds held and arising hereunder, in accordance with the terms hereof, obtaining and securing for such purpose such assistants, office space, force, equipment and supplies, and any other aid and facilities, upon such terms, as the trustees may deem necessary from time to time.

To hold, use, manage, administer and dispose of each and every of the properties which at any time, and from time to time, may be held in this trust, and to collect and receive the incomes, revenues and profits arising therefrom and accruing thereto, provided that said trustees shall not have power to dispose of the whole or any part of the share capital (or rights of subscription thereto) of Duke Power Company, a New Jersey corporation, or of any subsidiary thereof, except upon and by the affirmative vote of the total authorized number of trustees at a meeting called for the purpose, the minutes of which shall state the reasons for and terms of such sale.

To invest any funds from time to time arising or accruing through the receipt and collection of incomes, revenues and profits, sale of properties, or otherwise, provided the said trustees may not lend the whole or any part of such funds except to said Duke Power Company, nor may said trustees invest the whole or any part of such funds in any property of any kind except in securities of said Duke Power Company, or of a subsidiary thereof, or in bonds validly issued by the United States of America, or by a State thereof, or by a district, county, town or city which has a population in excess of fifty thousand people according to the then last Federal census, which is located in the United States of America, which has not since 1900 defaulted in the payment of any principal or interest upon or with respect to any of its obligations, and the

JAMES B. DUKE

bonded indebtedness of which does not exceed ten per cent of its assessed values. Provided further that whenever the said trustees shall desire to invest any such funds the same shall be either lent to said Duke Power Company or invested in the securities of said Duke Power Company or of a subsidiary thereof, if and to the extent that such a loan or such securities are available upon terms and conditions satisfactory to said trustees.

To utilize each year in accordance with the terms of this Indenture the incomes, revenues and profits arising and accruing from the trust estate for such year in defraying the cost, expenses and charges incurred in the management and administration of this trust and its funds and properties, and in applying and distributing the net amount of such incomes, revenues and profits thereafter remaining to and for the objects and purposes of this trust.

As respects any year or years and any purpose or purposes for which this trust is created (except the payments hereinafter directed to be made to Duke University) the trustees in their uncontrolled discretion may withhold the whole or any part of said incomes, revenues and profits which would otherwise be distributed under the "FIFTH" division hereof, and either (1) accumulate the whole or any part of the amounts so withheld for expenditures (which the trustees are hereby authorized to make thereof) for the same purpose in any future year or years, or (2) add the whole or any part of the amounts so withheld to the corpus of the trust, or (3) pay, apply and distribute the whole or any part of said amounts to and for the benefit of any one or more of the other purposes of this trust, or (4) pay, apply and distribute the whole or any part of said amounts to or for the benefit of any such like charitable, religious or educational purpose within the State of North Carolina and/or the State of South Carolina, and/or any such like charitable hospital purpose which shall be selected therefor by the affirmative vote of three-fourths of the then trustees at any meeting of the trustees called for the purpose, complete authority and discretion in and for such selection and utilization being hereby given the trustees in the premises.

THE DUKE ENDOWMENT

By the consent of three-fourths of the then trustees expressed in a writing signed by them, which shall state the reasons therefor and be recorded in the minutes of the trustees, and not otherwise, the trustees may (1) cause to be formed under the laws of such state or states as may be selected by the trustees for that purpose a corporation or corporations so incorporated and empowered as that the said corporation or corporations can and will assume and carry out in whole or in part the trust hereby created, with the then officers and trustees hereof officers and directors thereof, with like powers and duties, and (2) convey, transfer and deliver to said corporation or corporations the whole or any part of the properties then held in this trust, to be held, used, managed, administered and disposed of by said corporation or corporations for any one or more of the charitable purposes expressed in this Indenture and upon all the terms and with all the terms, powers and duties expressed in this Indenture with respect to the same, provided that such conveyances, transfers and deliveries shall be upon such terms and conditions as that in case any such corporation or corporations shall cease to exist for any cause the property so transferred shall forthwith revert and belong to the trustees of this trust and become a part of the corpus of this trust for all the purposes thereof.

Said trustees shall have and may exercise, subject to the provisions of this Indenture, any and all other powers which are necessary or desirable in order to manage and administer the trust and the properties and funds thereof and carry out and perform in all respects the terms of this Indenture according to the true intent thereof.

Any assignment, transfer, bill of sale, deed, conveyance, receipt, check, draft, note, or any other document or paper whatever, executed by or on behalf of the trustees, shall be sufficiently executed when signed by the person or persons authorized so to do by a resolution of the trustees duly adopted at any meeting and in accordance with the terms of such resolution.

JAMES B. DUKE

FOURTH

The trustees hereunder are hereby authorized and directed to expend as soon as reasonably may be not exceeding Six Million Dollars of the corpus of this trust in establishing at a location to be selected by them within the State of North Carolina an institution of learning to be known as Duke University, for such purpose to acquire such lands and erect and equip thereon such buildings according to such plans as the trustees may in their judgment deem necessary and adopt and approve for the purpose, to cause to be formed under the laws of such state as the trustees may select for the purpose a corporation adequately empowered to own and operate such properties under the name Duke University as an institution of learning according to the true intent hereof, and to convey to such corporation when formed the said lands, buildings and equipment upon such terms and conditions as that such corporation may use the same only for such purposes of such university and upon the same ceasing to be so used then the same shall forthwith revert and belong to the trustees of this trust as and become a part of the corpus of this trust for all of the purposes thereof.

However, should the name of Trinity College, located at Durham, North Carolina, a body politic and incorporate, within three months from the date hereof (or such further time as the trustees hereof may allow) be changed to Duke University, then, in lieu of the foregoing provisions of this division "FOURTH" of this Indenture, as a memorial to his father, Washington Duke, who spent his life in Durham and whose gifts, together with those of Benjamin N. Duke, the brother of the party of the first part, and of other members of the Duke family, have so largely contributed toward making possible Trinity College at that place, he directs that the trustees shall expend of the corpus of this trust as soon as reasonably may be a sum not exceeding Six Million Dollars in expanding and extending said University, acquiring and improving such lands, and erecting, removing, remodeling and equipping such buildings, according to such plans, as the trustees may adopt and approve for such purpose to the end that said Duke University may eventually include Trinity College as its undergraduate department for men, a School of Religious Training, a School for Training Teachers, a School of Chemistry, a Law School, a Co-ordinate College for Women, a School of Business Administration, a Graduate School of Arts and Sciences, a Medical School and an Engineering School, as and when funds are available.

FIFTH

The trustees hereof shall pay, apply, divide and distribute the net amount of said incomes, revenues and profits each calendar year as follows, to wit:

Twenty per cent of said net amount shall be retained by said trustees and added to the corpus of this trust as a part thereof for the purpose of increasing the principal of the trust estate until the total aggregate of such additions to the corpus of the trust shall be as much as Forty Million Dollars.

Thirty-two per cent of said net amount not retained as aforesaid for addition to the corpus of this trust shall be paid to that Duke University for which expenditures of the corpus of the trust shall have been made by the trustees under the "FOURTH" division of this Indenture so long as its name shall be Duke University and it shall not be operated for private gain, to be utilized by its Board of Trustees in defraying its administration and operating expenses, increasing and improving its facilities and equipment, the erection and enlargement of buildings and the acquisition of additional acreage for it, adding to its endowment, or in such other manner for it as the Board of Trustees of said institution may from time to time deem to be to its best interests, provided that in case such institution shall incur any expense or liability beyond provision already in sight to meet same, or in the judgment of the trustees under this Indenture be not operated in a manner calculated to achieve the results intended hereby, the trustees under this Indenture may withhold the whole or any part of such percentage from said institution so long as such character of expense or liabilities or operations shall continue, such

JAMES B. DUKE

amounts so withheld to be in whole or in part either accumulated and applied to the purposes of such University in any future year or years, or utilized for the other objects of this Indenture, or added to the corpus of this trust for the purpose of increasing the principal of the trust estate, as the trustees may determine.

Thirty-two per cent of said net amount not retained as aforesaid for addition to the corpus of this trust shall be utilized for maintaining and securing such hospitals, not operated for private gain, as the said trustees, in their uncontrolled discretion, may from time to time select for the purpose and are located within the States of North Carolina and/or South Carolina, such utilization to be exercised in the following manner, namely: (a) By paying to each and every such hospital, whether for white or colored, and not operated for private gain, such sum (not exceeding One Dollar) per free bed per day for each and every day that said free bed may have been occupied during the period covered by such payment free of charge by patients unable to pay as the amount available for this purpose hereunder will pay on a pro rata basis; and (b) in the event that said amount in any year shall be more than sufficient for the foregoing purpose, the whole or any part of the residue thereof may be expended by said trustees in assisting in the erection and/or equipment within either or both of said States of any such hospital not operated for private gain, payment for this purpose in each case to be in such amount and on such terms and conditions as the trustees hereof may determine. In the event that said amount in any year be more than sufficient for both of the aforesaid purposes, the trustees in their uncontrolled discretion may pay and expend the whole or any part of the residue thereof in like manner for maintaining and securing hospitals not operated for private gain in any other State or States, giving preference, however, to those States contiguous to the States of North Carolina and South Carolina. And said trustees as respects any year may exclude from participation hereunder any hospital or hospitals which the trustees in their uncontrolled discretion may think so

THE DUKE ENDOWMENT

financed as not to need, or so maintained and operated as not to deserve, inclusion hereunder.

Five per cent of said net amount not retained as aforesaid for addition to the corpus of the trust shall be paid to Davidson College (by whatever name it may be known) now located at Davidson, in the State of North Carolina, so long as it shall not be operated for private gain, to be utilized by said institution for any and all of the purposes thereof.

Five per cent of said net amount not retained as aforesaid for addition to the corpus of the trust shall be paid to Furman University (by whatever name it may be known) now located at Greenville, in the State of South Carolina, so long as it shall not be operated for private gain, to be utilized by said institution for any and all of the purposes thereof.

Four per cent of said net amount not retained as aforesaid for addition to the corpus of the trust shall be paid to the Johnson C. Smith University (by whatever name it may be known), an institution of learning for colored people, now located at Charlotte, in said State of North Carolina, so long as it shall not be operated for private gain, to be utilized by said institution for any and all of the purposes thereof.

Ten per cent of said net amount not retained as aforesaid for addition to the corpus of this trust shall be paid and distributed to and among such of those organizations, institutions, agencies and/or societies, whether public or private, by whatsoever name they may be known, not operated for private gain, which during such year in the judgment of said trustees have been properly operated as organizations, institutions, agencies and/or societies for the benefit of white or colored whole or half orphans within the States of North Carolina and/or South Carolina, and in such amounts as between and among such organizations, institutions, agencies and/or societies as may be selected and determined as respects each year by said trustees in their uncontrolled discretion, all such payments and distributions to be used by such organizations, institutions, agencies and/or societies exclusively for the benefit of such orphans.

Two per cent of said net amount not retained as aforesaid

for addition to the corpus of the trust shall be paid and expended by the trustees for the care and maintenance of needy and deserving superannuated preachers and needy and deserving widows and orphans of deceased preachers who shall have served in a Conference of the Methodist Episcopal Church, South, (by whatever name it may be known), located in the State of North Carolina.

Six per cent of said net amount not retained as aforesaid for addition to the corpus of the trust shall be paid and expended by the trustees in assisting (that is, in giving or lending in no case more than fifty per cent of what may be required for the purpose) to build Methodist churches under and connected with a Conference of the Methodist Episcopal Church, South, (by whatever name it may be known), located in the State of North Carolina, but only those churches located in the sparsely settled rural districts of the State of North Carolina and not in any city, town or hamlet, incorporated or unincorporated, having a population in excess of fifteen hundred people according to the then last Federal census.

Four per cent of said net amount not retained as aforesaid for addition to the corpus of the trust shall be paid and expended by the trustees in assisting (that is, in giving or lending in no case more than fifty per cent of what may be required for the purpose) to maintain and operate the Methodist churches of such a Conference which are located within the sparsely settled rural districts of the State of North Carolina, and not in any city, town or hamlet, incorporated or unincorporated, having a population in excess of fifteen hundred people according to the then last Federal census.

Expenditures and payments made hereunder for maintaining such superannuated preachers, and such widows and orphans, as well as for assisting to build, maintain and operate such Methodist churches, shall be in the uncontrolled discretion of the trustees as respects the time, terms, place, amounts and beneficiaries thereof and therefor; and he suggests that such expenditures and payments be made through the use of said Duke University as an agency for that purpose so long as such method is satisfactory to the trustees hereof.

THE DUKE ENDOWMENT

SIXTH

Subject to the other provisions of this Indenture, said trustees may pay, apply, divide and distribute such incomes, revenues and profits at such time or times as may in their discretion be found best suited to the due administration and management of this trust, but only for the purposes allowed by this Indenture.

In the event that any stock dividend or rights shall be declared upon any of the stock held under this instrument, the said stock and rights distributed pursuant thereto shall for all purposes be treated and deemed to be principal even though the said stock dividend and/or rights shall represent earnings.

No trustee hereby appointed and no trustee selected in pursuance of any powers herein contained shall be required to give any bond or other security for the performance of his, her or its duties as such trustee, nor shall any trustee be required to reserve any part of the income of any investment or security for the purpose of creating a sinking fund to retire or absorb the premium in the case of bonds or any other securities whatever taken over, purchased or acquired by the trustees at a premium.

The term "subsidiary" as herein used shall mean any company at least fifty-one per cent of the voting share capital of which is owned by said Duke Power Company.

The party of the first part hereby expressly reserves the right to add to the corpus of the trust hereby established by way of last will and testament and/or otherwise, and in making such additions to stipulate and declare that such additions and the incomes, revenues and profits accruing from such additions shall be used and disposed of by the trustees for any of the foregoing and/or any other charitable purposes, with like effect as if said additions, as well as the terms concerning same and the incomes, revenues and profits thereof, had been originally incorporated herein. In the absence of any such stipulation or declaration each and every such addition shall constitute a part of the corpus of this trust for all of the purposes of this Indenture.

JAMES B. DUKE

SEVENTH

The party of the first part hereby declares for the guidance of the trustees hereunder:

For many years I have been engaged in the development of water powers in certain sections of the States of North Carolina and South Carolina. In my study of this subject I have observed how such utilization of a natural resource, which otherwise would run in waste to the sea and not remain and increase as a forest, both gives impetus to industrial life and provides a safe and enduring investment for capital. My ambition is that the revenues of such developments shall administer to the social welfare, as the operation of such developments is administering to the economic welfare, of the communities which they serve. With these views in mind I recommend the securities of the Southern Power System (the Duke Power Company and its subsidiary companies) as the prime investment for the funds of this trust; and I advise the trustees that they do not change any such investment except in response to the most urgent and extraordinary necessity; and I request the trustees to see to it that at all times these companies be managed and operated by the men best qualified for such a service.

I have selected Duke University as one of the principal objects of this trust because I recognize that education, when conducted along sane and practical, as opposed to dogmatic and theoretical, lines, is, next to religion, the greatest civilizing influence. I request that this institution secure for its officers, trustees and faculty men of such outstanding character, ability and vision as will insure its attaining and maintaining a place of real leadership in the educational world, and that great care and discrimination be exercised in admitting as students only those whose previous record shows a character, determination and application evincing a wholesome and real ambition for life. And I advise that the courses at this institution be arranged, first, with special reference to the training of preachers, teachers, lawyers and physicians, because these are most in the public eye, and by precept and example can do most to uplift mankind, and, second, to instruction in chemistry, economics and history, especially the lives of the great of earth, because I believe that such subjects will most help to develop our resources, increase our wisdom and promote human happiness.

I have selected hospitals as another of the principal objects of this trust because I recognize that they have become indispensable institutions, not only by way of ministering to the comfort of the sick but in increasing the efficiency of mankind and prolonging human life. The advance in the science of medicine growing out of discoveries, such as in the field of bacteriology, chemistry and physics, and growing out of inventions such as the X-ray apparatus, making hospital facilities essential for obtaining the best results in the practice of medicine and surgery. So worthy do I deem the cause and so great do I deem the need that I very much hope that the people will see to it that adequate and convenient hospitals are assured in their respective communities, with especial reference to those who are unable to defray such expenses of their own.

I have included orphans in an effort to help those who are most unable to help themselves, a worthy cause, productive of truly beneficial results in which all good citizens should have an abiding interest. While in my opinion nothing can take the place of a home and its influences, every effort should be made to safeguard and develop these wards of society.

And, lastly, I have made provision for what I consider a very fertile and much neglected field for useful help in religious life, namely, assisting by way of support and maintenance in those cases where the head of the family through devoting his life to the religious service of his fellow men has been unable to accumulate for his declining years and for his widow and children, and assisting in the building and maintenance of churches in rural districts where the people are not able to do this properly for themselves, believing that such a pension system is a just call which will secure a better grade of service and that the men and women of these rural districts will amply respond to such assistance to them not to mention

JAMES B. DUKE

our own Christian duty regardless of such results. Indeed, my observation and the broad expanse of our territory make me believe it is to these rural districts that we are to look in large measure for the bone and sinew of our country.

From the foregoing it will be seen that I have endeavored to make provision in some measure for the needs of mankind along physical, mental and spiritual lines, largely confining the benefactions to those sections served by these water power developments. I might have extended this aid to other charitable objects and to other sections, but my opinion is that so doing probably would be productive of less good by reason of attempting too much. I therefore urge the trustees to seek to administer well the trust hereby committed to them within the limits set, and to this end that at least at one meeting each year this Indenture be read to the assembled trustees.

EIGHTH

This Indenture is executed by a resident of the State of New Jersey in said State, is intended to be made, administered and given effect under and in accordance with the present existing laws and statutes of said State, notwithstanding it may be administered and the beneficiaries hereof may be located in whole or in part in other states, and the vadidity and construction thereof shall be determined and governed in all respects by such laws and statutes.

It being the purpose and intention of this Indenture that no part of the corpus or income of the trust estate hereby created shall ever for any cause revert to the party of the first part, or to his heirs, personal representatives or assigns, it is hereby declared that: (a) Each object and purpose of this trust shall be deemed and treated as separate and distinct from each and every other object and purpose thereof to the end that no provision of this trust shall be deemed or declared illegal, invalid or unenforceable by reason of any other provision or provisions of this trust being adjudged or declared illegal, invalid or unenforceable; and that in the event of any one or more of the provisions of this trust being declared or adjudged illegal, invalid or unenforceable that each and every other provision

THE DUKE ENDOWMENT

of this trust shall take effect as if the provision or provisions so declared or adjudged to be illegal, invalid or unenforceable had never been contained in this Indenture; and any and all properties and funds which would have been utilized under and pursuant to any provision so declared or adjudged illegal, invalid or unenforceable shall be utilized under and in accordance with the other provisions of this Indenture which shall not be declared or adjudged illegal, invalid or unenforceable; and (b) in the event any beneficiary for which provision is herein made shall cease to exist for any cause whatever, then so much of the funds and properties of this trust as otherwise would be utilized for the same shall be thereafter utilized for the remaining objects and purposes of this trust.

IN WITNESS WHEREOF, the said JAMES B. DUKE, at his residence at Duke Farms in the State of New Jersey, has subscribed his name and affixed his seal to this Indenture, consisting with this page and the preceding and following pages of twenty-one pages, each page of which, except the following page, he has identified by signing his name on the margin thereof, all on the day and year first above written.

JAMES B. DUKE (L. S.)

Witnesses:
    CLARENCE E. CASE
    FORREST HYDE
    CLARENCE E. MAPES

STATE OF NEW JERSEY }
COUNTY OF SOMERSET } *ss*

BE IT REMEMBERED, that on this 11th day of December, 1924, before me,   a Notary Public of New Jersey, personally appeared JAMES B. DUKE, who, I am satisfied, is the grantor named in the within Indenture and Deed of Trust dated December 11th, 1924, and I having first made known to him the contents hereof, he did acknowledge that he signed, sealed and delivered the same as his voluntary act and deed, for the uses and purposes therein expressed.

WM. R. SUTPHEN,
Notary Public of N. J.

JAMES B. DUKE

We, the undersigned, being the persons designated in the within and foregoing Indenture as the trustees of the trust thereby created, do hereby accept said trust and undertake to act as trustees of the same as in said Indenture set forth.

NANALINE H. DUKE
GEORGE G. ALLEN
WILLIAM R. PERKINS
WILLIAM B. BELL
ANTHONY J. DREXEL BIDDLE, JR.
WALTER C. PARKER
ALEX. H. SANDS, JR.
WILLIAM S. LEE
CHARLES L. BURKHOLDER
NORMAN A. COCKE
EDWARD C. MARSHALL
BENNETTE E. GEER

OTHER TRUSTS CREATED AND BEQUESTS MADE TO ENDOWMENT AND UNIVERSITY

The properties of The Duke Endowment in some cases will be, and in other cases may be, augmented by provisions of the following instruments executed by Mr. James B. Duke:

1. By indenture dated December 11, 1924, and executed at Duke Farms in Somerset County, New Jersey, Mr. Duke created a trust which he denominated The Doris Duke Trust, which is to continue so long as any one or more of the following persons,

DORIS DUKE, his daughter; MARY DUKE BIDDLE, MARY DUKE BIDDLE II, ANTHONY J. DREXEL BIDDLE III, ANGIER BUCHANAN DUKE, JR., ANTHONY NEWTON DUKE, MARY LYON STAGG, ELIZABETH STAGG HACKNEY, MARY WASHINGTON NICHOLSON, JOHN MALLORY HACKNEY, JR., JAMES STAGG HACKNEY, STERLING JOHNSTON NICHOLSON, JR., MARY WASHINGTON NICHOLSON II, CLARA ELIZABETH LYON MCCLAMROCH, GEORGE LEONIDAS LYON, JR., MARY DUKE LYON, E. BUCHANAN LYON, MARION NOELL LYON, LAURA ELIZABETH LYON, WASHINGTON DUKE LYON, BAXTER LAURENCE DUKE, MABEL DUKE GOODALL, PEARL

THE DUKE ENDOWMENT

DUKE BACHMANN, MABEL DUKE GOODALL II, and MARTHA DULANEY BACHMAN,
who was living when the Indenture was executed shall remain alive and for the period of twenty-one years immediately succeeding the death of the last survivor of them, unless sooner terminated by its other terms.

Into this trust Mr. Duke placed $35,000 in cash and 2000 shares of Duke Power Company, a New Jersey corporation, and the will of Mr. Duke, hereinafter mentioned, by Item V bequeathed to this trust "All the shares of stock which I may own at my death of the Duke Power Company, a New Jersey corporation, and / or of any corporation fifty-one per cent of the voting share capital of which is owned by the said Duke Power Company at that time, if my said daughter Doris Duke or a lineal descendant of my said daughter be living at the time of my death: . . . The shares of stock to which said trust may become entitled by virtue of this item of my will shall be added to and become a part of the corpus of said trust." As Doris Duke was living when her father died this provision of the will takes effect. By it the trust will get 125,904 shares of the capital stock of Duke Power Company, 2 shares of the common stock of Southern Power Company, 2 shares of the common stock of Great Falls Power Company.

Two-thirds of the income of this trust is to be paid to his daughter, Doris, and her descendants if they survive her; one-third to his nieces and nephews, named in the Indenture, and their descendants in equal shares. Twenty-one years after the death of the last surviving beneficiary named in the Indenture, the principal of the trust is to be distributed in proportionate shares as designated, the remainder of such shares as may revert to the trust, by death or otherwise, going to the Duke Endowment.

2. The will of Mr. Duke is dated December 11th, 1924, and his codicil thereto October 1st, 1925. Both were probated in common form before the Surrogate of Somerset County, New Jersey, October 23rd, 1925.

Besides the bequest, hereinbefore mentioned, to The Doris

JAMES B. DUKE

Duke Trust by Item V thereof, it contains the following provisions in which The Duke Endowment is, or may be, interested:

By Item VIII there is bequeathed to

"the trust established by me by Indenture dated December 11, 1924, wherein said trust is denominated The Duke Endowment, the sum of Ten Million Dollars, to be added to and become a part of the corpus of said trust estate and to be held, used, managed, administered and disposed of, as well as the incomes, revenues and profits arising therefrom and accruing thereto, by the trustees of said trust under and subject to all the terms of said trust Indenture, except that: (a) said trustees shall use and expend as soon as they reasonably can after the receipt of said sum not exceeding Four Million Dollars thereof in erecting and equipping, at the Duke University mentioned and described in said trust, buildings suitable for a Medical School, Hospital and Nurses Home under the supervision of said trustees and in all respects as they may determine concerning the same, and the acquisition of such lands, if any, as may be needed for such purpose, said lands, buildings and equipment to be conveyed to and thereafter belong to said Duke University and operated by it; and (b) all the incomes, revenues and profits arising and accruing from the said Ten Million Dollars shall be utilized, paid, applied and distributed each year by said trustees upon, subject to and in accordance with all the terms of said Indenture with respect to the payment and distribution of a percentage of the incomes, revenues and profits of said trust to and for said Duke University."

By Item X a trust is created with the same trustees, and practically the same powers, as those of The Doris Duke Trust. Into this trust is placed "one-third in value of said residuary estate and, in addition thereto, such a portion of said residuary estate as will in the judgment of my executors certainly produce a net annual income of One Hundred Thousand Dollars from said portion."

As respects said "portion" it is provided:

"The trustees of this trust each year shall pay, apply and

THE DUKE ENDOWMENT

distribute the net amount of the incomes, revenues and profits arising and accruing from the said portion of said residuary estate to my said wife so long as she shall live, and upon the death of my said wife this trust shall cease and terminate as to said portion and any undistributed incomes, revenues and profits thereof, and said portion and all undistributed incomes, revenues and profits thereof, shall be paid, applied and distributed by said trustee into the trust created and established by me by Indenture dated December 11th, 1924 wherein said trust is denominated The Duke Endowment."

As respects said "one-third in value" it is provided:

"The trustees of this trust each year shall pay and distribute the net amount of the incomes, revenues and profits arising and accruing from said one-third in value of said residuary estate, or so much thereof as may not then have been distributed under the terms of this trust, to my said daughter so long as she may live and after her death per capita, in equal portions, to and among the lineal descendants of my said daughter who may be living at the time of the making by the trustees of each particular payment and distribution thereof, so long as this trust shall continue after the death of my said daughter and a lineal descendant of my said daughter shall be living, but in no event subsequent to the last day of the said twenty-one year period herein mentioned and described for the duration of this trust."

One-third of this portion of the trust is to be paid to his daughter when she is 21 years old, one-half of the residue when she is 25 and the remainder when she reaches 30 years of age. In case neither she nor any of her descendants survive, the remaining portion of this fund is to go to the Duke Endowment.

Item XI of Mr. Duke's will, as changed by the codicil, reads:

"The residue of said residuary estate not disposed of by Item X hereof I give, devise and bequeath, and I direct my executors to pay and distribute, into the trust established by me by Indenture dated December 11, 1924 wherein said trust is denominated The Duke Endowment, to be added to

JAMES B. DUKE

and become a part of the corpus of said trust and to be held, used, managed, administered and disposed of, as well as the incomes, revenues, and profits arising therefrom and accruing thereto, by the trustees of said trust under and subject to all the terms of said trust Indenture, except that the trustees of said trust shall use and expend Seven Million Dollars ($7,000,000) of the principal thereof in building and equipping Duke University and acquiring and improving property necessary for that purpose, according to such plans as may have been or may hereafter be adopted by them for such purpose, and except further that the incomes, revenues and profits arising from and accruing to said residue of said residuary estate shall be utilized, paid, applied and distributed each year by said trustees as to ninety per cent thereof upon, subject to and in accordance with all the terms of said Indenture with respect to the payment and distribution of a percentage of the incomes, revenues and profits of said trust to and for maintaining and securing hospitals, and as to the remaining ten per cent thereof upon, subject to and in accordance with all the terms of said Indenture with respect to the payment and distribution of a percentage of the incomes, revenues and profits of said trust to and for said Duke University."